D1418436

PRAISE FOR

ℱREE TO SOAR

The life of a pastor's wife is to be one of fulfillment and excitement.
Free to Soar will help every pastor's wife understand and embrace
the God-given life she is called to have each day. I highly encourage
you to incorporate this resource into your life today.

Ted Haggard
President, National Association of Evangelicals
Senior Pastor, New Life Church
Colorado Springs, Colorado

Free to Soar will both encourage and equip the pastor's wife.
If you desire to honor Christ more, add greater value to your husband
and love your local church more, *Free to Soar* is a must for you.

Dr. Jack Hayford
President, International Foursquare Churches
Chancellor, King's College and Seminary
Van Nuys, California

My best friend in life and ministry is my wife, Becky. There is no
doubt that Northland Community Church will never reach its
potential without her leadership. The message in *Free to Soar*
will energize your life and help you to fly above common
church problems we face today.

Dr. Joel Hunter
Senior Pastor, Northland Community Church
Orlando, Florida

My wife, Donna, has given birth and life to every new dynamic ministry
at Christ Fellowship Church. Without a doubt, *Free to Soar* is destined
to become the handbook for pastors' wives' ministries. I encourage you
to read and apply the principles of successful ministry today.

Dr. Tom Mullins
Senior Pastor, Christ Fellowship Church
Palm Beach Gardens, Florida

For more than 50 years, my wife, Joyce, and I have walked together in faithful and fruitful ministry. *Free to Soar* combines both the principles and the practical aspects of the pastor's wife's ministry. If you desire balance between your marriage and ministry, *Free to Soar* will help you achieve this.

Dr. Adrian Rogers
Pastor, Bellevue Baptist Church
Memphis, Tennessee

Every pastor needs to understand the vital roles of pastors' wives in order to reach his maximum potential as a leader. *Free to Soar* has been written and designed both to equip the pastor's wife and to enlighten the pastor. Read it and succeed.

Gary Smalley
Smalley Relationship Center
Branson, Missouri

Your God-given talents are valuable to the kingdom of God. *Free to Soar* will help you maximize your calling and bring fulfillment to your life.

Dr. Wendell Smith
Pastor, The City Church
Kirkland, Washington

Much of the success of the Church today can be attributed to the effective leadership of women in ministry and to pastors' wives. *Free to Soar* will help you find your God-given destiny and make a difference in your family and ministry.

Thomas E. Trask
General Superintendent, Assemblies of God
Springfield, Missouri

We often underestimate the value of the pastor's wife in the church today. *Free to Soar* will help every pastor's wife reach her God-given potential in Christ, as well as in the Church.

Bishop Kenneth Ulmer
Faithful Central Bible Church
Inglewood, California

FREE
TO SOAR

Global Pastors
Wives Network

Regal

From Gospel Light
Ventura, California, U.S.A.

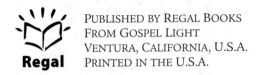

PUBLISHED BY REGAL BOOKS
FROM GOSPEL LIGHT
VENTURA, CALIFORNIA, U.S.A.
PRINTED IN THE U.S.A.

Regal Books is a ministry of Gospel Light, a Christian publisher dedicated to serving the local church. We believe God's vision for Gospel Light is to provide church leaders with biblical, user-friendly materials that will help them evangelize, disciple and minister to children, youth and families.

It is our prayer that this Regal book will help you discover biblical truth for your own life and help you meet the needs of others. May God richly bless you.

For a free catalog of resources from Regal Books/Gospel Light, please call your Christian supplier or contact us at 1-800-4-GOSPEL *or* www.regalbooks.com.

Library of Congress Cataloging-in-Publication Data
Free to soar / with Vonette Bright . . . [et al.].
    p. cm.
ISBN 0-8307-3790-1 (hardcover) — ISBN 0-8307-3792-8 (international trade paper)
1. Spouses of clergy–Religious life. 2. Christian women–Religious life. I. Bright, Vonette Z.

BV4395.F68 2005
253'.22—dc22   2005018116

1   2   3   4   5   6   7   8   9   10   /   10   09   08   07   06   05

Rights for publishing this book in other languages are contracted by Gospel Light Worldwide, the international nonprofit ministry of Gospel Light. Gospel Light Worldwide also provides publishing and technical assistance to international publishers dedicated to producing Sunday School and Vacation Bible School curricula and books in the languages of the world. For additional information, visit www.gospellightworldwide.org; write to Gospel Light Worldwide, P.O. Box 3875, Ventura, CA 93006; or send an e-mail to info@gospellightworldwide.org.

CONTENTS

PART ONE:

FREE TO SOAR THROUGH EMBRACING YOUR CALL

PART THREE:

FREE TO SOAR THROUGH NURTURING MARRIAGE, FAMILY AND RELATIONSHIPS

PART FOUR:

FREE TO SOAR THROUGH FOSTERING YOUR LEADERSHIP SKILLS

PART FIVE:

FREE TO SOAR THROUGH BUILDING HEALTHY MINISTRY

PART SIX:

FREE TO SOAR THROUGH EXTENDING YOUR MISSION

ACKNOWLEDGMENTS

Special thanks to our reliable transcribers: Yvonne Calahan, Angie Alongi, Ruth Bowman, Karla Leone, Maggie Wink and Angela Poma.

$\mathcal{P}$REFACE

"Balancing it all" is a heart cry of wives who share a ministry assignment with their husbands. According to *Just Between Us,* a magazine for women with a heart for ministry, balancing it all is the most pressing demand on wives who share a ministry assignment with their husbands. This is followed by the need to have a devotional life, the need to have a close friend, the need to handle conflict, and the need to deal with emotional issues and stress.[1] Many minister's wives today feel lonely and isolated, long for more time with their spouse, have concerns about their children's spiritual and emotional well-being, and struggle with unrealistic expectations.

For the last decade or so, Focus on the Family has attempted to come alongside and help meet the needs of clergy wives. Recently, Focus on the Family conducted an informal survey of more than 1,000 clergy wives, 18 percent of whom had been pastors' wives for more than 25 years and 29 percent of whom had served for 10 years or fewer. Though unscientific, the results from the survey were revealing: 56 percent felt personally called to ministry as a clergy wife, while 39 percent did it to support their husbands; 55 percent worked full- or part-time outside the home.

When the respondents were asked their greatest concerns about their husbands, most said pressures from ministry, followed by concerns about physical health, lack of finances, emotional well-being and spiritual health. When asked about their children, they listed at the top exposure to church conflict and the effect that conflict would have on their attitude toward the church. Yet 72 percent also felt the church had been a positive influence on their children.

These pastors' wives were frustrated over lack of adequate finances, inability to manage their time, and lack of time with their husband. They agonized over unresponsive congregations and felt they put too much pressure on themselves. Yet when all was said and done, though 73 percent said they felt discouraged over the last year,

85 percent of the wives who participated in the Focus on the Family survey generally enjoyed being a pastor's wife.

Being a pastor's wife has never been easy! But as the survey shows, you can find joy on the journey, and you will learn how to do just that within the pages of *Free to Soar*.

In addition to the issues revealed by these surveys, three crucial shifts have occurred in the pastorate recently that *Free to Soar* will help you to navigate. These include the training, teaming and timing of pastors:

Training. Since the last generation entered into full-time ministry, fewer leaders are being trained in the traditional seminary or Bible College setting. It is crystal clear that the local church rises and falls on leadership. *Free to Soar* is packed with godly wisdom from many of the leading lights in Christendom today who teach women how to adapt and complement their positions.

Teaming. In response to an ever-increasing demand from society, many full-time ministry wives now view themselves as partnering with their husband, not simply supporting him. A winning team is crucial in ministry; the team facilitates the God-given vision for the local church. When a pastor's home suffers, the whole church suffers. *Free to Soar* shows the power of husband and wife partnerships and illustrates how, in many places, pastors' wives are being given more of a leadership role in the local church. We believe that a biblical, ministry-oriented marriage can only fulfill its roles and goals when the husband and wife have a shared vision and passion for their assignment.

Timing. Pastors and their wives are now expected to achieve more in a shorter period of time. It is no longer deemed acceptable for the "man of God" to be simply given to prayer and the study of the Word of God. Today, many ministers work an additional job to provide for their families while they serve and grow their local church. When working in the church, the pastor is expected to be capable in raising funds, erecting buildings, hiring staff and increasing church attendance, and he is expected to show up well rested and smiling on Sundays with a fresh new penetrating message. Every pastor's wife knows that the work is never done. More than 90 percent of the 325,000 churches in North America have attendance under 120 people, so the pastor's wife has to fulfill many responsibilities that are not necessarily her strengths. *Free to Soar* will elevate the pastor's wife spiritually but will also enable her to face the reality of a most demanding responsibility.

Free to Soar provides ministry wings for wives who desire to reach their potential in Christ and in ministry, and we congratulate the pastors' wives who wrote it for gaining such insight and wisdom and for sharing it with you. Our hope is that this book will reaffirm the importance and value of your position and that you will use this book as a tool to fly higher than you ever have before.

We look forward to seeing you soar to a new level of service and fulfillment. We will be cheering you on as you reach new heights—a testimony to God's power in your life and your deep desire to see His Church increase. Most of all, we trust your marriage and family will be blessed by love and loyalty to one another. You were meant to live above the challenge. You were created to soar! May you be free to soar as never before.

James O. Davis
Cofounder/President/CEO
Global Pastors Network

H. B. London, Jr., Vice President
Church, Clergy and Medical Outreach
Focus on the Family

For more information on Global Pastors Network,
visit www.gpn.tv.

For more information on Global Pastors Wives Network,
visit www.gpwn.tv.

Note
1. Survey published in *Just Between Us,* Fall 2004 (Brookfield: WI).

PART ONE

FREE TO SOAR THROUGH EMBRACING YOUR CALL

CHAPTER 1

$\mathcal{A}$ GOD-GROWING CONFIDENCE

VONETTE Z. BRIGHT

We live in a noisy world, and noise pollution is everywhere. Practically everything that we own has a voice. Our cars speak to us and sometimes even give us directions. Our computers speak to us. Our household appliances speak to us. Frequently, we answer the telephone and a recorded voice speaks to us, and we cannot even talk back. I even received a digital camera at Christmas time. Would you believe that camera even talks to me? I wish it would tell me exactly what to do—it just lets me know when I am doing something wrong.

Voices

But then there are the beautiful voices that fill our lives with joy—our spouse's "Hi, Hon," our children's chatter, our Lord's loving words. How do we learn to hear those voices more clearly? I am going to share with you four basic principles that will help you safely navigate the noise you encounter each day—and that will enable you to hear the voices that really matter. These principles are listening to the voice of Jesus, discerning other voices, discerning the voice of the Holy Spirit, and understanding that your voice can make a difference.

Listening to the Voice of Jesus

As you seek to hear the Lord's voice, it is helpful to be clear about what exactly you are listening for. It is so difficult sometimes to know which words are from our own desires, which words are from God and which words are from the enemy. I can think of no better way to bring clarity to this issue than to share a story of the last days of my dear husband's life.

Although Bill was excited about going to be with Jesus, he was concerned about leaving me—and I, too, could not imagine life without him. A few days before his death, he initiated a conversation about voices that I might hear. We had discussed this subject a number of times before. He warned me that if I ever heard a voice telling me that I was weak, that I was not pleasing God or that I was a failure, I was to recognize that that negative voice was not of God. No, that voice of discouragement would be from the enemy. Bill assured me that God's voice would always be positive and assuring.

Not long after that conversation, I felt free to share with Bill the peace and confidence God had placed in my heart. The voice of God in His Word had assured me of His love and protection as he led me into a new phase of life. God ministered to me verse after verse, passage after passage. Almost every day, I gained some special truth that gave me greater strength. I was at peace in trusting God with Bill's future and with my future. I was still praying that God would heal Bill, although I felt led to give him permission to leave whenever the Lord was ready to take him home.

Now that Bill has passed away, how am I doing? I am not hearing negative voices. God's Word is still speaking to me loud and clear. Two of the most recent verses have been Isaiah 41:10 ("Do not fear, for I am with you; do not be dismayed, for I am your God. I will strengthen you and help you; I will uphold you with my righteous right hand") and Jeremiah 29:11 ("'For I know the plans I have for you,' declares the LORD, 'plans to prosper you and not to harm you, plans to give you hope and a future'")—what a promise! I rejoice in knowing that Bill is in the very presence of God—and that God is walking beside me.

Discerning Other Voices

Now, there are other voices in the world that we should heed. Yes, God has given us His Word, but He also speaks to us through other believers.

Some years ago, I heard the voice of Christian psychologist Henry Brandt speaking to a group of missionaries who had returned from the field. He was speaking about psychosomatic illness—bodily illnesses that have their root in emotional or mental disturbances. He made the statement that the largest number of people suffering from such illnesses are pastors' wives. Why? The pressure of living one thing and professing another can make us very ill or handicapped in some way. Dr. Brandt said:

> How can there be stability in one who thinks and feels evil but conceals his guilty conscience behind a pious look, who is filled with morbid misgivings rather that real confidence in God. Of all people, he is most miserable. Such a clash between inner self and outward manner results in faulty judgment and unpredictable behavior. This person seeks to protect himself rather than to minister to others. Instead of covering up sin, for this is what such behavior is, and pretending that it doesn't exist, we ought to confess our sins and through the atoning work of Christ be rid of it and there find courage and strength to face life. A peaceful walk is one that can be made only by faith in God's ability to provide for man's inability.[1]

I knew exactly what he was talking about. After I accepted Christ as my personal Savior, I was certain that life would be perfect, but I soon realized that I was not seeing evidence of Christ working in me. What was missing? I had heard about the work of the Holy Spirit, but I did not really understand how the ministry was related to daily living. I continued to be faithful with my prayer and my Bible reading, but I was not seeing spiritual fruit in my life.

So what is it that the voice of Dr. Brandt is really telling us? We need the Holy Spirit's control if we are to live a life pleasing to God and to effectively minister to others. Just as a woman taking on a new role as a mother must learn how to parent, once my position in Christ was assured, I had to learn how to live according to spiritual principles. There I was with a home filled with students and a husband who had boundless energy and more good ideas about expanding the ministry than we could accomplish in a lifetime. Wasn't that enough? No, I knew there had to be something more to this life in Christ, and I really wanted to know what it was. The daily demands of life had kept me so busy that I had subconsciously equated my busyness with my commitment to Christ.

When Bill began to understand the voice of the Holy Spirit, the Holy Spirit dramatically touched Bill's life, resulting in his call to establish the ministry of Campus Crusade for Christ. His call became mine as well. Some of you married your pastor-husbands, sharing his call from the beginning. Some of you found yourselves in the position of a pastor's wife long after you were married. Regardless of when you became a pastor's wife, remember that when God called your husband to ministry, He called you into ministry as well. Share your husband's call joyfully. Even in those times when you do not feel joyful about your call, ask God to give you a heart to respond with joy—and that is exactly what He will do for you. That is what He did for me.

Discerning the Voice of the Holy Spirit

We want to live consistently and victoriously the meaningful Christian life that seems to evade us. The key is to surrender to God and allow the Holy Spirit to work in and through us. In Romans 8:5-7, Paul says that those who are dominated by their sinful nature think about sinful things, but those who are controlled by the Holy Spirit think about things that please the Spirit. If your sinful nature controls your mind, there is death. But if the Holy Spirit controls your mind, there is life and peace. Romans 8:11 says that the spirit of God who raised Jesus from the dead lives in you, and just as He raised Christ from the dead, He will give life to your mortal body by the same spirit living within you.

But how do all these beautiful words of the Lord fit with our day-to-day tasks? Perfectly. George Eliot, in a criticism of Christians, said that Christians do not allow their celestial knowledge to affect their domestic action.[2] I now have a large plaque over my sink as a reminder to let my celestial knowledge affect my domestic action and to let the voice of the Holy Spirit speak to my daily concerns and duties. To try to live the Christian life apart from the Holy Spirit is like trying to run a car without gasoline—it just does not work. There is nothing strange about the Spirit-filled life. It is the way God intended for the Christian life to be. It is letting the Lord Jesus express Himself through my life. When I am filled with the Spirit, I am filled with Christ. Again, it is not how much we have of the Holy Spirit that counts, but how much He has of us.

Walking in the Spirit moment by moment is a lifestyle. It is learning to depend upon the Holy Spirit and His abundant resources as a way of life. As we walk in the Spirit, we have the ability to live a life pleasing to God. In Galatians 5:16 and 25, Paul tells us, "So I say, live by the Spirit, and you will not gratify the desires of sinful nature. Since we live by the Spirit, let us keep in step with the Spirit." As we walk in the Spirit, we experience intimacy with God and all that He has for us, namely, the fruit of the Spirit: love, joy, peace, patience, kindness, goodness, faithfulness, gentleness and self-control (see Gal. 5:22-23).

Understanding Your Voice Can Make a Difference

Now that we have looked at how to listen to the voice of Jesus, His followers and the Holy Spirit, we need to look at how you can use your voice to further the Kingdom. But first there are three important questions you need to ask yourself: Am I ready now to surrender control of my life to our Lord Jesus Christ? Am I ready now to confess my sins? Do I sincerely desire to be directed and empowered by the Holy Spirit? If your answer to all three questions is yes, please pray the prayer below to express to the Lord the desire of your heart to be one with Him and His Spirit—and to use your voice in His service.

Dear Father, I need You. I acknowledge that I have sinned against You by directing my own life. I thank You that You have forgiven my sins by Christ's death on the cross for me. I now invite You to again take Your place on the throne of my life. Fill me with the Holy Spirit as You commanded me to be filled and as You promised in Your Word that You would do if I ask in faith [see 1 John 5:14-15]. I pray this in the name of Jesus. I now thank You for filling me with the Holy Spirit and for directing my life. Amen.

Now you are ready to move forward—now you are really free to soar. As I think in terms of the voice that we have, if we are experiencing the Spirit-filled life, we women will be able to lead others to the Lord. Through our faithful witness of life and voice, we will see a dramatic answer to prayer in our nation. I believe that we, as Spirit-filled Christian women, hold the key to what this nation is going to be. I believe that the future of our nation is largely in the hands of Bible-believing, Christ-controlled women who have a heart for God and an authenticity that is obvious to the secular world.

We must win the victory for our nation by living what we profess. So many times we see people who profess to be Christians but act like they are controlled by the enemy. Friends, the world would have been won to Christ a long time ago if believers lived Spirit-filled lives. We must be the voice of forgiveness and compassion, leading others to Jesus Christ through lives lived in the power of the Holy Spirit! Let's begin today to allow our voices to be heard in our nation and in the world!

A Final Thought

I doubt that I have written anything here that is new to you, but it is important for us to be reminded of how we can live a Spirit-filled life amid the noise of the world. Is God's voice speaking to you? Where are you in your walk with the Lord? Is there sin in your life? Take time to do inventory. Is the Holy Spirit in control of your life? Is there some action that you need to take to make a relationship right? Take the opportunity now to hear the voice of the Lord. What is He is saying to you? Listen, and then act through the power of the Spirit.

Continue to depend on God's spirit moment by moment. I guarantee that you will experience a joyful intimacy with God and all He has for you: a truly rich and satisfying life—one that allows you to be free to soar.

Prayer

Oh, Father, thank You that you have made it possible for us to live above circumstances. You sent the Holy Spirit to help us cope with life. You have helped us to see that we can face any kind of impossibility with victory if we will but surrender to You and let You live Your life in and through us. Remind us not to struggle and not to fret about things around us but to take an eternal perspective and to trust You, obeying what You tell us to do. Oh, Father, give us a voice that is going to make a difference in this world. Give us lives that will cause others to want to know what makes us different—that they will want to know Jesus because they see Jesus in us. Father, we pray this in the name of Your precious Son and we ask You, Lord, to bring honor and glory to Your name through the lives of pastors' wives everywhere. Lord, we have devoted our lives totally and completely to You.

Yes, we have made lots of mistakes. Some of us have known exactly what it is to be Spirit-filled, but we have let the world creep in. We have become tired and weary. But today, Lord, we ask You to take total and complete control, and we thank You that You have answered our prayer. In Jesus' name. Amen.

Notes

1. Dr. Henry Brandt, speech given in 2005. Used by permission.
2. George Eliot, *Middlemarch* (New York, Penguin Books, 2003), n.p.

LIVING ON A SOLID FOUNDATION

MELANIE STOCKSTILL

As I reflect on what it means for me to be a pastor's wife, I can't help but recall how I fell in love with my husband when I was only 14 years old. We were having a youth function at our church and my father wouldn't allow me to attend unless I rode with the pastor's son. The necessary arrangements were made, but there was one small problem: I lived closer to the young man than did his girlfriend. That meant he had to pick me up first and drop me off last!

I'll never forget that night. He picked me up as planned, and then we picked up his girlfriend. The three of us went to the meeting together. Afterward, when we dropped off his girlfriend at her home, he and she got out of the car and walked to the door. Being a good little Baptist girl, I made up my mind not to watch as they said good night. But my female instincts kicked in and, of course, I looked! I watched as he brought her to the door, took her by the hand and then prayed over her before she went inside. I fell in love with Larry that night.

All these years later, I'm still in love with him and I still respect him so highly. Paul said in Ephesians 5:33, "Each individual among you also is to love his own wife even as himself, and the wife must see to it that she respects her husband" (*NASB*). If we could get that one little thing right, we would revolutionize both families and churches in America.

Laying the Foundation

In order for a pastor and his wife to live in love and respect, they must first lay a firm foundation. Couples build their foundations out of many different substances, but I believe there is no firmer foundation than that of a unified couple ministering together as one, fulfilling a specific and divinely appointed assignment.

I have the wonderful privilege of talking to pastors' wives all the time, and I have discovered how lacking this foundation is in the lives of so many of them. Many pastors' wives don't even know whether they have a call of God on their lives; or they know they have a calling, but don't fully realize what it is. I have compassion for these women, because I was just like them for so many years.

Discerning your calling is a quest—a journey of faith. Sometimes as a pastor's wife, you feel like a misfit in the congregation, like an ugly duckling. The truth is, however, that you are a beautiful swan waiting to discover your true identity.

Sharing in the Call

In Genesis 12, God called Abram out of Haran to go to a land that the Lord would show him (see vv. 1-3). We never see his wife, Sarai, mentioned in this initial calling, but we know she was very important in it because later we read of how God's divine protection was upon her (see vv. 14-17). You might say that God was her bodyguard, so essential was she in His plan.

In Genesis 15, God made a covenant with Abram. He said, "Abram, I want you to come out of your tent, and I want you to look at the sky. You see all those thousands upon thousands of stars? That's how many descendants you are going to have" (see v. 5). Again, Sarai's name is not mentioned. But we know that there's no way Abram could have all those descendants without a female counterpart in the plan!

It's not until Genesis 17 that God finally speaks of Sarai: "As for Sarai your wife, you are no longer to call her Sarai; her name will be Sarah. I will bless her and will surely give you a son by her. I will bless her so that she will be the mother of nations; kings of people will come from her" (vv. 15-16). This name change is of great significance. *Sarai* is a generic name for a leader, but *Sarah* means "princess." In this remarkable changing of her name, we see God elevating Sarai to an exalted position beside her husband, Abraham. That's because she was just as important in God's plan as was Abraham himself.

Like Sarah, your call is bound up in your husband's call. The call of God that is on him is also on you. When you married him you became one with him, so the mantle that rests upon him is now resting upon you. The enabling that's in him is also in you. The anointing that's on him is on you. The authority that resides in him resides in you. You share in all aspects of his life and ministry.

I have personally experienced the tremendous blessing of this shared calling. I am not a public speaker—it's definitely not one of my giftings—but my husband is. Through revelation, however, I realized that I could tap into his anointing and his enabling, so I speak when the opportunity arises. I don't wonder anymore about who I am and what my calling is. Instead, I have allowed the Lord to elevate me to that place where I belong—a place alongside my husband as a Sarah, a princess.

You, too, are a princess. Today my prayer is that God would give you a revelation of who you are and that He would elevate you to your rightful place alongside your husband so that you can effectively share in the calling the Lord has upon your lives.

Moving Forward in Faith to Fulfill Our Calling

Sometimes we refuse to embrace God's call on our lives. We fail to live by faith, bringing confusion and dissension into the home. This is what Sarai did, and this is exactly what we do too, sometimes. When Sarai's faith in God's promise weakened, she became hopeless. She knew there was a call of God on Abram, but she failed to realize that the call also rested upon her. She didn't think she could be the person needed to fulfill the call, so instead of pressing on in faith, she found a "solution" to her feeling of inadequacy. She presented Hagar to Abram, that Hagar might bear him a son. "Well, perhaps God will fulfill His promise through Hagar," she thought (see Gen. 16:1-2). In so doing and thinking, Sarai abdicated her place beside her husband and gave it to another woman.

I used to think this was preposterous. Why would any woman give another woman access to her husband? Yet one day the Holy Spirit spoke to me and said, "Melanie, you've done the same thing!" Let me explain: We as pastors' wives are the jacks-of-all-trades and masters of none. We work in the nursery; we work with the children's church; we do the janitorial work. We are the administrators and the accountants. We play the piano and sing in the choir. These are all great acts of service, but they are mere functions—they are not our purpose.

I, like many pastors' wives, had begun to make those functions my life. I was comfortable in my busy role, so when it came time for me to step up and share in my husband's call, I didn't want to. I feared that taking my place beside my husband would mean living in a fishbowl, and I was not about to give up my privacy. As a result, I said to my husband, "Um, here's Mrs. Hagar. Sister Hagar will take my place at pastoring the women. She's certainly qualified. She's been in the church for years, she's got lots of time on her hands, and she actually likes working with women. Here she is." So I gave a Hagar to my husband!

I thought I had found the perfect solution, but I came to see that when you give a Hagar to your husband, you are actually being unfair to the woman. As qualified as she may be, she does not share your husband's mantle. The anointing on him does not flow down on her. The authority on his head is not on her head. When you relinquish your rightful place to her, you are setting this woman up for failure because she is occupying *your* place.

You cannot surrender your place. If you don't fill it, no one else can, because God will not transfer that anointing. The Holy Spirit—and likely your husband—is waiting for you to take your place beside your husband so there can be a fulfillment of the calling of God in your life. That's what I discovered, and you are probably learning that same lesson as well.

When Sarai brought Hagar into the picture, she also invited dissension and strife into her house (see Gen. 16). This happens in our homes, too, when we reject our roles in the church. The Holy Spirit spoke this truth to me recently. He said, "Melanie, I am displeased with strife in the priestly home. The anointing cannot flow through the congregation if there's strife in the home. And the source of strife is unfruitfulness."

Sarai was contentious because she was unfruitful and couldn't find her place. She was hard to get along with, and so are we as pastors' wives until we find that place of fruitfulness and fulfillment beside our husbands.

Recognizing Our Call to Be Leaders and Mothers of Nations

God said that He would make Sarah the "mother of nations" (Gen. 17:16), and that is also His ultimate aim for you. My husband can preach, teach and expound on the Word of God like no one else, but he cannot mentor women. He cannot model to them how to be godly women, godly wives and godly mothers.

Two-thirds of a church's congregation is usually made up of women, and they need someone to mentor them in those things that uniquely apply to women. Who is that someone to be? It is you and I, pastors' wives. That's my place and that's your place. We have been called.

When I began to step out and fulfill my role as a mentor, I received a wonderful revelation: God wasn't trying to make me miserable by making me do something I didn't want to do. What He was trying to do was to help me reach my full potential: to become the mother of nations.

God is trying to bring you to that place as well. He wants to elevate you to that place where you'll be the mother of nations. You might be working in the nursery in your church, but that is not all God has for you. Or maybe you play the piano in your church. As wonderful as that is, that is not all God has for you. He has a place of mothering for you, a place of fruitfulness and fulfillment. He wants you to have a multitude of spiritual children in eternity.

When I began to surrender to this call on my life and started to mentor the women in our church, I made an amazing discovery. The very women whom I had been running from for 20 years, the ones I thought wanted to rob me of my last vestige of privacy, became my greatest allies. They became my friends. Now I know that these special ladies would die for me, and I would die for them. What an awesome realization!

Your mentoring of women will lead you down many exciting paths. Don't think it ends with leading the women's Bible study, as important as that is. God will stretch you further. You may be called to counsel women, to lead the women's choir, or to be a role model to the young women in your church. Like me, you may even be called to public speaking. I know what some of you are thinking: *Oh, no! God's not calling me to lead through preaching and public speaking!* I know exactly how you feel, because that's what I used to think. So fearful was I at the thought of public speaking that I couldn't even hold a microphone without feeling utter terror. But God had plans for me, and those plans included holding a microphone!

This is how it happened. One day my son was scheduled to give a talk to the women of our church. Shortly before the meeting, however, he called me and said, "Mom, I'm very ill. I'm not going to be able to preach tonight." Immediately I began wracking my brain for whom I could ask to take his place. I never once considered myself. Then, as I was trying to think of names of people to call, a message just came to me. I had never prepared a sermon, but suddenly a sermon simply dropped into my heart. I knew what that meant: The Holy Spirit had chosen a replacement speaker! An hour and a half later—after much spiritual kicking and screaming—I told my husband, "I believe I'll speak tonight."

And that's what I did. I really don't know what I said, but when I gave the altar call, I had one of the greatest experiences of my life. Women began to come to the altar to give their hearts to Jesus. At that moment, it occurred to me that I had never had this privilege before. With a grateful heart, I looked up to the Lord and said, "Jesus, I present these souls to You." What a thrill!

Immediately following that meeting, I announced that we were going to have a large evangelistic gathering for women and that I was going to do the speaking. I knew that I had to do this right away or I would never step into my rightful place of ministry. After I announced the gathering, however, fear began to grip me, and I prayed desperately, "Oh, God, do you need me somewhere next month? The mission field, maybe?" I wanted to be anywhere except at that meeting. I didn't know what I would speak on, and my fears grew daily.

Then one Sunday during worship time in the service, a vision came to me. I saw myself preaching an illustrated sermon. I saw the props. I saw the mayor's wife in the audience. I even heard myself give the invitation. The whole scene unfolded right in front of me. God in His goodness gave that vision to me, and that meeting was the easiest meeting I've ever led. All I had to do was follow what I had seen in the vision. I preached the sermon that I had been given, I used the props that I had seen, and the mayor's wife was indeed in the audience. It was a tremendous meeting, and once again, when I gave the altar call, the women streamed to the altar.

That night I learned a valuable lesson about success. I had been so pious that I had thought God wanted me to fail, that He needed me to fail so I would stay humble. Isn't that the stupidest theology you've ever heard? Probably some of you have held to that same theology. God, however, shattered that misconception when He spoke to me and said, "Melanie, if you never succeed, you never bring Me any glory; but when you succeed, you bring glory to Me."

A Final Thought

The thought of standing and ministering alongside of your husband may be farfetched to you. You may even laugh at the mere thought. But think back to the story of Abraham: Abraham laughed when God said he was going to have a child through Sarah (see Gen. 17:17) and Sarah also laughed when God told her she would have a child (see Gen. 18:12). In the end, however, God's Word came to pass, and Isaac (whose name means "laughter") was born (see Gen. 21:1-3).

In the same way, God wants to bring you to a place of life and fulfillment. He wants you in a place where all the contention and strife are gone from your home. He wants you one in ministry alongside your husband. But this can happen only when you embrace His call on your life, the call that you share with your pastor-husband, the call to minister and to have faith and to be the mother of many. When you finally answer that call and come alongside you husband, you will enter into the place of fruitfulness that God has planned for you.

Without a doubt, you are called. Your husband is a pastor, and you're called to be a pastor. You don't have to look and search for your calling and your place. You may have many functions in the church but you have one call: to pastor people and present them to Jesus whole and sanctified. That is your life's work.

The currency of the kingdom of God is faith. God will bring you to your place of calling if you surrender and step out in faith. It will happen no other way. An angel is not going to suddenly appear to lift you out of your comfort zone and set you on a platform of ministry and influence. The privilege of walking in your divine purpose will come when you finally say, "Okay, God, I don't know how I'm going do it, but I will obey your call." As you obey Him step by step, He will bring you into that place of fulfillment and fruitfulness, and you will become the mother of nations.

Blessing

Father, I thank You for all pastors' wives. I thank You that their hearts' desire is to obey You. I know they are searching for fulfillment and fruitfulness. I ask that Your Word bring light into their spirits, that they find their places beside their husbands and that they be fruitful and full of life. Lord, I thank You that You are going to accomplish this in their lives, just like You accomplished it in mine. Let their hearts be healed so that they can minister to others.
In Jesus' name, I pray. Amen.

$\mathcal{L}$IVING FOR A SUCCESSFUL FUTURE

ARLENE ALLEN

I guess the question that we should ask right up front is, *What is your definition of a successful future?* Does success have to do with the degrees that you have? Does success have to do with the kind of home you live in or the car you drive? Does success have to do with the size of church in which you minister?

What is your definition of success? Scripture tells us that each of us will stand before Christ one day and give an account on how we lived our lives here on Earth (see 1 Pet. 4:5-6). The account we give will have nothing to do with how many titles we had or how many possessions we were able to gain, but who we have become and how much we have allowed Jesus to make us into His image. Personally, when I hear my name called, I don't want to hear my Savior say, "Well, Arlene, I see you made it." More than anything, I desire to hear my Lord and Savior tell me, "Well done, My good and faithful servant."

Overcoming Limitations

I want to share with you a story of an eagle. An American Indian brave once found an eagle's egg and put it into the nest of a prairie chicken. The eaglet hatched with the chicks and grew up with them. All of his life, the eagle, thinking he was a prairie chicken, did what the prairie chickens did. He scratched in the dirt for seeds and insects to eat. He clucked and he cackled, and he flew no more than a few feet off of the ground. After all, that is what the chickens did. Years passed and the eagle grew old. One day, the eagle saw this splendid bird up in the sky that soared with scarcely a beat of its strong wings.

"What a beautiful bird," said the grounded eagle to his friend, the prairie chicken. "What is it?"

"That is an eagle," the prairie chicken clucked, "but don't give it a second thought—you could never be like him." So, the eagle never gave it another thought, and he died thinking he was a prairie chicken. What a shame—he had been born to soar, born to have a great future, but was grounded because of his self-imposed limitations.

So I ask you to understand that nothing is holding you back—except your own self-imposed limitations. I also want you to know that Satan knows every one of us. He knows the area he can put his finger on to make us feel unqualified. When I started doing retreats and speaking outside of my own church doors, I thought that I should first try to get rid of my Southern accent. So I signed up at a college, paid my $120 fee and attempted to lose the accent. Well, I failed the class and I didn't get my money back, but Satan knew that was an area in my life I felt I should be able to overcome. I think the reason I still have this accent is because God wanted to show me that He wanted me just the way I am.

Letting Go of the Past

So it is with every pastor's wife. God wants you just the way you are. He will then come alongside you and will bless your ministry. Second Corinthians 5:17 says, "If anyone is in Christ, he is a new creation; the old has gone, the new has come!" Don't base your future on the past. Don't base your future on bad things that happened in your past or people who have hurt you. If we hold on to the past hurts in our lives, we are going to be grounded by our own self-imposed limitations.

Letting Go of a Poor Attitude

All of my life, all of my ministry, I have been so privileged to have wonderful mentors and coaches who have helped me. Often, they didn't even know they were helping me. One such lady was Ann Wallace. Early in my ministry, I attended a pastors' wives conference where she shared this story:

Ann and her husband became saved after they were married, after they had two small children. Shortly after that, the Lord called Ken into full-time ministry. So they sold everything they had and bought a small travel trailer. They lived in that trailer for the next four years while Ken went to Bible college and she cared for their two little children.

Upon Ken's graduation, they got an invitation to pastor a small church in the middle of the cornfields of Illinois, and they felt so privileged to have that first chance, their first church. When they got there, they had no furniture, so they slept on mattresses on the floor. One morning after service, a lady approached Ann and said, "I have an extra sofa that I need to get rid of. Would you be able to use it?"

Ann said, "Oh, yes, I think I could." Ken brought home the sofa and put it in the living room—it was the only piece of furniture in the living room. So Ken sat down on one end of the couch, Ann sat down on the other end of the couch, and the two little ones sat in between.

At that moment, a mouse ran across the floor, followed by another. It didn't take long for them to figure out a nest of mice was living in their new sofa! So Ken just simply got up and said, "I am going to the hardware store." When he came back, he had four mousetraps—the old-fashioned kind. He took the traps out of the bag and then proceeded to paint one of their names on each of the traps. They made a game out of who could catch the most mice! They had such a good time that once the mice were all gone, the little girls cried, telling their Daddy, "Please get us some more."

Now, that is a good attitude! We need to learn early in our ministries that our attitude will control everything in our lives. The motto for many today has become "If at first you don't succeed, you are average—and that's OK." But we don't want to be average. That is not what God has called us to be.

Let's take a look at Matthew 28, where Jesus gives the Great Commission. He did not exempt anyone from that commission (see vv. 16-20).

He did not qualify the word "go" by excluding the extremely busy or the ill-prepared. This commission wasn't given just to pastors and evangelists—it was given to all of us. We are to go and tell the good news to others.

Making a Difference

We are born to soar. If you have given your heart to the Lord, I can tell you that by your new birth you are meant to soar and make a difference.

Discovering Your Gifts

Perhaps you struggle with feelings of inadequacy and think that the Lord hasn't gifted you to make a difference. Check out Romans 12 and 1 Corinthians 12. Paul tells us that each member of the Body of Christ is gifted for service and that it is up to each one of us to find that gift and get involved. If you don't know what your gift is, the local church is a safe place to step out of your comfort zone and try different ministries. Often when I speak about spiritual gifts someone will say, "When the Lord was handing out gifts, He passed over me." Not true—He did not. He has gifted every woman and every man. It is up to us to find what that gift is and to get busy using that gift for the kingdom of God.

As a national director of women's ministries, my heart is that every pastor's wife help every woman in her congregation understand that women's ministries is not about a monthly meeting. Women's ministries is about equipping every woman to understand that God wants to empower her and use her to make a difference in her family, in her neighborhood and in her church. Maybe He is going to give her a ministry that has never been thought of before, as she steps out and says, "Lord, I am scared to death, but I am going to step out of my comfort zone and take a chance. I am going to step out and become a woman You can use."

Using Your Gifts

Not long ago, the lights went off at my home, so I went to find our flashlight. I hadn't used it for over a year, so when I turned it on, it gave no light. I tried to get the batteries out, but they would not budge.

Finally, after some effort, they came loose. What a mess! Battery acid had corroded the entire inside of that flashlight. The batteries had been new when I put them in, and I had stored them in a safe warm place. But there was still one problem: Those batteries weren't made to rest in a warm, comfortable place; they were designed to be turned on, to be used.

The same can be said about every Christian. You and I were created not to be warm and safe and comfortable; we were made to be turned on, to put our love to work, to apply our patience in difficult, trying situations. We were made to let our light shine. We need to go back to children's church and learn what the song "This Little Light of Mine" means.

Soaring Into Your Successful Future

I hope that by now I've made my case that every pastor's wife does have an amazing role to play in life—and an amazing future awaiting her. So now let me share with you three facts that you need to know in order to understand what it means to soar into a successful future.

The need is more than you can imagine. Whether next door or across the world, the need of present-day humanity is overwhelming. God needs men and women to respond to the urgent needs around them. Who are the people and what are the situations in your life that are earnestly calling for your attention? What is holding you back from really getting involved? God needs women to be His hand extended. He needs women who purpose in their hearts to be women of purpose.

God is more than you imagine. Have you ever asked God, *Why did you allow this difficulty to come into my life?* only to get to the other side where you could see how you grew through that situation? He is all present, all powerful, all knowing. He is transcendent, He is eternal, He is unchangeable, He is perfect, He is holy, He is good, He is compassionate, He is patient and slow to anger, He is faithful, He is just, He is truthful. God is also all loving and is continually working on our behalf. This is the God we serve. God deserves that you understand what He can do through your life as you yield to Him. He told Moses, "I AM WHO I AM"

(Exod. 3:14), and that means whatever you need, that is what He will be to you. He is a personal God—He knows where you are. So resist the temptation to narrowly define Him with your limited understanding. He is greater than our minds can conceive. Psalm 145:3 says, "Great is the LORD and most worthy of praise; his greatness no one can fathom."

You can be more than you've ever imagined. I would like to encourage each of you to imagine just how God can use you. Early in my ministry, I was very comfortable in church in the children's department. That is where I excelled. But a couple of women in our church kept asking me to teach a Sunday School class for women. When I told them I was comfortable with the kids, the two women would walk away. But then the Holy Spirit began to speak to me: "If you taught that class, what would you teach on?" It began to be a what-if situation. I began to imagine what it could be like, and then that day came when I stepped out of my comfort zone. When you get out of your comfort zone, you are growing and maturing in the Lord.

If you are comfortable with what you are doing right now, I encourage you to *step out* of that comfort zone and get involved in something new. That is when you will grow. By stepping out of your comfort zone, you allow the Lord to stretch you and grow you. When we make the choice to be our best, to live our best and go for the best, we discover that the power of God is present to enable that noble choice to become a reality. But remember, your horizon will not expand until you start walking toward it. Otherwise, you will always see what is just in front of you. Philippians 3:13-14 tells us, "One thing I do: Forgetting what is behind and straining toward what is ahead, I press on toward the goal to win the prize for which God has called me heavenward in Christ Jesus." Look forward to a fuller, more meaningful life and future because of your hope in Christ.

A Final Thought

I ask you, *What is holding you back?* There shouldn't be anything, you know. God's love is sufficient to bring us salvation, to give us a future, to purify our hearts of anything that makes Him sad. "Search me, O

God, and know my heart; test me and know my thoughts. *Point out anything in me that offends you,* and lead me along the path of everlasting life" (Ps. 139:23-24, *NLT*, emphasis added). Now, I am a mother of two boys and there were times when they offended me and made me sad. If you are parents, you know what I'm talking about. During their teenage years, there were times that I did not even like them! But I never, ever stopped loving them, and I always would have been willing to give my life for either one of those boys.

So consider your heavenly Father: Are there times when you have offended Him and made Him sad? I think every one of us would have to say yes. We make Him sad when we fail to grow and mature. We make Him sad when we fail to talk to Him daily. We make Him sad when we need an attitude adjustment and we do nothing about it. We make Him sad when we don't read His Word. We make Him sad when we don't develop a servant's heart. We make Him sad when we don't use the gifts He has given us. We make Him sad when we allow Satan to ground us because of our own self-imposed limitations.

So how do we please God? By doing what is expected of us and embracing the future He has in store for us, beginning today. So let's grow and mature. Let's adjust that bad attitude. Let's live in His Word, finding its power as we hide His truth in our hearts. Let's learn that "service" doesn't mean "serve me." Let's take Jesus' example of servanthood and follow it. Let's work to discover our gifts—and then use them. Let's realize that with God, there are no limits, except those we devise. Let's realize that in a time of great need, we have an awesome God who has given us an unimaginably beautiful and successful future.

Blessing

Today, Lord, I thank You for the opportunity to share with pastors' wives. Lord, I pray that when any pastor's wife is tempted to be grounded because of her self-imposed limitations, she will remember the story of the eagle and she will step out knowing that You will empower her and that You will not ask her to do anything without first coming alongside her and equipping her to do her God-given task.

I pray also, Lord, that something I have written has stirred her heart to see that You want to use her today, not in the future, today. As she steps out today, You will give her a successful future. Thank You, God, thank You for every pastor's wife. I pray in Jesus' name. Amen.

LIBERATING A GOD-GIVEN CALL

LOIS I. EVANS

"He who began a good work in me is faithful to complete it. He is faithful to complete it in me and in you." I sang that song all my life, but it became real when I became a pastor's wife.

I grew up in a Christian home, and all I knew was ministry. But at the age of 15, I realized that I had a specific call for my life, so I walked down the aisle at a Christian camp and said *yes* to ministry for Jesus Christ. But my *yes* was not unconditional. I remember praying, "I surrender all, but please, Lord, I don't want to be a pastor's wife." I met Tony Evans shortly thereafter, and we started talking about ministry (God had just called him into the ministry as well). I remember standing under a starlit sky with a large moon one night, and Tony and I were talking about ministry, about what God had called us to do. I said, "I surrendered my all to the Lord, Tony—except being a pastor's wife." Then Tony told me, "I surrendered it all too, Lois—except I'm not going to be a pastor."

But in Tony's last year of seminary, he came home with this bright idea: God had called him to pastor. I said, "Tony, what about that moon and that starlit sky we saw that night? Remember we said no pastor, no pastor's wife?" Well, anyway, we soon started our church with 10 people in our home. Ten people. How was that possible? After your husband has gone to school for eight years after college, you expect him to find a real church, with some real folks and a thriving ministry! So I had to adjust to just 10 people in our church, and I struggled daily with the idea of being a pastor's wife. But one day my husband looked at me, and he said, "Lois, I know you are used to ministry and I know you are accustomed to it, but God probably is taking you outside of yourself so His supernatural power can show up in your life. He wants to do something in your life. And I just want you to be yourself." I said, "Are you sure the folks are ready for me to be myself?"

But we continued on our journey. And in my confusion I realized that God really wanted to use who He created me to be. The call that He had given to me at the age of 15 He was now exploding and expanding, and I really could be myself in an uncomfortable situation because He who began a good work in me was sufficient to keep me. I could bring all the familiar things I was comfortable with to the situation. This made me think of Jeremiah. He was busy doing what was normal for him. He was a part of the priesthood. He was born into a family of priests. And all he knew was what he was familiar with: taking care of the people in the Temple. He was accustomed to that, and he couldn't hear God calling him because he was so busy with taking care of the needs of the people. But God continued to call him, and call him, even in those difficult times in the history of Judah when there was constant rebellion, moral decay, total compromise and idolatry.

Answering Your Call

Does that sound like today? Think about the chaos and moral compromise of our times. Can you believe that we're dealing with legislation as it relates to whether Adam and Steve should be "married," rather than pursuing better legislation for Adam and Eve? You and I are ministering in a difficult and tough time. But God is telling us that He has a specific calling on our lives. He wants to take us higher in our ministry. We've been doing things a particular way—ways we've become accustomed to—but God wants to do something different in our lives.

Think about how God called Jeremiah: "Jeremiah, you have to understand, before I formed you in your mother's belly, I knew you, I set you apart, I sanctified you, I consecrated you, I selected you, I ordained you, I appointed you to be the spokesperson right now in the Kingdom" (see Jer. 1:5). Jeremiah should have known something was coming, because the meaning of his name is "the Lord throws." And the Lord threw Jeremiah into ministry for 40 years. You might feel thrown into ministry. But I want to tell you that the God who called you before you were even placed in your mother's womb is able to take care of you and to meet your needs. You're in God's calling, and God will take care of everything you need for the ministry He has called you to. God is sufficient to take care of the role you have, to ignite your role with His purpose.

Perhaps you feel like running from your call. Well, you wouldn't be the first. Jeremiah was conflicted when it came to his calling, just like some of us were. He said, "Lord, I can't. I know You might have put me in my mother's belly, but I can't speak. I can't" (see Jer. 1:6-8). Yes, he had plenty of excuses: I'm too young. I don't have the experience. I'm not equipped. I am an introvert, not an extrovert. Jeremiah was the weeping prophet—the brother could cry! He just cried and cried. By Jeremiah 9, he was totally depressed.

First Corinthians 1:27 says, "But God chose the foolish things of the world to shame the wise." If you have a God calling, God will equip you for what He is calling you to do. God doesn't always call the qualified, but He qualifies the call. Are you ready for Him to qualify you? Look in God's face to hear directly from Him. He wants to speak to your heart—to tell you where He wants to take you in ministry.

Again, I mention that you might have been doing ministry a particular way for a long time, but God probably wants you to soar to a different level in your ministry. Position yourself in His secret place. Jeremiah 1:8 tells us, "Be not afraid of them [their faces]" (*AMP*). The faces of the people will scare you to death. You and I would do well in ministry if it wasn't for people. But don't focus on their faces; focus on the face of the Lord. The heavenly Father of your life, and of this Church, has your direction for your life.

The Scripture goes on to say that if you are afraid of the faces of the people, you'll stand alone (see Jer. 1:17-19). Are you and I standing alone today in ministry because we're looking at the faces of the people? I'm here to tell you that there are some carnal people in our churches. I know we are teaching faithfully every week, but some folks need to grow up. You've got some folks in your church that still need to find Jesus Christ as their personal Savior. Don't let their faces determine where God wants to go in your God-given call. He's got a plan—He wants to work out His salvation in your life and in your ministry.

You need to get back to ministering within your call as a gifted woman, married to a pastor. Get back into your call. Jeremiah 1:18 says that He will give you His strength. Whose strength are you operating on? Is it God's strength? Whose ministry are you doing? Stop and take inventory. God wants to touch your heart. He wants to restore your marriage and your ministry. He wants to restore you so that you can clearly see your God-given call.

In Jeremiah 1:11, God asks Jeremiah what he sees. Jeremiah answers, "I see the branch of an almond tree." What that means is that God will hasten to perform His works and word. God was telling Jeremiah that He was going to perform His work and word through him. God was telling him that almond trees grow very quickly and produce fruit very quickly.

In Jeremiah 1:13, God again asks Jeremiah what he sees. Jeremiah replies, "I see a boiling pot." What does this mean to us? It means that you and I will have tribulation in this world. But we've got to be of good courage, because we are overcomers through the blood of the Lamb. In ministry you are going to have good times and bad times. What God is telling us through the story of Jeremiah is that His power is sufficient for us to withstand any trial (see vv. 17-19).

In Jeremiah 1:17, God tells Jeremiah he needs to be dressed. You have to be dressed for ministry. *THE MESSAGE* says, "But you—up on your feet and get dressed for work! Stand up and say your piece. Say exactly what I tell you to say. Don't pull your punches or I'll pull you out of the lineup." God is calling you to work—in His might and in His power. Ephesians 6 talks about being dressed for spiritual success so you can go to work to fulfill God's call in your life. You must have on the belt of truth and your breastplate. You must do what's right, not what's popular (see Eph. 6:14-15). So stop this preoccupation with what's popular and do what God has called you to do. Have on your shoes. Be ready to move when God calls you into action.

A Final Thought

Let's get on with what God has called us to do. Walk forward in faith, because He who began a good work in you is faithful to complete it (see Phil. 1:6). God has given you a call—a specific call on your life. Look in His face and get about the business of answering that call. How can you do that? By being free to soar, by flying ever higher in His power and in His strength and in His might.

Prayer

Dear Lord, please help me to keep my focus on Your face and Your voice. Do not allow me to be distracted by the noise of the world or the various opinions of church members. Let me remember that I serve You—and You alone. Help me to move forward in faith. Strengthen me and empower me to do the work that You have called me to do. I thank You, Lord, that You have heard my prayer. Amen.

SUPERNATURAL COMMISSION

DIANA HAGEE

As pastors' wives, we acknowledge that we have been called to fulfill the Great Commission (see Matt. 28:16-20). Well, what happens to the Great Commission when we are out of commission? If you're like me, you feel out of commission much of the time. You know how things are after your honeymoon with the Lord and the ministry is over and reality sets in. Reality has its ups and downs, and we must learn to cope with them.

Being the Pastor's Wife

When I married my husband, John Hagee, I had no idea what the responsibilities of a pastor's wife were. The only woman in the ministry whom I could relate to due to my Catholic background was a nun. Then I met the "church ladies." The conversation I had with them was rather one-sided and went something like this:

> Oh, you're the pastor's wife! Oh, you must sing? No? Oh, then you play the piano? No? Oh, then you play the organ—you must be a gifted organist. No? Oh, then you must have a dynamic teaching ministry. Oh, no, really? Um . . . well, we're sure you'll work out just fine.

After that not-so-great beginning, I told my husband that I had the perfect solution. I would go to another church, get training in the ministry and return as the perfect pastor's wife—I was sure I would not be missed.

This is how I began my career as a pastor's wife. It was not much fun, but I had a husband who loved me for who I was and who knew my destiny in Christ. He wanted me to love him, establish our home, have his babies and raise them in the fear and the admonition of the Lord Jesus Christ. He knew who I was in Christ long before I did.

Struggling with Low Self-Esteem

I have always had a problem with low self-esteem. I saw myself as ugly, inadequate and unworthy. One Sunday, my husband was doing a teaching on the righteousness of the Lord Jesus Christ. I mentally shut the door on his teaching—righteousness was not for me. I was not worthy to go to the altar, and therefore I was not worthy of any form of righteousness—it was something I could not achieve. At that same moment, my husband could sense that most of our church was not receiving the fullness of righteousness and the beauty of its message. Determined to convey the importance of God's gift to His people, he shared an amazing illustration that I would like to borrow to counter any feelings of inadequacy that you may also be feeling.

Picture yourself at the cross of Christ. You come with all your sin and bring your dark past, impure thoughts and evil deeds. The Lord Jesus Christ then meets you at the cross, forgives you and redeems you. He takes off His beautiful, white, spotless robe and puts it over your shoulders. The robe that He earned. All of your sin is covered with Christ's robe of righteousness. The robe that was His is now yours.

When you go to the Cross after your salvation, Satan goes with you and reminds you of all the sinful deeds that you committed—sins that have brought the Lord pain and shame. He tells you that you are not worthy to receive favor from the Father. But when you arrive at the Cross, our Father says, "All I see is the white robe of My Son; I see nothing else. All sin is hidden under His righteousness."

What a beautiful illustration! When my husband finished teaching, I knew that I had the righteousness of the living God. So do you, not because of what you or I have done, but because of the Great Exchange Christ made at the Cross—His righteousness for our sins.

Putting to Rest That Sense of Unworthiness

During my journey, I came to realize that I was worthy. When I read the *Prayer of Jabez*, I was inspired by the story of a man's tour of heaven. The man came upon a room that was filled with beautifully wrapped presents. The room had the man's name on the door. As he admired the gifts, the man asked, "Who do these gifts belong to?" The angel told him that they were his. These gifts were prepared by the Lord for him—but because the man never felt worthy, he had never received them.[1]

This illustration really hit home for me. I thought about my five beautiful children whom I love to buy special gifts for. What if I were to choose a lovely gift for each of my children, wrap those gifts in exquisite paper and silk ribbon, and then present the gifts to them—but only to have them refuse to open those gifts, telling me, "No, mom I don't deserve them—you should give these gifts to someone else." Oh, I would be crushed; and it dawned on me that I had crushed the heart of the Lord Jesus Christ every time He had attempted to present a gift to me in order to bless me. I had said, "No, I am not worthy." In that moment, I determined that when I went to heaven, my room would be filled with empty boxes and beautiful ribbon on the floor.

I am determined to open every gift that the Lord Jesus Christ has for me, and so should you. Remember this truth: Jesus wants to bless you with amazing gifts. Through His free gift of salvation, you are worthy to receive every one of those gifts. So don't delay—start your opening gift boxes today!

Discovering Your Gift

When it came to discovering my gift, I knew I had one—I just didn't know what it was. I knew that God wouldn't call me to ministry and then not equip me to fulfill my mission; however, I knew that gift wasn't in music, in singing or in teaching. I searched but couldn't find my gift.

Gradually, I began to realize that my gift was hospitality. I didn't recognize it as a gift because it came so easy for me. I am Hispanic and hospitality surrounds our culture. But dear sisters, when it comes easily, guess what it is? Your gift! It took me a while to figure that out.

Once I realized that my gift was also something that I could enjoy, I began to use it often, and I loved it. Soon, I was content in my comfort zone.

But what happens when we're in our comfort zone? That's right—God decides we're ready for something new, so out of the zone we go! My husband came to me one day and said, "Diana, I want you to help me with the women's ministries. Our church is growing and we need strong leadership for women." I said, "Great, I'll pray about it and see who you should choose to lead them." And then he told me what I didn't want to hear—the leader would be me. I protested, telling him that I'd only recently been saved. To this he replied, "You're 38 years old—you were saved when you were 19! That is half your life!"

So I went to the Word of God. I opened it and began to weep because I was so overwhelmed. The Word of God, written by the living Savior, transforms lives, brings salvation to the lost, gives healing to the sick, restores those who are brokenhearted and delivers those who are in bondage. This was the powerful Word that I was supposed to teach. I was so intimidated, yet I plunged deeper into the Word of God, studying His truth, preparing for the next step in my journey with the Lord.

I am no longer intimidated by the Word of God—it has become an inseparable friend. It accepts me for who I am and who I will become.

Learning to Let His Light Shine Through Our Brokenness

I have a dear friend, Patsy Claremont, who shared the story of a vision she had in her teaching "God Uses Cracked Pots."

> I had a vision in which there were two pots. One pot was beautiful and flawless. The Light of the Lord was in the pot. But suddenly a hand covered the mouth of the pot and the Lord asked, "Patsy, where do you see My light shining from." I said, "From nowhere." Then He showed her another pot—it was ugly and full of cracks, He put His light in it and His hand covered the opening. He asked, "Where do you see My light shining from now?" I replied, "I see it shining from the broken places."[2]

We all have broken places in our lives. Maybe it's abortion, maybe it's divorce, maybe it's sexual abuse. You need to allow the light of the Lord Jesus Christ into your life so that when His light is seen shining from the broken places of your past, people will come from far and near just to watch you burn with the Shekineh glory of the living God. So don't be ashamed of your broken places. You'll never be effective in fulfilling the Great Commission until you are real—until you are willing to show your true self to the world.

Proclaiming the Favor of God

I want to close with a little encouragement, so keep these words close to your heart on days when you are feeling a little out of commission!

You are the best teachers that the sheep who have been put under your guidance will ever have, and in turn, you have the best teacher in the person of the Lord Jesus Christ. Nothing is impossible to you. You are the King's daughters. You have the favor of the King. You have a great inheritance. You need to claim your inheritance. You need to know that you have a destiny in Christ. You will accomplish the Great Commission and make a difference in the lives of the people our Lord has put before you as soon as you recognize who you are and what your destiny is in the living God. Proclaim the Word over yourself in this proclamation:

> In the name of Jesus, I am the righteousness of God; therefore, I am entitled to covenant kindness and favor. His favor surrounds the righteous; therefore, it surrounds me. Everywhere I go I will expect the favor of God to be in manifestation. Never again will I be without the favor of God.
>
> Satan, my days in the lode bar cease today. I am leaving that place of lack and want. I am going from the pit to the palace because the favor of God is on me. It profusely abounds in me and I will experience the favor of God, immeasurable, limitless and unsurpassing. The favor of God goes before me and my life will never be the same. Amen.

Prayer

Dear Lord, I ask Your special blessing on the pastor's wife.
She loves You, Lord, and she is seeking to do Your will in her life.
Help her to claim her inheritance in Christ Jesus. Help her to see that
the Great Commission is also her commission. You have called her to
fulfill a unique role in the Kingdom. Strengthen her and empower
her that she might step out in faith and fulfill her destiny.
Grant her a double portion of Your blessing and favor, Lord.
I ask this in the name of Jesus, amen.

Notes

1. Bruce Wilkinson, *The Prayer of Jabez* (Sisters, OR: Multnomah Publishers, 2000), p. 25.
2. Patsy Claremont, teaching based on *God Uses Cracked Pots* (Colorado Springs, CO: Focus on the Family Publishing, 1999).

LIBERATING A GOD-GIFTED CONDUCT

SERITA JAKES

Even though you and I, dear reader, are probably from different backgrounds and have different denominational affiliations, I want you to understand that I know exactly how you feel. That may seem odd because you see my husband and I where we are today: overseeing some 30,000 church members locally. But don't forget how we started on the back side of the mountain.

In order to appreciate the glory that God has bestowed upon our lives, you need to understand that I was born a coal miner's daughter in a very rural part of West Virginia—a very small town located across the creek, around the corner and down the road from the coal mine. Because of where I came from, I was able to walk the steps that God had ordered for my husband and me. Not because I thought I was so much, but because God called me from the back side of the mountain and because He knew that transparency is so essential in ministry. So my message may not be grand or wonderful, but it will be from the heart.

Giving Your Best

I'm sure you're all familiar with the story of the little elderly lady who gave her last two pennies to the Temple collection (see Mark 12:41-44). It was remarkable because all around her people were giving much more—they had lots to give, but all she had was two coins. I don't know about you, but have you ever felt like you've given all that you have but everyone around you seems to be able to celebrate because they have so much more to give than you? Jesus looked over at the little lady and said, "This poor widow has put more into the treasury than all the others. . . . She, out of her poverty, put in everything—all she had" (vv. 43-44).

Don't you sometimes feel that you have given everything you have to your ministry, and you wonder, *When are they going to acknowledge that I've done the best I can?* Some of you, like me, started ushering in your church. I was the first president of the usher board. Then I was the praise team leader, and I also taught the juniors in Sunday school. But somehow it never seemed to be enough for some people, and I had given all I had. But I thank God, because one day He said, "Don't even worry about it, Serita; I know that you've given the best that you had."

I'm afraid I haven't always lived in that moment. Sometimes the saints got on my nerves, and I wouldn't want to teach Sunday school, and I didn't want to hear them testify, and I didn't want the choir to sing. I wanted to take my kids and go home. (Now if that's not your testimony, live on.) Some years later, every now and then, I still have those moments when I just want to go home. But then I look around and I see how so many people depend on me, how I'm right where God has called me to be.

Acknowledging the Gift

All of you ladies reading this book, God has given you a gift. He's given you a mandate to grab hold of and use to minister to His people. He has called you—fully aware of who you are and what is on the inside of you. As pastors' wives, we have the tendency to apologize for our inadequacies and what we can't do: "I can't sing and I don't have the finest apparel and I don't play the piano." But God is telling you through this little ol' coal miner's daughter that you have a gift—and that you, yourself, are a gift. Realize that He who has begun a good work in you is faithful to carry it through to completion (see Phil. 1:6). Trust Him.

A Final Thought

Some of you have been caught up in some messy situations in your lives and in your ministry; but God said that only someone who doesn't need the forgiving power of the Savior can throw the first stone (see John 8:7). We need to stop judging ourselves and each other. We're in this thing together. We're here to build each other up for the good of the Kingdom.

Let me encourage you, if you are still in the desert, weeping endures for a night—but joy comes in the morning (see Ps. 30:5). And know that the dawn is coming. Keep your head up. God is in control!

Blessing

Dear Lord, I pray that You would abundantly bless the pastor's wife who is seeking Your tender embrace. Let her feel Your love for her, Lord. Let her know that she is important to You and that the role she plays is important to You and essential to the Kingdom. Inspire her to give her best, even in the tough times. Let her be filled with comfort, knowing the desert times don't last forever, knowing that even the difficult times are part of Your plan. I pray this in Jesus' name, amen.

FINDING THE LOST

CHERYL A. RECCORD

I wonder if we as Christians realize there are people all around us desperately hoping that we're going to come and rescue them. Sometimes they may not even be aware that they need rescuing, and we might not even recognize who they are.

But they're waiting to be rescued. Think about what these people are *really* saying:

- Svetlana: "This country isn't my home. My job is okay. But American cities are hard places. I walk down the street and look for a kind face. I try to meet people. I'm so lonely."

- Margaret: "Ted always said we would spend our retirement together, but he gave everything to his job. Then his heart just gave out. The kids never come to visit, and there aren't any grandbabies. I feel deserted. Are these my golden years?"

- Bethany: "I always did what my parents told me to do. I studied hard. Now I make plenty of money. I have a fine house and a great car. My kids go to private school. I don't need anything. Why am I not happy?!"

You Are Called to Share Jesus with the World

Svetlana, Margaret and Bethany have different complaints but the same need: They need Jesus Christ. All three, without knowing it, are waiting for you to tell them about the new life you've found in Him.

If we're going to follow the mandate that Jesus gave us (see Matt. 28:16-20), we're going to have to cast off false notions, such as "I'm not gifted for evangelism" or "I can't equip others to spread the gospel." Remember, ladies, Jesus would not have called us to share Him with the world without equipping us to do it.

Begin with Prayer

If we love Jesus and want to be like Him, then we must look at His mission statement: "The Son of Man came to seek and to save what was lost" (Luke 19:10). If we aren't fishing, then we probably aren't fully following Him. We need to get busy doing what God called us to do.

How are we going to do it? Colossians 4:3-6 reminds us to begin with prayer: "Pray for us, too, that God may open a door for our message, so that we may proclaim the mystery of Christ, for which I am in chains. Pray that I may proclaim it clearly, as I should. Be wise in the way you act toward outsiders; make the most of every opportunity. Let your conversation be always full of grace, seasoned with salt, so that you will know how to answer everyone."

We must pray for three things. First, pray for opportunities that happen naturally. We can't force the gospel message on people! Second, we need to pray that we proclaim the gospel clearly. The lingo in our culture changes all the time. We need to keep up with those changes so that we can communicate effectively. Third, we need to pray that we will live wisely and have a heart that truly cares about people. We want our lives to reflect Jesus Christ and His love.

Tell His Story

When we witness to others, we can do it with God-ordained confidence. Romans 1:16 reminds us, "I am not ashamed of the gospel, because it is the power of God for the salvation for everyone who believes: first for the Jew, then for the Gentile." We simply boldly proclaim Christ in the power of the Spirit and leave the results to God.

Keep It Biblical

We need to make sure that we're sharing a biblical message. We are reminded in Scripture that "salvation is found in no one else, for there is no other name under heaven given to men by which we must be saved" (Acts 4:12). Jesus, Himself, told us, "Whoever believes in the Son has eternal life, but whoever rejects the Son will not see life" (John 3:36). The message you've been given to deliver is not about Christianity being the one true religion; it's about having a *relationship* with Jesus, the One who saves us from the death penalty of our sins. So let's be sure that we're sharing the authentic gospel.

Have a Purpose

We need to be intentional. I'm sure that every woman reading this would say she wants to know every good thing that Jesus has in store for her. Well, Philemon 6 is your verse: "I pray that you may be active in sharing your faith, so that you will have a full understanding of every good thing we have in Christ." The meaning is clear: God's purpose for you and others is worked out when you reach out with His Word.

A Final Thought

At a recent convention in Interlocken, Switzerland, on a sunny, clear day, my husband and I were awed by the paragliders winging their way into the park. I went from awe to amazement when my husband, Bob, looked at me and said, "I think I want to do that at the end of the week. And I think you need to do it with me." It took me a while, but I got up the nerve to experience this grand adventure with him. Frankly, I did it mostly because I wanted my kids to be impressed with me!

Later in the week, as we made our way up the mountain, I began to chicken out. At the top, I heard the instructor say, "This is what we need to do. You're going to run in tandem with me, and then we'll run straight off the mountain." Then he told me, "Just sit back, relax and enjoy the ride." And what an awesome ride it was!

You know what, ladies? That's what our Lord Jesus Christ is calling us to do: "Run in tandem with Me. Join Me in My priorities. Get ready to fly off the mountain. Then just relax and enjoy the ride!"

Prayer

Lord, please help me to be aware of those around me who are in need of rescuing, who are in need of Your love. Let me be Your loving embrace to those who are sad or lonely. Let me bring Your life-giving Word to those who are lost. With Your Holy Spirit working through me, I will answer Your call to bring the good news to the world. I thank You for the gift of salvation, Lord. I love You. Amen.

PART TWO

FREE TO SOAR
THROUGH ENCOURAGING
PERSONAL GROWTH

$\mathcal{L}$EARNING PRACTICAL PRINCIPLES OF GROWTH

ANNA HAYFORD

As we consider ways that we can grow in our Christian walk, we often forget to return to the basics. We all need to start with first things; we need to begin every day of our Christian life with the basics. And what are those? Prayer and Bible study. But what do we do with that firm foundation? How do we live out our Christian walk in practical terms?

Finding the Lord in the Mundane

I used to spend my days cooking, cleaning, ironing, vacuuming and taking care of the children. But I didn't see those tasks as without merit. I realized that I didn't need to use my brain to get the chores done, so I would usually pray during that time and just fellowship with the Lord. I would sing praises while I was vacuuming and ironing; I would be present with the Lord in my heart while my body was busy with a million and one other things.

When I reflect on what our practical responsibilities are, I am always encouraged by the words of Vonette Bright. She said, "God values a wife's ministry of everyday responsibilities as much as He values that of a pastor's ministry." We often berate ourselves and say that we're not all that important; we're not doing that great. You know what we say: "I just make the bed every day. I just cook for my family and do the dishes every day. I change diapers—I do all those things." Thankfully, I no longer have the diaper situation! At any rate, a lot of the things we do are mundane kinds of things. Yet they are tasks that need to be taken care of—and it's our responsibility to see that they get done.

Oneness: Called to Ministry

Matthew 19:5 says, "The two will become one flesh." Many people have questioned what I do in ministry because I'm not a front person; I'm not a speaker per se, I don't teach a Sunday school class, and I definitely don't play the piano. But let me explain to you what I *do* do.

One summer, when my husband, Jack, was speaking at a summer camp, I got a word from the Lord through another gentleman who was speaking at the camp—his name was Brian. After Brian prayed over me, he told me that the Lord had a word for me: Jack was to be my ministry. And what a good call that was on God's part, because Jack is an amazing man of God—but he needs me! He's kind of helpless without me. If I'm out of town, he doesn't cook—he takes our daughters and the grandkids out to eat. He doesn't remember to do the thousand and one things that keep a household running. That's just not his style. You see, Jack is an extremely spontaneous person. I, on the other hand, was raised in the Midwest. (When I was growing up, our schedule was to rise at 7:00 in the morning, do our chores, get dressed, get ready, go to school, come home, do our chores, do our homework, have dinner, go to bed. At 10 o'clock we were in bed.) So I marry a man who is extremely spontaneous, and I never know what's going to happen on any given day. But God is so wise to have made one flesh out of the spontaneous man and the practical woman—by bringing us together, by calling us together, by causing our home and ministry to thrive.

Sharing in the Qualifications

In 1 Timothy and in Titus, we see the qualifications of a bishop, or pastor (see 1 Tim. 3:1-13; Titus 1:5-9). Because we are one flesh with our husbands, those qualifications rest upon us, too, in our daily life.

ANNA HAYFORD

59

Blameless

One of the qualifications for pastors is to be blameless (see 1 Tim. 3:2). That doesn't mean we're perfect; it just means we're growing. And as long as we continue to seek the Lord first, then we will continue to grow and the Lord will make that provision in our lives for us.

Monogamous

I'm very happy about this qualification because it says that a pastor should be the husband of one wife (see 1 Tim. 3:12). I think that's a very good arrangement; however, I thought if that other wife could be the one who did all the vacuuming and that kind of stuff, it might be kind of nice for me to have a helper!

Not a Lover of Money

It says that we're not supposed to be lovers of money (see 1 Tim. 3:3). I don't think many of us have to worry about that; however, I want to give you a little illustration from when Jack and I were young in ministry. We had five dollars a week to spend on food—we got a bit more once the first two kids came along. I was praying one day because we were at the point where we had to watch every penny. I said, "Lord, why is it that we have given You our lives; we've given You everything we have; we're serving You; we live for You; and we pay tithes and give our offerings; and still we have to watch every penny? I mean, there are people in the world who seemingly have all the money they want—they don't have to worry about a thing financially." At about that point I felt the Lord whisper to my heart, "They don't get to trust Me either." And I thought, *Oh, Lord, that is really a privilege—thank You, thank You, thank You.* With that word I knew God was going to make every provision for us!

Have Faithful Children

The next qualification is that the pastor has faithful children (see Titus 1:6). I think this is one of our biggest practical duties: to raise our children to be faithful to the Lord, to be secure in themselves, to not resent the ministry but to grow up loving Jesus with all their heart. The Lord, in this case, helps us as pastors' wives to grow in grace, trust, faith and wisdom. We learn to trust in Him—to trust Him with our children. He's more concerned about their well-being than we are. He loves them more than we do, and He knows the plans He has for their lives.

Hospitable

Scripture goes on to say that pastors must practice hospitality (see Titus 1:8). Speaking of my own life, I have had no choice in this area because my husband is extremely hospitable. I mean, I never knew how many we were going to have for dinner. He would call me up five minutes before he got home and say, "So-and-so is coming home for dinner with me"; and so another potato would go in the pot and we would be ready when the guests arrived.

I want to urge you to entertain in your homes. There is no greater blessing than to welcome people into your home, to invite them to share in your life, if only for a short while. So many times pastors' wives think they have to have china, silver and crystal before they can entertain. But people who come to your home don't expect that. They want to come and enjoy fellowship with you. They want to come and just enjoy the warmth of your home. It is important for people to know you in your own natural habitat. And so it is extremely important that we give ourselves to hospitality.

Self-Controlled

The next qualification is that pastors be self-controlled (see Titus 1:8), and that's where the kids come in again. I don't know about you, but my kids have not always been perfect. Yes, mine are very good children. But they're not perfect children; they haven't reached perfection any more than I've reached perfection. So we have to have a great deal of self-control in dealing with our kids and addressing their failures and rebellion with honesty and compassion.

Transparent

Scripture tells us that pastors should have a good reputation (see 1 Tim. 3:5). What's the best way to protect a good reputation? Through transparency that requires accountability. Jack and I have always been extremely transparent with our congregation; sometimes that has been a great embarrassment to me because he's not afraid to tell them if we have had an argument on the way to church. And he will say, "Isn't it just like the devil to cause some kind of friction on the way to church?" And it's not just our arguments that he shares. I mean, he and I have taught seminars on sexuality; and, well, let's just say there were moments when I wanted to crawl under my seat. I thought, *Nobody knows we ever do those things; why is he sharing them?* But he has always been very transparent, not only about our relationship but also about how God deals with him. And so I have come to learn that the more you grow in the Lord, the smaller the things that are being corrected in you. As a result, you need to respond to those very small things all the more.

It's not just for our sake that we are transparent with our congregation. When you are transparent in the presence of the church, your members can say, "What a comfort! If they have to face those things and come out victorious, so can I." So it's important that we open ourselves up and let our congregation know us. They can see us for who we are: real people with real flaws who are allowing real faith to transform our lives.

Faithful to the Word and Able to Teach

It should come as no surprise that pastors are also called to teach (see Titus 1:9). When we consider how this qualification applies to us, we should remember that it doesn't mean that we're teaching a Bible study all the time. It means that we live before our congregation as a teacher because they watch everything we say and do. I always make the extra effort and go the extra mile for the sake of the congregation.

Teaching also plays a huge part in raising your children to be faithful. When our children were small, we taught them some of the rules of our household. One of the rules was that as soon as they heard us call, they were to respond right away. We were teaching them not only to respond to us but also to respond to the Lord when He spoke to them. We also taught them, "We are Hayfords, and so we don't do that." We never taught our children, "We are Christians, and so we don't do that." We felt that it would make them resent the Church and

Christians if they thought that rules stemmed from Christ and His Church. But by approaching our discipline the way we did, our children saw that if our rules stemmed from our being Hayfords, there was no way out. I mean, they couldn't stop being Hayfords, could they?

Obedient

And of course, pastors and their wives are called to be obedient to the Lord (see Titus 1:16). Learning to obey is an ongoing struggle. Not very long ago, I learned a very important lesson regarding obedience.

I don't know if any of you feel the way I do, but I feel that if we sing a song three times, that's enough. And so if the song leader kept singing after three go-rounds, I would stop singing and just wait for the choir to get done. One day I did that and the Lord said, "You know, you are quenching the Spirit in the whole congregation because you're not being obedient to what the leader is telling you to do." So there I was, wanting to crawl under my seat again! Seriously, even though that was a small thing, it was an important thing, too. We need to learn to be obedient in all things. The Lord will constantly guide us if we will listen to His voice.

A Final Thought

I want to tell you a story of one of our trips in Israel. The year was about 1981. We had moved into a new house in November and had hosted the big family Thanksgiving dinner at our house. Then I had decorated the house for the tour of homes, which we put on through our women's ministries. Jack was busy with new duties at work, as he had just become president of our college. It was just overwhelming to have so much going on. And if all that weren't enough, we left for Israel on December 28. During the trip, I would often just sit on the bus and not get off to see the sights—I was just too tired.

There was one sight that I did see—a little beach on the Sea of Galilee. I'm sure you remember the story of the disciples' unsuccessful fishing trip there, when Jesus caught and cooked plenty of fish for them (see Luke 5). But this time Jesus was in the boat and I was on the shore. He called to me and said, "Do you have any bread?" I replied, "No. I don't have any bread at all." He responded, "I have lots of bread. I have enough bread for you to satisfy yourself, and I have enough bread for you to share with others." What an amazing consolation!

My dear pastors' wives, Jesus has all the bread you need to meet all of your practical and spiritual needs and to help you through your ministry challenges. Jesus has enough bread not only for you but for all those with whom He wants you to share it.

Blessing

Heavenly Father, I just ask You to bless the dear women who are reading this book—women who are seeking freedom to soar. I pray that You would meet their needs and enable them to meet the needs of their spouses. Lord, give these dear women a sense of purpose. Show them the vital role they play in their families and in the Church. Be near these pastors' wives, dear Lord. Hear their hearts; answer their prayers. I ask these blessings in the precious name of Jesus, amen.

ℒIVING WITHIN A SCRIPTURAL FRAMEWORK

KAY ARTHUR

Beloved, God created you to soar, and He has predetermined the place, the plan, the purpose and the power for you to soar. If you want to soar, you must pursue a biblical mind-set and live within the framework of God's Word. Why? Because outside of the framework of Scripture, we don't soar—we thud. The framework of Scripture is defined by God's character—by who He is. When you plumb the depths of the Word of God, you interact with the mind of God, see the character of God, glean the wisdom of God and understand the grace of God. In other words, you get to know God. And God tells us through Daniel that "the people who know their God will display strength and take action" (Dan. 11:32b, *NASB*).

God Is Sovereign

The first truth you must know about God—the cornerstone of all knowledge and the very foundation of the universe—is that God is sovereign. God is God. Read Isaiah 45:5. God says, "I am the LORD, and there is no other; besides Me there is no God" (*NASB*). And, Beloved, if He is God, that means you are not. Whenever I forget that God is sovereign, I have big problems. I find myself thinking that I can help God do things, help Him achieve things. But God is God. He doesn't need my help. I am not His helper; I am His servant. Read on through verse 7. This is hard for us to accept, but here it is. God says that He is the "One forming light and creating darkness, causing well-being and creating calamity" (Isa. 45:7, *NASB*). Through Isaiah, God tells Israel about the disaster that is going to come upon them and that not only is He aware of it, but He is also in charge of it all. Yet, in God's sovereignty, calamity is never without hope, because everything He determines through His sovereignty He carries out against the backdrop of His love.

God's love and sovereignty go hand in hand. God holds you in His hand, and everything that comes into your life—everything, even the good, the bad and the ugly—is filtered through His fingers of love. No one can say a *word* to you and no one can do a *thing* to you without God's permission, because God is God and there is no other. David, the man after God's own heart expressed it beautifully, "The lovingkindness of the LORD is from everlasting to everlasting . . . and His sovereignty rules over all" (Ps. 103:17a,19b, *NASB*). So whatever comes into your life is part of His purpose for your life.

God's Will, Your Worth

Now, because God is sovereign, there are no accidents. You are not an accident. You exist because God, the Sovereign Ruler of the universe, the Alpha and the Omega, the Beginning and the End, ordained your existence and numbered your days before you were born. The notion that you are an accident or that you are worthless is a lie. You are on the face of this earth by the will and plan of God. The throne room of Heaven reverberates with this truth to the praise of Almighty God: "Worthy are You, our Lord and our God, to receive glory and honor and power; for You created all things, and because of Your will they existed, and were created" (Rev. 4:11, *NASB*). Because God is sovereign, and you exist by His will, your life has a purpose.

A Purpose

Beloved, you were created for a purpose, and not just any purpose, but a glorious purpose. Turn to Ephesians 1:3: "Blessed be the God and Father of our Lord Jesus Christ, who has blessed us with every spiritual blessing in the heavenly places in Christ" (*NASB*). You are the recipient of His blessing, and not just a few blessings, but *every* blessing. As you read on through the chapter, the blessings unfold. Keep reading through verse 6: "Just as He chose us in Him before the foundation of the world, that we would be holy and blameless before Him. In love He predestined us to adoption as sons through Jesus Christ to Himself, according to the kind intention of His will, to the praise of the glory of His grace" (Eph. 1:4-6, *NASB*).

I want you to know how precious you are in His sight. I want you to apprehend the depth of God's love and the magnitude of His purpose for you. Before He spoke light into the universe, He looked out from eternity past, across all time, and set His heart on you. Before He formed you in your mother's womb, He loved you and chose you. At the right time, He sent His Son to redeem you and adopt you as His very own daughter. It is God's timeless plan that in Christ you would be holy and blameless. It is His eternal purpose that as His child your life would be a living demonstration of His glorious grace. Your life has an eternal purpose. Right now that purpose is showcased in your marriage as you strive to be the best wife that you can be, to be your husband's companion and friend, his counterpart and complement, his partner in the task that God has given him to shepherd His flock.

Salvation

Did you ever ask, *If my life has a purpose, why did God take so long to get me there*? I used to weep about my past and ask God, "Where were You when I was a teenager? Why didn't You save me sooner? Why did I have to go through all of this?" Then, God took me to Paul's words in Galatians 1:15-16a, "But when God, who had set me apart even from my mother's womb and called me through His grace, was pleased to reveal His Son in me so that I might preach Him among the Gentiles" (*NASB*), and He showed me that He saved me when it pleased Him to save me, not when I was pleased to be saved. He said to me, "If you will quit crying about your past and quit moaning about where you've been, I will take all of that and use it for My glory." Salvation is of the

Lord and comes to us on His timetable. If God is God, and He created you by His will, and your life has a purpose, then He saves you when He is pleased to reveal His Son in you.

Sealed with the Spirit

When God saved you, He also sealed you with the Holy Spirit. Ephesians 1:13-14a says, "In Him, you also, after listening to the message of truth, the gospel of your salvation—having also believed, you were sealed in Him with the Holy Spirit of promise, who is given as a pledge of our inheritance" (*NASB*). God sealed you with the Holy Spirit as the seal of His ownership and the pledge, or down payment, of your inheritance. He is in you. He will never leave you. He will never forsake you. So, no matter what comes your way, you have been filled with power from on high. You soar, not by might, not by power, but by His Spirit.

Redeemed from Our Past

It is impossible to soar if you are chained to your past. So I want you to know that God, your Redeemer, has redeemed you from your past. Read 2 Corinthians 5:14-17.

> For the love of Christ controls us, having concluded this, that one died for all, therefore all died; and He died for all, so that they who live might no longer live for themselves, but for Him who died and rose again on their behalf. Therefore from now on we recognize no one according to the flesh; even though we have known Christ according to the flesh, yet now we know Him in this way no longer. Therefore if anyone is in Christ, he is a new creature; the old things passed away; behold, new things have come (*NASB*).

You have been redeemed from your past. How? You died. You were crucified with Christ and you are a new creation, walking by faith, empowered by grace and controlled by the love of Christ. In this new life it is the love of Christ that controls us and keeps us pure regardless of our past. Now you might be thinking, *I know God sees me as a new creation, but what about others who know about my past?* Thinking biblically means seeing each other as God sees us. According to 2 Corinthians 5:16, no child of God is appraised through the prism of her past but through the lens of Christ's love. Beloved, when your past comes roaring back to taunt you, put it away. Live by the Word of God and keep soaring.

Nothing Wasted

Because He is your Redeemer and because your life has a purpose, Romans 8:28-30 says, "We know [with absolute certainty] that God causes [keeps on causing] all things to work together for good to those who love God, to those who are called according to His purpose" (*NASB*). He does not say all things will be good. But because He is God, because He is the Redeemer, because He has a purpose for your life, He takes all the pain and suffering, all the trials and betrayals, all the problems and failures, and He—the Sovereign Ruler of the Universe—causes them to work together for good. In verse 29, we discover what "good" He is talking about, "For those whom He foreknew, He also predestined to become conformed to the image of His Son" (Rom. 8:29, *NASB*). When did He foreknow you? Before the creation of the world. Before He wove you in your mother's womb, He foreknew you and predestined you to become conformed to His image. That's what His purpose is for your life, to become conformed to the image of His Son; and He will never stop working in your life until He completes the work He has begun in you (see Phil. 1:6). We soar on the knowledge that everything that comes into our life, whether it seems to us good or bad, is for our good and His glory.

Uniquely Gifted

Because God has created you and redeemed you and called you according to His purpose, He has uniquely gifted you. "We are His workmanship, created in Christ Jesus for good works, which God prepared beforehand so that we would walk in them" (Eph. 2:10, *NASB*). Would

God create the eagle to soar and not give him wings? Of course not. And neither would He create you to serve without gifting you to serve. God has placed you in the Body of Christ and has given you the spiritual gift that He wanted to give you (see 1 Cor. 12:4-7,18). You don't *choose* your gift; you *use* the gift He has chosen to give you. "As each one has received a special gift, employ it in serving one another as good stewards of the manifold grace of God." (1 Pet. 4:10, *NASB*). So, if you are thinking, *God, I don't have a spiritual gift*, or if you are wishing for a gift other than the one He has given you, then you are living outside the framework of Scripture and you will never be able to soar. You must soar on the wings He has given you.

Just One

Because God is the One who created you and redeemed you, called you and gifted you and freed you to soar . . . you soar for Him. This one truth has helped me so much. You have an audience of only one. In Galatians 1:10, Paul says, "For am I now seeking the favor of men, or of God? Or am I striving to please men? If I were still trying to please men, I would not be a bond-servant of Christ" (*NASB*). Your church has plenty of people who think that you should please them. They have plans for your time, your life, and your children, not to mention your husband. But you do not exist to please them; you exist to please God. What does God's Word say? If I were trying to please people, I would not be a bondservant of Christ. No matter what people think or what they might say, you must remember that you have an audience of only one, and that One is God. Beloved, if you are a pleaser of God, it doesn't matter what people think, because you have pleased the Sovereign Ruler of the whole universe who created you for His pleasure.

A Final Thought

Now you know that in order to soar, you must live within a scriptural framework. But how do you know if you're doing that? Your friends can't tell you; church members can't tell you; your pastor can't tell you.

You can't find out from books or commentaries. God's Word tells you.

In closing, I want to take you to a familiar story. Jesus is visiting in the home of Mary and Martha. The story opens with Martha running around like a chicken with her head cut off to serve Jesus. While Martha is sweating and stewing, Mary—calm, cool and collected—is sitting in the parlor listening to Jesus. The Bible tells us that "Martha was distracted with all her preparations" (Luke 10:40, *NASB*). That word "distracted" means that she was pulled away from Jesus instead of toward Jesus. Exasperated, she complains to Him, "Lord, do You not care that my sister has left me to do all the serving alone? Then tell her to help me" (v. 40, *NASB*). When you are not walking with the Lord, you think He doesn't care. You think that you are bearing your burdens alone. But the Lord answered and said to her, "Martha, Martha, you are worried and bothered about so many things; but only one thing is necessary, for Mary has chosen the good part, which shall not be taken away from her" (vv. 41-42, *NASB*).

Martha was serving, but she wasn't soaring. She failed to soar, not because she did the wrong thing but because she neglected to do the necessary thing. Beloved, if you want to soar, you must take the time to know God's Word—all 66 books. Everything you and I need is in God's Book. God has spoken, and the psalmist says, "For You Yourself have taught me" (Ps. 119:102, *NASB*). When you open His Book and read His Words, God, Himself, will teach you.

So remember, only one thing is needed, and it's a choice. Make that choice and you'll know these truths and be able to live according to all that He has commanded you. Then you will hear, "Well done, My good and faithful servant" (see Matt. 25:21). Now, that's soaring.

Prayer

Father, I thank You that our adequacy is of Jesus. Father, You know every thought of our readers, these dear wives of the shepherds of Your flock. You know the past of each of these women. You know the future of these women. You know what they are battling. Father, I ask that You would hear the cry of their hearts and speak to each one, face-to-face. I pray this in the precious name of Jesus, amen.

DEFEATING DEPRESSION

RHODA S. GONZALES

Depression is not something we catch like a virus. If we are suffering from spiritual and emotional depression, we probably have brought it on ourselves by wrong thinking and wrong choices. When the cause is not organic or chemical, depression is a strategy for coping with our disappointments. But this man-made coping mechanism is a temporary solution for dealing with our pain, and it leads us away from God's solutions. This makes it part of Satan's program of deception.

As Christian women, we can overcome depression by facing our disappointments, seeing God as all-sufficient, facing our fears and changing our thinking about who we are in Christ. We are totally victorious through His death and resurrection (see 1 Cor. 15:58).

Understanding Depression

Our Emotions

Let's look at emotions first. Unfortunately, the world teaches us that emotions are not necessarily valid. We often hear people say, "Oh, she is so emotional." My sisters in Christ, please know that God is a God of feelings; He is a God of sentiment. If He weren't, He would not have sent His Son to save you. He loves you and He feels your pain. Your emotions are God-given; they are spontaneous responses to life's events.

Emotions are part of what it means to be human. But you do have a choice in how you handle your emotions. You can respond to your emotions in one of three ways.

1. Allow your emotions to escalate so they affect everyone around you, usually in a negative way.
2. Accept or deny the validity of your emotions.
3. Direct your emotions in a manner that is appropriate and healthy in a given situation.

Our Hearts

Our heart is the center of our emotions. It is also the spiritual center of love, calling, drive, motivation and purpose (see Prov. 4:20-27).

Because of the essential role our heart plays in our lives, we are to guard our heart. We are to protect our heart with the Word of God so that when difficult times come our way, we will be comforted by God's voice. Sometimes we are confused by the voices that surround us, but His is the only voice that matters. If we know God's Word, we will then recognize His voice—and follow Him.

If you are suffering from depression right now, ask yourself, *Have I given my whole heart to the Lord, or am I holding something back?* Remember, God desires fellowship with you; but for your part, you must be vulnerable and honest in order for that to happen. "You are not your own" (1 Cor. 6:19). If you desire to have fellowship with God and to be a woman after His heart, allow the Holy Spirit to guide your life, and walk with Christ (see John 16:13-15). The Holy Spirit is much more effective—and cheaper—than a psychotherapist!

Causes of Depression

As we seek to live Spirit-filled lives, we should be aware of the physical and spiritual causes of depression. We need to be careful not to set ourselves up for a bout of depression. So consider this preventative medicine.

- *Physical causes of depression.* These include lack of sleep, improper diet, vitamin deficiency, exhaustion, low blood sugar and chemical imbalances.
- *Spiritual causes of depression.* These include disappointment when expectations are not met, an unbiblical self-concept, covetousness (always wanting what others have), rejection by

others (especially church members), a sense of hopelessness or helplessness ("nothing I do really matters"), anger and hurt that lead to self-pity, and lack of apparent progress.

Take inventory of your life. Are you getting enough rest? What is your diet like? Do you take vitamins each day? And what about your spiritual house—your heart? Are you harboring anger toward anyone in the church? Do you have unrealistic expectations for yourself and others?

If there are any physical or spiritual risk factors present in your life, discuss with your spouse what you are struggling with. Then ask the Lord for help and healing. He desires to make you whole.

A Final Thought

The main thing is to avoid stinkin' thinkin.' You cannot go forward if you are your worst enemy. So if you are thinking negative, defeatist thoughts, you have got to change the way you think. Your attitude will determine how far you go in ministry and in life, so make a decision today to make a change in your attitude and you will see a change in the rest of your life.

Prayer

*Dear Heavenly Father, awesome and living God, I thank You because
You are so good and Your truth endures throughout all generations.
Father, right now I want to thank You for allowing me to see in Your
Word that I belong to You. Help me to change my attitude. Lord,
I come against spirits of depression in the name of Jesus Christ of
Nazareth. I ask that Your Holy Spirit would bring healing and that
Your Word would transform my mind. Lord, do not allow the voices,
the expectations or the fears of rejection to press in on me.
Lord, help me to be victorious so that I can be greatly used
by You. In Jesus' name, I pray. Amen.*

CHAPTER 11

*L*EADING IN CHRISTIAN TRUTHS

GAYLE HAGGARD

Those of us who are pastors' wives know what it's like to have people watching us; but rather than allow that to be a negative aspect of our role, we should see it as an opportunity to use our influence to help and encourage others. Understanding this truth has helped me grow to love being a pastor's wife. In fact, I join with many others in believing that it's time we as pastors' wives rise up and embrace the role God has given to us. It is a role of tremendous honor and value to the Body of Christ. We are called to walk alongside our husbands to be a strength, an encouragement, a help and a glory to these godly men as together we serve God by serving His Body.

Our Role Is Simple (but Not Easy)

I want all of us who are pastors' wives to see clearly how simple our role really is. It's not always easy—life on planet Earth rarely is. The Scriptures tell us that we will have trials; we will have difficulties. But our lives can be very simple because our role as a pastor's wife boils down to the fact that we are Christians. Becoming a Christian was our first step in the process that led us to where we are today. We were believers in the Lord Jesus Christ, growing in a vital relationship with Him; then we met a man and fell in love with him—and he too was a believer whom God called into pastoral ministry. Thus we should see our lives as pastors' wives as our continuing Christian walk, our Christian journey in God. It's that simple.

When I first became a pastor's wife, I told everybody that I loved being a pastor's wife; however, I was scared to death. I was afraid that I wouldn't live up to people's expectations, that I didn't know enough Scripture, that I wouldn't have answers for people if they asked me questions. Worst of all, I was scared to death I would be asked to speak publicly. That was 26 years ago, and I've learned a few things over the years.

I've learned that being a pastor's wife (or simply being a Christian) involves learning to hear the voice of the Spirit and responding to Him. Allowing other people to watch you in this process is the honor of influence. It is simply about our maturing in Christ and allowing other people to observe us and to mature with us. Doesn't that take the pressure off of trying to be something we aren't? I mean, we all want to grow in Christ, and that's what God calls us to do as pastors' wives. In Scripture there's not a lot said to pastors' wives specifically other than that we should live our lives worthy of respect. And isn't that something every Christian woman should aspire to do? So let's embrace our calling and live it well so that we can be a positive influence on the lives of others.

The Secret to Freedom

Our calling is not meant to be burdensome. How many of you reading this book right now want to be free? Think about it; do you know that God wants us to be free—pastors' wives included? He wants us free of the burdens that weigh us down, the sin and the unnecessary expectations as well. He wants us to enjoy life in Him; He wants us to enjoy our husbands, our children and those He's added to us in our churches. I find a path to this kind of freedom revealed to us in Romans 12.

Our Lives Are Not Our Own

Romans 12:1 tells us, "Therefore, I urge you, brothers, in view of God's mercy, to offer your bodies as living sacrifices, holy and pleasing to God." This means that we must be determined that our lives are not our own; they belong to Him. If we can settle this, we are a long way down the road of freedom. Accept the fact that your life is not your own. Verse 1 goes on to say that this is your spiritual act of worship. It is your response to His mercy and grace toward you. Once you settle that you belong to Him and offer yourself to Him as a living sacrifice, you enter into freedom from worldly bondages.

If we keep reading, verse 2 says, "Do not conform any longer to the pattern of this world, but be transformed by the renewing of your mind." How do we do this? By reading the Word and thinking about it and allowing the Holy Spirit to teach it to us as we ponder and meditate on it. This process transforms us and imparts wisdom to our lives. And what does wisdom do? Wisdom teaches us; wisdom protects us; wisdom rewards us. (See Proverbs 1—4.)

"Then you will be able to test and approve what God's will is—his good, pleasing and perfect will" (Rom. 12:2). How often do we ask the question, "What is Your will, God?" I speak a lot to young women, and that's the question on their minds: What is God's will? Where do I go to college? Should I marry? Whom should I marry? What should I do in life? I always tell them that the way to know God's will is to be renewed in your mind by reading the Word and then allowing that wisdom to come into your life and teach you. In my own life, wisdom has taught me; wisdom has protected me. Now, I'm reaping rewards of wisdom in my life. I have a rich life; I feel very blessed in God, in my family and in my church. But it's all because God renewed me as I read His Word, and then He imparted that wisdom to me that allowed me to know His will for my life. This is an ongoing process in my life.

We Should Not Think Too Highly of Ourselves

The next verse, Romans 12:3, is, in my opinion, one of the greatest secrets to freedom: "For by the grace given me I say to every one of you: Do not think of yourself more highly that you ought, but rather think of yourself with sober judgment in accordance with the measure of faith God has given you." Do not think more highly of yourself than you ought. Sometimes we hear how important we are and that we just need to be separated from everybody else in the congregation so they'll respect us. But that "importance" is a tremendous burden to carry. There's nothing heavier than a façade; and when we try to carry around facades, we are not free. We really can't help other people to be free in Christ until we are free ourselves.

What we've got to do is recognize the fact that we are members of a Body, and each part of the Body has its role to play (see Rom. 12:4). Thinking more highly of ourselves than we ought separates us from other people; it leads to isolation and loneliness, and that is no fun in life or in ministry. But when we accept the fact that all of us are members of this one Body and that each of us has our part, then we are free to be ourselves, to form friendships, to welcome others into our lives and to experience the joy of sharing our work with others.

My husband and I pastor a church of 11,000 people. You would think we would need to separate ourselves from the congregation—to have time away from all the people in our church. But I have seen over the years—and I have learned this from my husband—that God never gives us more than we can carry. Sometimes we give ourselves more than we can carry because we think more highly of ourselves than we ought; but when each of us just does what the Lord has given us to do and has gifted us to do, then we experience freedom. That freedom allows us to enjoy life and ministry. Ted and I love the life and work of being pastors; and we do not feel overwhelmed, because we have many others around us sharing in the work of ministry. In fact, my husband has taught the members of our church that they are all ministers. This allows us to be home most nights of the week with our family.

Once we recognize the vital role each member of the Body plays, it gives our brothers and sisters in Christ freedom to fulfill their God-given gifts and function in the Body, which brings tremendous value and satisfaction to their lives. "Just as each of us has one body with many members, and these members do not all have the same function, so in Christ we who are many form one body, and each member belongs to all the others" (Rom. 12:4-5). When we let other people do their part in serving the Body, and we don't try to do it for them, it sets them free to experience the joy of being a vital, functioning member. This is what helps them mature in Christ.

I have received so many letters from people in our church body thanking me for not singing—I'm not sure how to take that—for not trying to lead the choir, for not trying to play the piano, for not leading every ministry in the church—in other words, for not trying to do everything. I realized that I had my part to do and that's all I had to do; and I try to do it well. In my case, that part is loving my husband, caring for our children and leading the women of our church. That is real freedom for me, and freedom is what God wants for every one of us.

We Need to Be Sincere

The final verse I want to share with you from Romans 12 is the ninth verse, which says, "Love must be sincere." Sincerity is another key to freedom in our lives. And I don't mean, "Let's be real." Somehow those words carry a negative connotation that if we're going to be real, we're going to reveal the worst stuff about ourselves. How about if we be real and reveal the best stuff about us? How about if we can be sincerely good, sincerely in love with Christ, sincerely seeking to please Him with our lives? It is true freedom when we can express our love for the Body with that kind of sincerity. Of course, these actions do not mean we're perfect; rather, they mean we're sincerely growing toward maturity in God, which is expressed through love.

A Final Thought

So why should we even have to think about these things just because we are pastors' wives? The final Christian truth I would like to share with you is that God has added you to your husband to help him. This is not a loss of your identity or value as a human being, rather it gives definition and direction to your life, including all your dreams and gifting. I always encourage wives to bring their dreams and gifting into the context of helping their husbands. In time they will experience the expression of their own heart's desires. There is so much I could share on this point, but let me just share with you the why of it all.

First Corinthians 11:7 talks about men being the glory of God and women being the glory of man. When I first truly studied that verse, my response to it was "No way. I mean, yes, I'm happy to be a glory to my husband—I want to be a glory to my husband—but I also want to be a glory to God. What does this mean, that I am a glory to man?" What the Lord showed me was that, indeed, every one of us in the Body of Christ is a glory to Him. We are all His glory on the earth; but He is communicating something specific in these verses that He really wants us to get. We have to understand this verse in light of Genesis 2, where we are told that after God created man, He said, "It is not good for the man to be alone" (v. 18).

I don't think that was the first time God ever thought about creating woman. I don't think we were an afterthought. We know that God knows the end from the beginning, and so He had to have a reason for creating man and woman the way He did. I believe God waited to create woman to picture for Adam God's own desire for a companion, God's own desire for someone with whom He could share all of His thoughts and His wondrous works. Eve pictured for Adam God's desired companion. That is what we reflect, ladies. Men reflect in their masculinity who God is; in all their masculine traits, they are a glory to Him. We as women are a glory to man in how our feminine traits complement them.

It is true that we are equal in our humanity—both men and women are created in God's image and told to rule over the earth. We have similar capabilities. We also have equal access to God in our relationship with Him and are together heirs to His promise. But I believe God wanted to communicate something specific about His own desire for a companion and how He wanted His companion, the Church, to relate to Him. And so He created man first and then woman. He had Adam first and alone, and then He created woman and brought her to man. And what did Adam say? "This is now bone of my bones and flesh of my flesh" (Gen. 2:23).

This is the picture that God has for us to help us understand our value as women. It gives purpose to our femininity and our relationship with our husbands. Single women find their expression of this directly in their relationship with God, but married women also express it in their relationship with their husband (see 1 Cor. 7:34).

So let's grab hold of this understanding of God's plan. Let's embrace who we are as women so that we can stand alongside our husbands. Seeing God's plan, it makes perfect sense that we're called to help. God wants to communicate to us the fact that our femininity does not make us the lesser creature. It means that we have been given real purpose in the world: to represent God's desired companion in how we relate to our husbands. I can't think of a greater role than to be my husband's helpmate. And I am so thankful that God made me a woman so that I can come alongside my pastor husband and be a glory to him in the same way God wants the Church to be a glory to Him. And if by watching me, other women are helped in their growing relationship with God and in learning to be a glory to their husbands, then having this role as a pastor's wife is an honor.

Prayer

I pray, Father, that I may be a glory to my husband and ultimately a glory to You. I pray that I might have the freedom to not think more highly of myself than I ought, to function in a Body that I love and to love the other members of the Body sincerely. When I walk down the halls of our church on a Sunday morning, I pray that I won't be filled with animosity and fear that I am somehow not living up to people's expectations. Instead, Lord, I pray that with Your grace I will walk down the halls of our church with tremendous joy because I love our church. Let me see the members of our church as beloved, and let me see myself as being blessed to be the pastor's wife. Amen.

$\mathcal{L}$EADING IN CHARACTER TESTS

BOBBIE HOUSTON

We all know that there are many seasons to life. We recognize the ebb and flow of these seasons and that there are times when we perhaps need to move on. But what the earth needs right now is for the Church of Jesus Christ to stand strong and secure, to be faithful to her post and to be impassioned more than ever to bring truth to a world that is searching for something genuine.

I don't know if you have noticed, but the earth is not well. Yes, wonderful things are happening and God's goodness is manifest across the earth; but in many, many places the earth is under challenge and the human heart is not flourishing. It is definitely a time for those of us in ministry to rededicate ourselves to our calling. We have an integral role to play on the earth today. We have a job to do.

In Australia, we believe in women—we believe in the powerful contribution they bring to this table called life and to the Church. At our church, Hillsong, our congregation is healthy and flourishing in many ways because we esteem women as having great value.

Leadership Is All About Example

Leadership without doubt is about example. As pastors' wives, we know that people are watching us, whether we like it or not. And more than that, many are actually following the pattern and the manner of our lives.

In Hebrews 13, the author of the letter writes to the people who, in essence, are in our sphere of influence. He writes to the congregation and exhorts them, "Remember your leaders, who spoke the word of God to you. Consider the outcome of their way of life and imitate their faith" (v. 7). Here the Word of God is telling our congregations to look at you and me—to see how we are living our lives. These people watch our love affair (or not) with God, with our husbands and family and with our churches. They observe the way we respond to and raise our children; and they watch the way we negotiate relationships—the good, the bad and even the ugly.

Members in our congregation also watch to see what we give priority to in our lives. If something is not important to you as a leader, it is not going to be important to them. If we come in late to church, they'll more than likely come in late. If we sit down during the worship, are easily distracted and don't enter in, more than likely they will have that same attitude.

They watch us in season and out of season. They watch us in the good times and the bad; and to be honest, none of this is wrong, because this is what leadership is about. Jesus never said it would be easy and He never said the conditions would always be perfect. In fact, He doesn't even demand perfection from us—just our best effort.

Leadership Is All About Character

Leadership is also about responsibility. In the process of fulfilling our responsibilities, we build character. Character is forged in the journey— there are no shortcuts. We can fast-track ourselves into the wisdom of God and we can save ourselves a lot of pain; but character is forged in the journey.

In an effort to help you on your journey as a pastor's wife, allow me to share with you three defining moments that have laid a foundation in my life as a young pastor's wife.

1. His Fruit Is Your Fruit

I got saved at 15 years of age and fell madly in love with Jesus. When I was 22, I was feeling like the young, inadequate, completely ill-equipped pastor's wife. My husband, Brian, who had been in the church, was stepping into his ministry beautifully. I didn't know where I fit. I loved God and wanted to serve Him no matter what that meant; but at that point in our young life and ministry, I felt completely insecure and lacked confidence. I didn't know my place in the equation. Like many of you, I also didn't sing, play piano or lead Bible studies. I was just married to a pastor—ironing his shirts, having his babies and seeking to be the best support I could be.

I was struggling with an identity crisis meltdown. And do you know what I heard, exactly when I needed to hear it? The Spirit of God spoke and whispered, "Honey, Brian's fruit is your fruit also." Wow. That one word from God totally released me—it released me to release my husband to his ministry and to his calling, and it also released me to grow in confidence.

So many ministers' wives struggle and condemn themselves, because they feel inept and ill equipped. Again, the responsibility is upon you and me to actually grow as leaders, to learn to position ourselves wisely. And how do we do that? By taking the Word of God and applying it to our lives so that we have His strength to draw upon. You cannot give away what is not within you yet. But the choice to learn His Word and to get moving is yours.

2. The Church Is Not the Enemy

Let's be very clear on this point: The church is not the enemy. Have you ever noticed that when people begin to backslide and become cold of heart, they suddenly change their language? Suddenly the church did this and the church did that, and a sense of "them and us" begins to surface. It's very unhealthy. Sadly, many pastors' wives (especially younger ones) see the ministry or the church as the enemy. To them it encroaches on their time, their finances, their lifestyle, their children's lifestyle and their relationship with their husband.

We all have to become wise. When we are tired or struggling or frustrated, that's when this nasty little attitude can so easily creep in. And you know that our attitudes are the testing ground of life. Sometimes we think that we get tested on the really big issues—the big crises, the big dramas—but you know it's actually the everyday stuff. Our heavenly Father watches our heart as we go through our daily routines. He sees when that attitude is prevailing and we are falling prey to resentment and a woe-is-me philosophy of life. So we must be on guard against seeing the church as the enemy, because once we believe it, soon we will speak it: "Out of the abundance of the heart [the] mouth speaks" (Luke 6:45, *NKJV*). It may lie dormant for a while, but it will eventually come out of your mouth.

Further, what comes out of your mouth will color your world and your leadership. Over time, it will prevent you from walking into those wide open spaces. So watch your heart, notice any change in your attitude and be on guard, because resentment against the church will be your demise.

3. Just Be Your Lovely Self

We are not the Church of the dark ages; we are not the Church of 50 years ago. We are the Church of the twenty-first century, and we have permission to be ourselves. Across the landscape of the Church there is room for diversity, individuality and personality. The last thing this earth needs is for us to be religious clones of one another or to get stuck in old wineskins. So relax and be your lovely redeemed self.

A Final Thought

I have also realized that I need to stay young, current and healthy so that I can relate to the "now" generation that God is giving us. I want to encourage you to ask the hard questions when it comes to your leadership style. Let's not become overly familiar or complacent with ourselves or the way we do church. As a pastor's wife, you will be called to new places and you will be asked to accept new challenges. Be available and willing to grow and to find new talents you didn't know you had. Be prepared to pass new character tests. Step up to the call. Let's walk forward together on this leadership journey.

Blessing

Father God, I just thank You for every pastor's wife in every church,
in every community, in every nation. I pray that You will continue to
speak to the hearts of these beautiful women, that You will cement
Your goodness and Your will in their lives. They love You, Jesus.
Bless them abundantly. I ask this in Jesus' name, amen.

$\mathcal{L}$EADING IN CHALLENGING TIMES

ELISABETH TSON

I was blessed to born by the Lord into a Christian family. My parents were very faithful and devoted people. At a very young age, I learned that being a Christian means being hated by the world but loved by God—with that amazing love only He can give.

Planting the Seeds

I grew up in Romania. My father, a Baptist pastor and pioneer church planter, was among the first evangelicals in Romania. Many blessings came along with this job—and one of those blessings was intense persecution. This meant that he was often arrested, sometimes beaten by the police—and once he was even court-martialed because of his faith. However, due to the providential intervention of a merciful general, the charges were dropped and he was released.

As a child, I knew what it meant to be persecuted for one's faith in the Lord. Growing up in this environment, I watched my parents react to this hostile treatment with courage, faith and unwavering commitment to the Lord. Our home was filled with love and joy despite the constant perils we faced. My parents' example helped me immeasurably later in life when my husband and I were confronted with persecution.

Tending the Vine

When I was in my twenties, I attended a wedding in which the groom was already the pastor of a Baptist church. I looked at his young bride and thought, *Does she have any idea of what she's getting into?* At the same time, I never dreamed of the possibility that one day I would become a pastor's wife. Little did I know what God had in store for me. Looking back, I see now that the Lord took me through a variety of different experiences in order to train me for the high calling of being a pastor's wife. He was with me through all these precious learning experiences, preparing me for the life He had in store for me alongside my husband, Joseph.

When Joseph and I married in September 1959, Joseph was not, at that time, a pastor. He was a high school teacher. But on January 21, 1968, my husband had a special encounter with the Lord. As a result, he decided to make his recommitment to the Lord publicly and to return to public ministry.

The Separation

The Lord graciously rewarded Joseph by making it possible for him to go to Austria and from there to England. Through a series of incredible miracles, he had been able to enroll in a yearlong course in theology at Oxford University. After he received the first scholarship from Oxford, Joseph sent me an invitation to join him in England, but the Romanian authorities denied my application for a passport. They wanted to keep me hostage in Romania to ensure Joseph's return. The fact that we would be separated—a separation that ended up lasting for more than three years—came as a very painful shock to me.

I felt completely devastated. I fell to my knees before the Lord and begged Him to make His will clear to me. I wanted to be perfectly sure that both Joseph and I were in His will and His care. Shortly after my prayer, the Lord gave me some Scriptures to ponder. From them I understood that God wanted Joseph in England—and He wanted me to wait for Joseph in Romania. The Lord made it very clear to me that He had a special plan for us.

What was my response to this revelation? I accepted His will, I trusted His Word and I received His perfect peace. I prayed for the Lord to give me courage to stand strong during those long, difficult years in which I was separated from Joseph. But over and above the courage that God had given me, He also filled me with unspeakable joy. I lived every day in a wonderful communion with the Lord. I talked with Him throughout each day, and He walked with me through everything I did. I consulted with Him as you would a best friend. I constantly shared with Him every problem, every heartache and every success.

Learning Generosity

The Lord taught me many, many lessons in those times—those 3 years, 6 months and 21 days. One of those lessons was that I must do unto others first that which I would like them to do unto me: If I wanted to make friends, I needed to reach out. One of the things I always liked to do, and which brought me great joy, was to greet the people at the church and to shake hands with as many people as I could. I would try to reach those who looked sad. By making an effort to reach out, I discovered people who had very special needs. I would talk with them and they would share with me the burdens they were carrying; then we would often pray together. I felt that the Lord had given me this ministry of outreach, and I felt that His peace and His joy were being transmitted through me to the people whom I greeted.

My path to learning the Lord's ways was not always an easy one. One Sunday morning, someone at the church had offended me rather badly. I said to myself, *At the end of the service today, I'm going to walk straight out of here without saying a word to anyone. After all, let me see if anyone cares enough to stop me to ask how I am doing. I want to see if anyone loves me or cares about me.* And that is what I did. I walked out of the church and all the way to the bus, expecting all the while that someone would come after me to see what was wrong. But no one did. No one approached me at all. When I got off the bus, I heard a voice softly saying to me, "My dear child, how poor you were today." I understood instantly what my Lord was trying to say to me. I answered Him, "Yes, Lord, I was a beggar today. I did not allow You to work through Me, to give Your joy to anyone else. I myself was empty and had nothing to give. When I let You lead me, Your Spirit thrives in me; but today I tied up Your hands and scourged Your Spirit."

As I stepped into my apartment, I knelt down and immediately asked the Lord to forgive me for having allowed my fleshly desires to rise above His holy will for me. I confessed my sin; I repented with many tears. Then I felt the Lord's forgiveness and complete reconciliation wash over me. I have never forgotten that experience. The next day, the person who had hurt me came to me and asked for forgiveness.

That is how our God works. We have to recognize our sin, ask for forgiveness and receive the Lord's forgiveness. Then the Lord is faithful to work out the restoration of relationship between us. When this happened to me, it was wonderful to see Him at work, restoring peace to my heart and resolving my entire problem. He taught me that it *is* so much more blessed to give than to receive.

Keeping the Lord First

In those years without my husband, the Lord revealed Himself to me in a way in which I had never known Him before. He became so close to me that no one was closer to my soul than my precious Lord was. I had my eyes firmly fixed on Him, and He was always the first and the last person with whom I would discuss my problem.

Nevertheless, one Sunday morning, as I was returning home from church with the lady who was staying with me, she asked me why I was rather quiet; and so I started telling her something about what was bothering me. After I arrived home, I knelt down to pray, as was my custom. But before I had uttered a word, I heard a clear voice asking me, "Do you have anything left for Me?" Oh, it was very painful to hear those words from my Lord. "Please forgive me, Lord," I prayed. I felt that I had betrayed my best and most faithful friend. This was another lesson that I would never forget. Never again did I place anyone else above the Lord. He was my all.

Learning Trust in His Will

Through those years of aloneness, the Lord prepared me for the time when Joseph would come home. Of course, the events that followed his return were totally new to us. What made it possible for me to get through those new challenges in a way that honored the Lord was the faith in God that had already been engraved in my mind and heart during those lonely years. I had learned by then to trust in His sovereignty and to rest in His almighty power. I had learned that nothing, absolutely nothing, was beyond His great power or outside of His perfect will. My part was to accept His judgment and His will with all my mind and all my heart. Whenever I accepted His will in this way, with my whole being, I would be filled to overflowing with joy.

Bearing Fruit

In 1972, Joseph returned home from England. Despite our fears, he was not arrested or imprisoned; instead, he received a position as a professor of theology at the Baptist seminary in Bucharest. Two years later the secret police succeeded in removing Joseph from the seminary, moving us to Proiest, where my husband became a pastor in a Baptist church. My responsibility as a pastor's wife started right there. I must confess that I went to Proiest with great fear in my heart, because the church there had been plagued by many conflicts and problems. I had prayed that the Lord would not send us to Proiest, yet His will for us was to begin a ministry in that troubled church. So then I prayed, "OK, Lord. I see that this move is Your will. Now I ask You to give Me the strength and the wisdom to do the work that You have for me to do there."

Surrendering to the Lord's Will

Of course the Lord was faithful: He gave me wisdom to know how to show love and respect toward all the people, especially to all the ladies, in the church. During the three years we spent leading the Baptist church in Proiest, we lived under house arrest for many months, and Joseph endured hundreds of hours of interrogation. Our lives were constantly threatened, and the police were always watching our home. It was a time in which we had to place our lives on the altar of the Lord. We had to accept the reality that we might be called to die for Him. I surrendered the life of my husband and my own life to the Lord. Without this conscious surrender, we would not have been able to survive, because one cannot live in constant fear. The only way to keep one's sanity is to accept whatever the Lord wills, even though it may mean literal death.

My husband and I came to understand that to lose one's life for God is the greatest privilege and honor. The Lord never asked us to carry more that we could bear, and His grace was sufficient every single day. He helped us to accept His will, no matter how much it would cost us. In spite of the threats of imprisonment and death, we were peaceful and full of joy.

We also gave our infant daughter, Dora, to the Lord, asking that He might be her mother and father. We knew that we might well be killed by the secret police. In surrendering our only child to the Lord, we experienced something that one rarely experiences. I felt that eternity was at my right hand and that heaven had come down to us. It was within our reach. I felt so detached from all physical, earthly things. I told my husband that if I would touch him, I would not feel his body. I have never felt the Lord so close to me, nor heaven so near. Those were unforgettable moments of union with Christ and of renunciation of all that this world has to offer. During this experience, I learned that what is of the greatest importance in this life is that my will be in complete harmony with the will of God. My greatest treasure is in knowing that my Lord is fulfilling His plan in my life. There is no greater grace than knowing that we are in His will.

Answering the Call to Be a Pastor's Wife

Afterward, with my whole being, I dedicated myself to my new calling as a pastor's wife—because that was the Lord's holy will. To be a helpmate for my husband—that was what He was asking of me. God was teaching me that the role of a wife is a great responsibility but also a great privilege and grace. When I can help Joseph to be faithful to God in every situation, to be upright and honest in all he says and does, to be joyful, even in the midst of hardship, I feel fulfilled and complete. When I am obedient to God's will, I can see Him working through both Joseph and me.

My passion and my joy have been to do my best to serve others and to help my husband in whatever way was necessary for him to be able to fulfill his own calling from the Lord. My husband and I were a team because his calling was also my calling. My part was to watch over my husband, to make sure that he was happy so that he could fulfill his duty without any hindrance. To that end, I was very careful to have no unresolved conflicts, misunderstandings or differences of opinion between us. When we disagreed on a certain matter, I always went on my knees to ask God to reveal to me where I had been wrong and to help me to see what my husband had seen but I had not. I never wanted to feel that Joseph and I were not on the same page.

In that time of persecution, unity was of utmost importance. We insisted upon unity and clarity in our thinking, and we would not allow conflicts to divide us in any way. Unity was as necessary to us as the air we breathed, because where there is division, there is no power. Divided we would not have been able to stand.

Embracing Death for the Lord's Sake

The persecution went on. While on an evangelistic trip to Bucharest, Joseph was arrested and savagely beaten. The secret police general told Joseph that his license to be a pastor had been revoked and that he would receive a secular appointment somewhere else. Joseph was told to accept the secular job or else face deportation to the labor camp. The secret police officer had frightened Joseph to his very core. Joseph came home and simply told me that he would accept the secular job because he did not see any reason why he should go to the labor camp.

I was shocked. I realized that Joseph was going through a deep spiritual crisis. There was absolutely nothing I could say to him to change his mind, even though I pleaded with him over and over. "Joseph, by giving in to the Communist authorities, you establish a precedent. Others will follow your example and give in to them as well; but did you not say, many times, that you are ready to die for the Lord? Now is the time to do it! Joseph, we will die together." Yet he would always reply, "No, it is no use. I will take the secular job."

I was in a desperate position. I called an old friend of ours who had spent five years in the labor camp. Joseph looked up to this man as a spiritual father and counselor. I asked him to come quickly to our city and meet Joseph and me at the home of an older deacon of our church. There I explained to him Joseph's state of mind and his crippling fear and discouragement. We prayed together, and after that our friend went to see Joseph. He went into Joseph's study, sat down and looked at him with pity. "Joseph, let me tell you what you have done. One day you picked up a flag and told us all to follow you. We did follow you and it was great, but recently you have become frightened. You put your flag down on the ground and hid in a bush. You are telling others that the flag is there for the taking. Maybe someone else will pick it up, and we will follow him."

The vivid picture our friend painted stung Joseph. He saw himself down in that bush, cowering with fear. At that moment, life came back into him. He answered, "You are right, my friend. My problem has been fear. When the officer beat me, I became terribly afraid of their savagery and brutality. I did not dare say no again for fear they would take me back there and beat me again. But now it is all over. I will not lay that flag down. I will not accept the secular job they offered me. I will continue to preach even without license. But you know they will not let me go; they will kill me. Now, please stay with me this afternoon and help me to prepare for death."

A few days later, Joseph went to speak with the secret police officer. Joseph said, "Sir, I know that you will kill me for this, but I have no choice. I must do what my Lord wants me to do and that is to preach. So if you want to kill me, you should know that I'm ready to die." The officer was incredibly moved when he heard Joseph's decision. His facial expression and tone of voice instantly softened as he said, "Mr. Tson, who is talking about killing here? You will not die." From that day on, that secret police officer became Joseph's protector. For four years, Joseph pastored the church in Aradia and preached throughout Romania without a license, but no one touched him.

We realized that this experience had been a test from the Lord. The Lord wanted to do a special work in us. He wanted us totally and completely surrendered to His will, even if it cost us our lives. Once Joseph had been freed from the fear of death, he received a new fullness of the Holy Spirit. The Spirit worked through him in those years with tremendous, newfound freedom. Joseph had placed absolutely everything on the altar before the Lord. At that same time, the Lord gave me another ministry, the ministry of counseling. Joseph was very busy overseeing the church's construction projects, so it became my task to minister to the believers' needs. When believers came to our home for counseling, I asked them to tell me what was their burden. While they were telling me, I was praying for an answer from the Lord. The Lord was always faithful to give me the words to say.

A Final Thought

As I think back upon my life as a pastor's wife, I count it a privilege and grace to be Joseph's wife, and I love him more than my own life. The fact that I am such an intimate part of his life and his calling means that all his accomplishments are also my accomplishments, all his victories are my victories, all of his glories are mine—and all of his joys are my joys. What a gift! And for this, I thank the Lord.

Blessing

Dear pastor's wife, perhaps you are struggling right now with some kind of hardship in your life and/or your ministry. Perhaps there is a member of the congregation who is causing your husband heartache. Perhaps you are feeling the strain of meeting your church's and your family's needs. Perhaps you have begun to doubt whether you can weather the storms and fulfill God's calling on your life.

But Jesus tells you, "Take courage; I have overcome the world" [John 16:33, NASB]. What a comfort! No matter what the hardship, He can give you the grace and strength to overcome. Whether you face minor annoyances or life-threatening persecution for your faith, He is faithful. May He bless you as you continue to heed His voice and walk in His ways. I pray this in Jesus' name, amen.

$\mathcal{H}$OW TO COMMUNICATE WITH CONFIDENCE

CAROL KENT

I went to school thinking that I was going to be an elementary school teacher. I wound up majoring in the subject that I had feared most: public speaking. Now I want you to know, if I could get over the fear of speaking, surely you can too. What we do deserves excellence, because we represent the King of kings and the Lord of lords. What we do for His glory we want to do to the best of our ability every time we have an opportunity to speak.

Some of us are "wingers." We've been able to stand in front of a crowd since we were toddlers. We never mind introducing the guest speaker, emceeing at a meeting, teaching a class or guiding a discussion—it's a natural gift. Some of the rest of you may fit into the category that I like to call "the plodder." That is a word I have made up for the person who goes into cardiac arrest just thinking about standing in front of a group or even introducing somebody else. As a pastor's wife, you know you should be able to do some basic public speaking, but it's downright hard.

However, once a plodder begins to learn how to communicate, miracles happen. Plodders would never stand up without having all of their points organized. They know what their aim is; they know what their illustrations will be; they know how they're going to wrap it up; they even know how long it will take them to say what they have to say, because they've practiced. That means you're going to get quality material from a plodder, whereas the winger just stops wherever she ends up when it's time to go.

Steps to Success in Preparing a Talk

A Main Point

How many of you can talk for three days without communicating what your main point is? I believe it is the Word of God that transforms our lives, so make this precious book the foundation of whatever topic you're speaking on and make sure you have a biblical basis to substantiate what it is you're talking about.

Fleshing Out Your Idea

Once you figure out your main point or idea, take an inventory of your general knowledge to see what you know about the topic. Most of us have a whole lot of general knowledge that we're going to be drawing from. One weekend I had a dynamic African-American woman in my seminar. She came rushing up to me after the talk and said, "Carol, I'm so excited! You just gave me the theme for my testimony. I have relatives who came to this country on slave ships, and in my own personal life, God has brought me from slavery to sin to freedom in Jesus Christ."

Think about anything having to do with your nationality or roots. How about your education or your lack of it? What about your job experiences? Do you have any favorite quotes that might be helpful? What illustrations can you draw from your past or your present that teach a valuable spiritual lesson?

Regarding the use of personal experiences as illustrations, I have a funny story to share. A few years ago, I wrote a book entitled *Secret Passions of the Christian Woman*. I brought the book with me on an airplane trip and had it tucked under my arm as I sat down and buckled my seat belt. The gentleman sitting next to me looked over in my direction and said, "Well, what do you do for a living?" I said, "I'm a Christian public speaker and I do a little bit of writing." He said, "Do you write books?" I said, "That's right." He said, "Tell me, what's the name of your latest project?" Without making eye contact with him, I gulped, blinked, paused, and then said, "*Secret Passions of the Christian Woman*." He gulped, blinked, paused, and then said, "*Secret Passions of the Christian Woman?!* Now that's a topic I could get interested in." So while I had a tough plane ride, I gained a great story. Look for illustrations everywhere you go, and write them down as they happen or you'll lose them.

Identify Your Audience

As you sort all of your information and stories, the first thing you need to do is consider who your audience is. How spiritually mature are they? Are they ready to open their Bibles just as soon as you start to speak? Something that has grieved me greatly is that more and more people are biblically illiterate. How many of you are ministering in very seeker-sensitive churches where most of your members are initially biblically illiterate? In that situation you'll need to keep your message simple. You want the audience member with the least amount of Bible background to be able to understand what you are talking about.

Have an Action Step

Next, consider what your aim is. Whenever you prepare a Bible study or topical talk, ask yourself, *What do I want my audience to do as a result of hearing this message?* In other words, what action step do you want your audience to take? Although I have been tremendously inspired by some phenomenal speakers, I haven't always known what to do with what I heard. If I am delivering a message, I want the audience to know in their hearts what action step they are going to take because of what God's Word has said. Remember, if you don't know what your aim is, neither will your audience. Be as specific as you can. Write it out. Have it involve a change in attitude or a measurable behavior. Start getting into the nitty-gritty of what the follow-through steps are.

Create an Outline

The next step is basic outlining. Make your outline simple. An outline is a systematic listing of your most important talking points on a given topic. And here's a very important truth I learned about outlining: If I can't remember my outline, my audience won't remember it.

As you fill in your outline, you'll want to include illustrations. You might consider using a word definition, an anecdote or a personal experience. Let's take a little time looking at that last item, because a personal experience is probably the most powerful illustration you could use. Here's something I recommend when you have a day or even an hour alone with God: Write down every lesson God has ever taught you. Then write down a key Scripture or favorite quote that could be used to help reinforce in the minds of a listener what that Bible-based lesson is.

After you've outlined the body of your talk, figure out your introduction. How many of you have ever wasted a couple of hours trying to figure out how to start a talk? I pray this way: "Lord, You know who is in that audience. Help me to know how to begin." He will be there to inspire you! And remember that a well-prepared introduction or "rapport step" is for the purpose of creating warmth with your audience and introducing your subject. If I'm trying to raise funds for missions, I would like people to get their checkbooks out at the end of the talk and write a check—I want to motivate them. And I want to start out with an introduction that's going to get them excited about the mission. So remember, as you gain the attention of your audience, you are increasing their ability to *hear* what you say and you are ensuring that they are ready to *move toward action*. After you gain the attention of your audience, you want to lead them into the subject of your talk with a good transitional statement.

Once your outline is finished and you are ready to get up in front of that crowd, be confident and step out in faith. God wants to use your uniqueness. Wouldn't it be horrible if we were cookie-cutter communicators, all sounding alike? If you're funny, be funny; if you're dramatic, be dramatic. God is going to use the uniqueness of your personality for His kingdom glory as you make yourself and your gifts available to Him.

A Final Thought

Now that we've covered the basics of how to prepare a talk, I'd like to leave you with a few pointers on how to deliver that talk. After all, it's the actual public speaking that tends to be the tough area for a lot of people. But have confidence; God intends to work powerfully through you. He has called you to ministry through the spoken word. He wants to save the unbeliever and comfort the doubter through you!

There's a wonderful verse in Proverbs 15: "A happy heart makes the face cheerful" (v. 13). We need to remind ourselves of that often. You see, 55 percent of our communication is nonverbal. Our body language says far more to the audience than our words do.

Show some energy and enthusiasm. Have a spring in your step and a smile on your face. Stand straight and tall! You have every reason to be confident. "And the things you have heard me say in the presence of many witnesses entrust to reliable [women] who will also be qualified to teach others" (2 Tim. 2:2). As you begin to speak up with confidence, God does a wonderful thing through you.

Blessing

Oh, Lord, I get so excited when I think about what these pastors' wives are doing in their part of the country or their part of the world! God, I pray that they will know that it isn't about how impressive they are or how perfect they are; it's about getting equipped and then doing the job with passion as they share with others the way You have transformed their lives. God, I pray that You would help them to give fresh faith, renewed courage and eternal truth to the people they have the privilege of impacting. Lord, I pray that each of them would further Your kingdom agenda while they still have time. In Jesus' name I pray, amen.

$\mathcal{H}$OW TO LIVE IN A PERSONAL REVIVAL

JERI HILL

When we began our lives in ministry, we were all in hot pursuit of God. But I wonder if we realized that our desire for the Lord was not the only power working in our lives. I'd like to share with you some reasons why our first passionate pursuit of God must be renewed daily.

The Devil Is in Hot Pursuit of Us

The devil is in hot pursuit of us, seeking to destroy us. He does everything he can to keep Christians from making the mark. He's going to pull us away; he's going to try to get our attention away from God. Does that mean that we have to be afraid that the devil is out there? No. But we do have to be on guard. In 1 Peter 5:8, we are told, "Be self-controlled and alert. Your enemy the devil prowls around like a roaring lion looking for someone to devour."

He's not only after Christians to bring them down, but he's also after sinners. He does everything he can to keep sinners from seeing the light. Second Corinthians 4:4 tells us, "The god of this age has blinded the minds of unbelievers, so that they cannot see the light of the gospel of the glory of Christ." The enemy is doing everything he can to keep the sinner from seeing the light of the glorious gospel. Where is that sinner going to see the light of God's Word? Through us—through the witness of our lives.

God Is in Hot Pursuit of Us

God really doesn't need us, but He wants to use us. And this brings us to an important truth: God the Father, Jesus Christ the Son and the Holy Spirit are also in hot pursuit of us sinners (see Titus 2:11-12). Most of us have had personal experience of the Lord's pursuit of our hearts and lives.

Thirty years ago, He was in hot pursuit of me, but I didn't know it. I was an unlikely candidate for Christianity, or so I thought. I'm the oldest of five children; my mom was raped when she was 18 years old, and I was born as a result of that rape. She married in order to give me a dad, not because she loved him. They had a son in that marriage, but there was no love there. That wasn't enough to keep them together—she wasn't a Christian at the time—but after the rape, her whole life had been thrown into a tailspin. Then her third child was conceived during an affair. She married the father, but five years later, she was a single mom, struggling to raise us on her own. And we were very poor. I remember times when we would eat oatmeal for three weeks straight. But Mom loved us.

When I was 10, my mom remarried; she had two more children in that marriage. At first it was awesome: I was calling her new husband "Dad," and everything was really great. We finally had a dad, somebody who was taking care of us; my mom didn't have to work; we weren't on food stamps anymore. It was really awesome. But after about six months, all hell broke loose. We found out that he was an alcoholic and a child abuser. The fighting, the beatings and the verbal abuse continued until I turned 18. I became a very bitter, hard and hateful person, and my heart was closed to God. Amazingly, during that time my mom got saved. As I began the whole partying, drinking and drug scene at the tender age of 12, my mom began to pray for me.

But I was running from God. Actually, I didn't think much of Him—I wondered what He did all day. I couldn't see that He did much good for anyone I knew. That all changed at age 18, while sitting in jail. God spoke to me in an audible voice, and the voice I heard was my mother's voice. I was the only girl in that jail cell. He said, "Jeri, don't you understand that I love you?" It blew my mind. When I got out of jail a week later, I asked my mom if she remembered saying those words. Sure enough, that previous week she had been fasting for me and at the exact moment I had heard those words, she had been leaning against the sink in the kitchen, calling out in desperation, "Jeri, don't you understand that I love you?" And I knew it was God.

A week later, I passed a billboard that had John 3:16 printed on it, as if God were saying loud and clear, "For I so loved *you*, for I so loved *you*." Every time I drove by that billboard, I'd turn my head and say, "God, leave me alone; I'm not worth it." Later in the week, I had a dream: Jesus was standing at the foot of my bed with His hands outstretched; He spoke to me and said, "I died for *you*." It so jolted me awake that I sat up and was holding my knees, crying out, "God, why are You after me?"

We Need to Rid Our Lives of the Devil's Works

What keeps us, as pastors' wives, from pursuing God? Often it is hurt, pain, anger, disappointment, criticism—all the offenses that others have committed against us—that stand between God and us. We have to remove those rocks from our lives. We have to renew our relationship with God—to constantly live in revival with Him.

Our need for revival is ongoing. Though we have plans, things are going to come up that we didn't plan for—things that are part of God's plan but weren't on our agenda. Whether or not you're a youth pastor, things come up; whether or not you're a missionary, things come up; whether or not you're doing evangelistic work, things come up. There are always going to be obstacles. God is constantly tilling the soil of our souls so that we might be receptive to His Word and be ready to do His will (see Luke 8:15).

Is God waiting for us to undergo revival and bear fruit? Yes, He is. Look at the story in Luke 13:6-9 of the man who was caring for the fig vineyard. Year after year a particular tree bore no fruit; still, the farmer

JERI HILL

103

cared for the tree. He refused to cut it down—he wanted one more year to till the soil around the tree's roots. Notice that the tree wasn't dead—the soil was just too hard.

We can be spiritually dead when the traumatic events in our lives make us hard. We don't want to pray; we don't want to read the Word; we don't want to get into the Spirit. The water of the Word keeps us soft and receptive; and the Spirit of God fertilizes us and keeps us soft so that we can minister to others. We need to constantly take care of the soil in our lives so that God can use us, speak through us and minister to others through us.

We Should Be in Hot Pursuit of God

Jeremiah 29:13 tells us, "And ye shall seek me, and find me, when ye shall search for me with all your heart" (KJV). Because I want God's anointing on me, I pursue Him. I spend time with Him. I want my relationship with Him to be more real than it was 30 years ago; I want God to be more alive to me today than He was yesterday. I don't want my walk with Him to become mediocre. I don't want to just float through life. I want to be near Him. And if we draw near to Him, He will draw near to us (see Jas. 4:8). God is not far from any of us—He is with you in your church and He wants to pour out His Spirit there.

We Need to Be in Hot Pursuit of Others

We need to bring God's salvation to others. This is where the last part of my testimony comes in. I was an angry teen who had no interest in getting to know the Lord. And yet when I was 16, an Assembly of God minister came to the house, knocked on the door and invited me to church. "No thanks" was my response. But by the next Saturday he had found out my name: "Jeri, Jesus loves you and has a plan for your life." "That's nice—bye." The next week he was back again—and it was getting irritating. Every Saturday for two years he came to my house just to tell me that Jesus loved me. Did I want to hear him tell me, "Jeri, Jesus loves you and has a plan for your life"? No. Toward the end, I was slamming the door in his face, telling him that God didn't care about me.

At about the time I was running from God—and He was in hot pursuit—I went to live in the country. My pastor friend didn't know where I was for six weeks, but he prayed: "God, I've had a burden for this girl for two years and I am not going to give up on her. And I know You're not giving up on her." So God told him where I was. I was so shocked to see that persistent pastor at my front door. God had been making His presence so clear to me in those preceding weeks, and out of nowhere came this pastor who hadn't given up on me. In that moment, I knew that God wasn't going to give up on me either.

How many of us have done that for anybody? How many of us have been such faithful witnesses of God's love for the lost? This pastor was an incredible testimony to me—he saw no fruit but he kept going after it. God wants us to have fruit, too, but we've got to go after it. If we don't go after it, we won't get it. So tend that soil—and trust God for the harvest.

A Final Thought

When we left Brownsville in the middle of 2000, we had just built a brand-new house. My husband and I had been married 26 years and had owned three houses. We lived in the first one for a year and a half. We lived in the second one, which is the one we built, for seven months. Wasn't that nice of my husband to give me seven months in a house that I had designed? We moved into my dream house in November; and in February, my husband informed us we were leaving. Yes, we had thought to settle in Florida—we loved it there. But then God made changes. The move reminded me who was in charge: God.

We moved to Dallas, Texas, where I lived with our three children and two dogs in a second-floor apartment. Then my husband left on his first crusade two weeks after we moved into that little apartment. I had to drive around a city I wasn't familiar with and find out where I could get my kids their shots, enroll them in school and so on. I managed somehow. I remember that one day shortly after the school year started I was out on the porch stirring up the dog food and complaining. I was not a happy camper. We hadn't found a church yet, and so I gave vent to my complaint: *God, I feel like I have left the river and You have dumped me in the desert.* As clear as a bell, I heard God say, *What? I am your river in the desert. Revival is in Me—not in a church or a prayer meeting.* I started weeping, and I saw myself being carried, in my spirit, down His river.

We will never be discontent if we are floating in God, being carried by Him and by His Spirit. We will lack for nothing in our spirit if He is removing the rocks that come up in our lives, if He's taking care of the thorns. When we are yielding to Him, He is everything we need.

Blessing

Jesus, I pray for each woman reading this book—that she will come against the attacks of the enemy on her life. Jesus, I pray that You will anoint her, that she will go after You with all her heart. I pray that her anointing will reach the people in her church, that You will be glorified. Don't ever let her consider her daily duties insignificant—everything is significant when it's done for You, Jesus. Amen.

ℋOW TO MAKE THE REST OF YOUR LIFE THE BEST OF YOUR LIFE

MARY JO WILLIAMS

We each have been given this fragile gift of life. I thank Him for it; it is no little thing that He has given us. I've realized more the preciousness of life since I turned 50 in June. My thoughts were, *God, is this possible? I was 20 just yesterday!* I then began to wonder how many days I had left on Earth—and it made me take an account of my life. I realized that I had already spent most of my life. I asked myself, *Am I happy with it?* Truthfully, I am not—I am not where I wish I was. I have determined in my heart that I am going to make the rest of my ministry the *best* of my ministry.

I want to share with you three things that I think can help all of us make the rest of our ministry the best of our ministry. We will consider the following:

1. What is our attitude about sin?
2. What is our attitude about ourselves?
3. What is our attitude about God?

Attitude About Sin

What is our attitude about sin? Do we take sin lightly? Do we realize that it really is an enemy? Do we heed the words of Hebrews 12?

Therefore then, since we are surrounded by so great a cloud of witnesses, [who have borne testimony to the Truth], let us strip off and throw aside every encumbrance (unnecessary weight) and that sin which so readily (deftly and cleverly) clings to and entangles us, and let us run with patient endurance and steady and active persistence the appointed course of the race that is set before us, Looking away [from all that will distract] to Jesus, Who is the Leader and the Source of our faith [giving the first incentive for our belief] and is also its Finisher [bringing it to maturity and perfection]. He, for the joy [of obtaining the prize] that was set before Him, endured the cross, despising and ignoring the shame, and is now seated at the right hand of the throne of God (Heb. 12:1-2, *AMP*).

This passage in Hebrews is talking about a race. God has called us to a race. I am passionate with all of my heart that I am going to finish my race. Satan is not going to keep me back and hinder me with weights of fear, judgmentalism, anger or unforgiveness, because those attitudes are not my friends—or yours. They are something the devil has laid as bait, but we don't have to bite. The choice is up to us.

God's Word

Sometimes it takes a great deal of energy to fight temptations that are trying to get your attention. Maybe somebody did something nasty to you, and it might take a lot of energy to resist that thing that is trying to get you. But you don't have to give in. If you make a habit of memorizing Bible verses, storing God's Word in your heart, then when those thoughts that shouldn't be there start coming, such as rehearsing an old hurt, you can replace it with Scripture concerning those issues and watch the truth set you free (see John 8:32).

Even though we are born again, we must constantly renew our minds. Ephesians 4:23 says, "And be constantly renewed in the spirit of your mind [having a fresh mental and spiritual attitude]" (*AMP*). Set the computer of your mind according to God's Word. Let's get our minds in alignment with God's Word. It is worth every bit of energy we have to learn to think with the mind of God.

Unforgiveness

What happens when we don't put on the mind of Christ? We can easily slip into old habits and patterns—like the sin of unforgiveness. We dredge up old hurts and tear off scabs. We cause ourselves incredible pain, and in doing so, we foster sin in our lives. But that's not what God wants for us. He wants us to be free to soar.

So let go of thoughts about what other people have done! You will find such freedom when you really embrace God's Word. It is so exciting when you realize that through God's grace, you can let go of people who have hurt or offended you. That is true freedom. Can you see Jesus on the cross, saying, "Father, forgive them, for they do not know what they are doing" (Luke 23:34)? That is love. I want to be like that.

Selfishness

One of the most miserable ways to live is to be self-centered. The happiest people are those who forget about themselves. They trust God to take care of their needs and they focus on other people and help to make their dreams come true. As a result, unbelievable joy begins to pour into their lives.

Years ago, before my husband became pastor at Mount Hope Church, he was head of a ministry called Good Ground Evangelical Association. He felt that God was speaking to his heart, telling him, "I want you to bury those dreams and surrender your time to Pastor Snook; help make his dreams come true." So he went to Pastor Snook and said, "I am going to help you make your dreams come true." And that's exactly what he did. My husband was willing to answer God's call, even though it meant putting aside his own plans. And what has been the result? God has raised him up and just lifted him to a great place of prominence in ministry—and I believe it started with his surrendering his life to the Lord.

Ungrateful Attitude

Replace grumbling and complaining with thanksgiving. We all have so much to be thankful for. I have seen such a good change come to me as I change from a grumbling heart to a grateful, rejoicing heart. It is as if a feast of rejoicing is going on in my heart. I am grateful that I'm alive, grateful for my husband, for my children, for the ability to serve Him, for my home—and the list goes on and on.

Problems that once seemed so big are really not as big as they seem. God is more than enough to help me through every single one of them. Some of my problems look so scary sometimes. I don't know how He is going to resolve them, but I know He is going to come through. God loves me so much and wants to constantly bless me.

In fact, I've come to realize that God is chasing after me with these blessings. I believe that God chases after all of us, but sometimes we are so blinded with grumbling and a lack of gratitude that we block those things from coming into our lives. He delights, just like you do with your kids, in blessing us and giving us so many good things—that's His way. He wants to bless us and make us happy.

Concern for Our Reputation

Another thing that can be a hindrance is being concerned about our reputation. Do we constantly wonder what other people are thinking? You aren't going to go anywhere if you worry about trying to please people, because some people don't even know what they want. One day they want the music loud, but maybe tomorrow they want it soft. They may not like your makeup, but the next day they may suggest that you should wear more makeup. The fear of man brings a snare (see Prov. 29:25). Don't be a people pleaser.

There are no two pastors' wives who are exactly alike. There is no mold or model. When I became a pastor's wife 23 years ago, I would have liked a manual or instruction book; but there is no such thing, because there can't be. We are all so uniquely different. God has put different things in me than He has put in you. So be who God made you to be and let His light shine bright through you.

Lord of Your Schedule

We need to give our schedule to the Lord. I thought I had done fairly well when it came to releasing my schedule, but I realized a while back that I still had kept some control of it. I found myself thinking, *Hey, I gave all these hours to the Lord and the ministry, and now it is my time.* It is never my time; it all belongs to Him. We have been crucified with Christ; it is not ourselves but Christ who lives in us (see Gal. 2:20).

Sometimes it's hard to be open to the Lord's leading when we've made plans, programs and schedules. On many days, I might have a plan, but nothing works out because of interruptions and unplanned circumstances. I am learning that sometimes all of those interruptions are what God really had planned for me that day, and I don't want to miss them. Recently, I was hustling through the church, late for a meeting, when a woman's voice called out, "Can I talk to you for a minute?" I thought, *Great, just what I don't need.* When she began to pour out her story—it was just so sad that I could have cried. I told her, "I'm sorry if I seemed like I was in a hurry." Silently, I said, *Who cares if I'm late for the meeting; I want to be available for people in need.* I'm learning. It's not always easy, but people are why we are here.

It is just like God to give back to us when we give to others. It is a new thing to put into the computer of our mind: "Give, and it will be given to you. A good measure, pressed down, shaken together and running over, will be poured into your lap" (Luke 6:38). The less I think about myself, the happier I am. I mean that sincerely. Anytime I begin to feel sorry for myself and have self-pity, God shows me somebody I can help. It is like medicine to my sick soul. When I reach into somebody else's life, that joy comes back to me.

Fear

One of the biggest traps that Satan lays for us is fear. But 2 Timothy 1:7 says, "For God has not given us a spirit of fear, but of power and of love and of a sound mind" (*NKJV*). Further, Hebrews tells us, "Let us lay aside every weight, and the sin which so easily ensnares us" (Heb. 12:1, *NKJV*). Fear is a snare that wants to grab us.

The things about which the devil will try to just freak you out are really nothing. So how do we begin to overcome our fears? Refuse them. It takes effort and energy, but we need to look away from our fears and look to Jesus. We have to remember that He has not given us a spirit of fear (see 2 Tim. 1:7). Let Him be in charge of your life and don't worry about it.

Have we set aside those things that have weighed us down so that we can really be free to soar to those places that God has destined for all of us? Let's make a start today to ask Jesus to free us from those sins that try to keep us from victory.

Attitude About Ourselves

Feelings of Inadequacy

Do we feel inadequate for our role as pastors' wives? We probably all do. I hope there is no pastor's wife who really feels qualified, because that would trouble me. Recognizing our inadequacies makes us rely on Jesus for His power and sufficiency. We step up to the plate, answering our call, expecting God to show us—and He does. So it's not about us; it's about us allowing His Holy Spirit to flow through us.

"I can do everything through him who gives me strength" (Phil. 4:13). Can we heal anybody? We know that we can't. Can we conjure up a word of knowledge or the gift of faith? No and no, but God will let them flow through us as we make ourselves available to Him. Second Corinthians 12:9 says, "My grace is sufficient for you, for my power is made perfect in weakness."

So what is our task? To be bold in obedience to God and watch Him show up. We just plunk out our simple efforts and God shows up and does the impossible; but we still need to show up. So never feel like you are inadequate; none of us is adequate. Just be there, show up and watch what God will do.

Feelings of Discouragement

Maybe you are struggling with discouragement over past failures. Discouragement is one of the biggest obstacles that keep people from being where they need to be. You may be hurting and tired; but don't give up. Through Christ there is more in you than you can believe. Psalm 145:14 says, "The LORD upholds all those who fall and lifts up all who are bowed down." You may have fallen down, but you need to get back up. God did not send you here to quit. Don't ever give up. He will send you encouragement and the help you need to get the job done.

Your attitude, not your aptitude, will determine your altitude. "Be strong in the Lord and in his mighty power" (Eph. 6:10). You can do a whole lot more than you think.

Deceptive "Limitations"

What does God want to do with us? How have we limited Him in our lives? What more will He do if we will just step out in simple faith? Probably most of us have heard the story about Roger Bannister, the guy who broke the world record for running the four-minute mile. Well, it was believed at that time that it was an impossible thing for the human body to do, but he believed that he could do it. He worked hard, he trained and he visualized himself doing it until he really believed it—and he did it. After Roger Bannister broke the four-minute mile record, two months later it was broken again. So it wasn't impossible to do—people had simply believed that it was.

In a similar way, the devil has told some of us that some things are just not possible. But we can break those barriers with faith in God's Word. If God said it, we can do it—with God all things are possible (see Mark 10:27). Isaiah 40:29 says, "He gives strength to the weary and increases the power of the weak."

Attitude About God

The third attitude we need to take a look at is our attitude about God. This is the most important attitude, since what we believe about God determines what He can do through us. Do we really believe that God is who He says He is—the healer, our comforter, the One who will never leave us or forsake us?

Realize that He is a truly personal God. He knows you so well. He knows what you're going through. He knows that you are looking for help. He will be there to help you. Watch for His presence, because He is there for you—He is so real. He is right here and He is able to take you through any challenge you might be facing. Praise the Lord for His goodness!

A Final Thought

If I can leave you with one thought, it would be this: Let the Lord be your main pursuit. As pastors' wives, our schedules can be demanding, but don't let your quiet time with the Lord ever escape you. He needs to be our passion. Read the Bible and meditate on it often. Listen to the Bible on audiocassette. Keep pouring the Word of God into your heart so that you can pour it out to others.

Do you doubt that you can share His Word and His love effectively? Doubt no longer. The Spirit who dwells in you will uncover your gifts and make you fruitful in service. Don't leave the power, the gifts He has given you, your talents—all that He has put in you—unused! Pray that God would stir up those gifts in you. Pray that you would have a heart that is passionate for the things of the Lord. Make the rest of your ministry the very best of your ministry!

Prayer

God, I pray that we, your daughters, would be passionate for what is on Your heart and that we would be true heroes. That is what I want our lives to be. Help us to die to selfishness, to fears, to those things that try to entrap us and keep us from being fruitful for You. I pray that these beautiful women can reach the people in their congregations— those people to whom they are meant to minister Your love. I pray this in Jesus' name, amen.

ℒEARNING POWERFUL PRAYER FOR GROWTH

JOYCE ROGERS

Does God always answer prayer? Should we ever give up praying? What do you do when you're waiting on God? Is the pastor's home exempt from trouble? Is the main purpose of prayer to get the things we want? Well, not exactly. The main purpose of prayer is to have such an intimate relationship with Jesus that we find out what He wants and then ask for it.

The greatest thing that God desires for your life and for my life is that we grow into the likeness of His Son, Jesus. And He will make all things work together for our good (see Rom. 8:28), because He's a good God. But you have to be convinced of this truth, even in your darkest hours.

Learning from David's Sorrow

If we are looking for an example of steadfast faith, we need only look to Psalm 18 and to David. He cried out to God, and God enlarged his life through powerful prayer and trust.

Praising God

Before David enumerated his troubles in prayer, he praised God: "I love you, O LORD, my strength" (Ps. 18:1). The first thing David did, and what we should do, was to make a declaration of love to God—before anything else. Praise is twofold: It's telling God how much you love Him, and it is expressing your gratitude to Him for who He is. When trouble knocks at your door, do you just throw up your hands? Do you go into hysterics and say, "Oh, my, what am I going to do?" Well, that's not what we ought to do, is it? We should first of all declare our love to God, to Jesus, no matter what our trouble is or what the outcome is going to be.

After David declared his love to God, he then explained to God what He meant to him. "The LORD is my rock, my fortress and my deliverer; my God is my rock, in whom I take refuge" (v. 2). That's the second time that David mentioned God as his strength. David just ran into his high tower—into God. And we, too, should focus on the Lord and not on our troubles. That's easier said than done, isn't it? But because David knew God personally, he was able to focus on God first instead of on his troubles.

Crying Out for Deliverance

After David had praised God, he cried out to Him for deliverance from all his distresses. In verse 3, he said, "I call to the LORD, who is worthy of praise, and I am saved from my enemies." David was intentional in his prayer. It was powerful prayer. And his prayer life wasn't just a "think so," "maybe so,"—no, he had a confidence in God that God was going to save him from his enemies because he knew God intimately, and so should we have that same confidence.

Then David went into a description of all his troubles. He poured out his heart to God. "The cords of death entangled me, the torrents of destruction overwhelmed me. In my distress I called to the LORD; I cried to my God for help" (vv. 4,6). I don't know whether all these troubles were literal or symbolic, but whatever they were, David had been in a mess of trouble. But he didn't hesitate to share his problems and his distress with God.

We can do that, too, can't we? God knows our troubles, but we can still pour out our heart to God. The only thing we shouldn't do is blame God for our troubles. Instead, count your blessings and name them one by one—it will surprise you to see all that God has done in your life.

Will troubles come to the pastor's home? Will times of darkness come? Will tragedy, sorrow and disappointment knock on your door, even when you're doing your best to serve God? Yes, yes and yes. But don't despair. Instead, tell God all about your troubles. God wants to hear about them. He is waiting to embrace you, to comfort you, in your time of need.

God's Timing

As we watch the story unfold in Psalm 18, we're probably thinking that it's time for David to be delivered. But guess what happened in David's case? God delayed deliverance, and the darkness set in. "My cry came before [God], into his ears. The earth trembled and quaked, and the foundations of the mountains shook" (vv. 6-7).

Have you ever been in trouble and then it got worse? Most of us have. What do you do when God delays an answer to prayer and then the darkness sets in? Set aside what you may have done in the past. Today when troubles come, lean in on Jesus. And then offer up your heartache as a sacrifice to God.

Deliverance at Last

What happened in the end? David's deliverance finally came. "He reached down from on high and took hold of me; he drew me out of deep waters" (v. 16). Sweet deliverance!

God will bring deliverance. Now, it may not be exactly as you wanted, but you know, ladies, He will deliver you and enlarge your life. David said in verse 19, "He brought me out into a spacious place; he rescued me because he delighted in me."

A Final Thought

As you look to the Lord for deliverance, keep in mind the conditions for having your prayers answered.

- Clean house before you pray (in other words, be sure there is no sin in your life).
- Ask according to God's will.
- Ask in Jesus' name.
- Agree in prayer with other believers.
- Pray continually.

0

Prayer

*God, enlarge my life. Help me to grow as a result of trials,
heartaches and powerful prayer. Allow me to know You more
intimately than I ever have before. Help me to hold on to You,
and You alone. I trust that You will bring deliverance.
I pray this in the mighty name of Jesus, amen.*

ℋOW TO APPLY THE SEASONS OF A WOMAN'S LIFE

LOIS I. EVANS

The Lord has just kind of given me a passion to share with women that you can really experience the full measure of the blessings that God has for your life. The world tells us that we can't, and we as Christian women have bought into that lie. I travel quite often and hear what's going on in the hearts of women, especially in the hearts of pastors' wives. I get to hear their frustration and disappointment in life. They always ask the same question, "Will it always be this way?"

You know what? I asked the same question when I had two kids and a lot of diaper bags and strollers and highchairs and a new ministry. I thought, *My goodness, these are gifts from the Lord, but will this nonstop, hectic way of life ever change? Will it always be this way?* I can give you a resounding answer of hope. If you are in a difficult season, it too will pass. God will make a way.

When difficult times come, I remember the words of my mother: "I am going to hang in there for His name's sake." So when life becomes overwhelming for me—and it does—I hear my mother's voice. You and I have to remember that we are here for His name's sake. We are here to bring Him glory. My life verse is John 15:5: "I am the vine; you are the branches. If a man remains in me and I in him, he will bear much fruit; apart from me you can do nothing." We need Him.

Esther: A Woman for All Seasons

If there is any godly woman who can relate to our difficulties in facing the seasons of life, it is Esther. God had an amazing plan for her life, but she wasn't always aware of that. There were moments when she struggled. Yet in the end, she persevered: She answered God's call; she entered into victorious living.

The Silent Years

As the book of Esther opens, we see Esther investing in God's plan for her life. Although she was not sure what God intended to do through her she was guided by Mordecai, a godly man (see Esther 2:10-11,19-20). So she served the Jewish people, day in and day out. I'm sure she sometimes wondered, *Why don't they take care of themselves?* She couldn't understand what God was doing. These were the silent years of her life. She wanted to get on with things, with her call, with her ministry; but nothing ever changed. Job voices her lament, I think, "No matter where I turn, He is not there; but He knows my way, the path that I take. When He has tried me, I shall come forth as pure gold" (see Job 23:8-10).

Yet God was working in her, preparing her for the challenges that lay ahead. Perhaps God is doing the same with you. He is working; maybe you should be working, too. During this silent time, invest in your Mordecai—your pastor-husband—and invest in your family. So often in the midst of church-related activities and demands, you might forget that your family is the ministry God has given you. Delve right in and forget what the world has told you. You don't know God's plan for your life. He is working it out in your life each day. He is developing you. He wants to help you grow into His plan. So make the most of the silent time by ministering to your husband and your family. Be the best pastor's wife you can be.

People in the church ask me what I do. The answer is simple: I am Executive Personal Assistant to Tony Evans—that is my title. You have the position of a pastor's wife. You are the helpmate to the pastor.

The Leadership Years

Once God had stretch Esther through the routine of ministry, she entered into her leadership role. She walked right into the next season and right into the palace. Once she made it into the palace, she was put away for 12 months (see Esther 2:12-14). I know she must have thought to herself, *Come on. I have been through this before, serving all these years!* But God put her away for 12 months so she could be properly prepared to walk in to see the king.

Has God led you to a place of leadership, only to put things on hold for a time? Then perhaps He is trying to tell you something. God might put you in this situation so that you can reflect. You might be waiting for 12 months. Some people might be waiting for 20 years. Through it all you have just got to trust in God, that He is doing something. He is taking you through that season in your life to show you that you can trust Him.

Harvest Time

After her period of preparation, God moved Esther into the harvest season. After a time of prayer and fasting, she was victorious through the power of the Lord (see Esther 5—7). The evil Haman was killed on the gallows that he had prepared for Mordecai. God had taken care of the enemies of His people—and He did it by working through Esther's life. What would have happened if Esther had not persevered through the challenging seasons? She would not have found victory and blessing in the Lord.

I can tell you today that we need to open our mouths and learn to bless the Lord at all times, even in the midst of difficult situations. If you invest now, in the silent years, I promise you that the Lord will lead you into the harvest time. So make the most of the silent years, too. You have a beautiful life in the Lord. Live it!

A Final Thought

Dear pastors' wives, I have one piece of advice to leave you with: Do like Esther did. She was not supposed to walk in and see the king, but she did anyway (see Esther 4:11; 5:1-2). She stepped out in faith, with prayer and fasting. And what happened? The king looked at her and said, "What do you want, Honey? I can give you half the kingdom" (see Esther 5:3). You and I didn't get half the Kingdom when the Lord saved us—we got the whole Kingdom. Whatever is His is Yours. You are in Him. So walk in Him and He will be beside you during this season. Hold your head up high and say "Halleluiah" anyhow!

Blessing

Dear Lord, I ask You to bless the woman who is reading this book, looking for guidance, desiring to walk in Your ways. If she is in a difficult season of her life, I ask that You would strengthen her and encourage her. Let her see the beauty in her life—the joy amid the struggles. Let her see that You are walking with her each step of the way and that everything in her life is part of Your plan for her— Your plan to give her a future and a hope [see Jer. 29:11]. Just bless her, Lord. I thank You for her. I pray this in Jesus' name, amen.

ℋEALTHY LIVING

JOYCE ROGERS

Generally, Christians make an effort to honor their bodies by living a healthy lifestyle (see 1 Cor. 6:19-20). But what does it mean to live a healthy lifestyle? Most of us who are Christians believe this means that you shouldn't smoke, drink or do drugs, but we do plenty of bad food. Or if we don't, it's because we want to lose weight, look better or live longer. Now there's nothing wrong with these goals, as long as they are by-products of the right motivation: glorifying God with our bodies.

As I began to study God's Word for myself, I found out that it contained nutritional principles and guidelines. Of course, the Bible isn't a cookbook—it doesn't have charts for fat grams and calories. Nevertheless, you'd be surprised how many biblical and nutritional principles there are in the Bible, and I want to share some of them with you.

God's Food Groups

The book of Deuteronomy speaks of seven good things that the Israelites should eat and drink. God told the children of Israel that these good things to eat and drink would be in the Promised Land. I really believe that if we ate this way today we would enter into our own promised land of healthy living and eating. I want to share briefly about these seven food groups.

Water

We cannot live without water—it is essential to life. Therefore, it should come as no surprise that God's people would have an abundance of water. In the book of Deuteronomy, we are told that the Promised

Land was "a land with streams and pools of water, with springs flowing in the valleys and hills" (8:7). Water is one of God's most wonderful provisions, and it's amazing how we undervalue it. We think we have to add some carbonation, some caffeine, some flavor, some sugar. So we're going to have to make a deliberate choice to return to plain old-fashioned water—8 to 10 glasses a day, to be exact.

Whole Grains

The second food mentioned is whole grains. Deuteronomy 8:8 says that this good land is the "land with wheat and barley," and I'm sure they had other wonderful grains. The natural whole grains were part of the good land that God promised, and they were literally the staff of life for these people. They didn't understand vitamins and minerals and protein and fiber and all those things, did they? But neither did they know about the refining processes that rob the whole grains of most of their vitamins, minerals and fiber. Did you know that it wasn't until the 1900s that the refining process was discovered? Up to that point, grains were milled locally and bread was baked at home. So what's the message here? Put aside the processed grains and get back to nature. Eat whole grains!

Honey

The third food mentioned is honey (see Deut. 8:8). Proverbs 24:13 says, "Eat honey, my son, for it is good; honey from the comb is sweet to your taste." There are numerous honey flavors, so find one that fits your taste. The stronger tasting ones have the most nutritional value. There's a spiritual application to eating honey; it is compared to wisdom. If you find wisdom, you'll have a wonderful future full of hope (see Prov. 24:13-14).

Milk

The fourth food is milk. Deuteronomy 6:3 says that this land was a land flowing with milk and honey. If you've read much in the health world, there is controversy about milk. I believe that if we had the kind of milk they had back in biblical times (and I had my own cow in the backyard) then that would definitely be wholesome milk. Milk is one of the most easily digested foods and is said to be one of the chief sources of calcium, which is so essential for building healthy bones. Other people claim that calcium and other nutrients in cow's milk are not adequately absorbed into your body. I myself drink milk; you'll have to weigh the evidence and make up your own mind about whether "modern" milk is appropriate.

Fruits and Vegetables

The fifth food item is fruits and vegetables. Deuteronomy 8:8 speaks of a land of vines and fig trees and pomegranates. We need to eat fruits and vegetables, because they are rich in vitamins, minerals, fiber and enzymes. Of course, they are best in their raw state. But if you cook them, use steam (cooking them lightly with very little water). You want to keep those vitamins that help regulate metabolism, help convert fat and carbohydrates into energy, and assist in forming bones and tissues. So fruits and vegetables, particularly raw ones, are very rich in all these things.

Remember when your mama told you to eat more fruits and vegetables? Well, the cry of the health world today is, eat more than you think you need! Recent studies indicate that people who eat the most daily servings of fruits and vegetables have half the cancer rates of those who eat the least.

Oil

The sixth food group is oil. According to Deuteronomy 8:8, the Promised Land was a land of olive oil. And this brings us to the immortal question: Fat—good or bad? For a long time, nutritionists were telling us that fat was good for us; then they changed their mind and said it was bad. We went through the fat craziness; I got on that bandwagon and counted my fat grams religiously. I got down to almost zero fat grams at one time; and then I looked at my hands, and they were so dry. I realized that maybe I needed some fat in my diet after all.

The truth of the matter is that there are some good fats and some bad fats. The good fats are called the EFAs, or the essential fatty acids. They're probably the most important and the least understood of all fats. They're necessary for energy production, growth and tissue repair, blood pressure regulation and fat metabolism. But the typical

American diet is not rich in EFAs. The foods that are rich in EFAs are certain nuts, walnuts, seeds, oils and cold water fish like salmon and tuna. An inadequate intake of these and an overconsumption of bad fats will create an imbalance in your body and lead to disease. The worst of the bad fats are the saturated fats. So be aware of what kinds of fat you're eating—and know that your beloved junk food that tastes so good isn't so good for you.

Meat

The seventh food group is meat. I am a meat eater, and I do believe that the Bible will back me up as I promote eating meat. In fact, Genesis 9:3 says, "Everything that lives and moves will be food for you." I do, however, follow the Old Testament dietary laws; I don't eat pork and I don't eat shellfish (that's something that you have to decide for yourself). But God gave us permission to eat meat; still, we've done a lot of bad things to our meat, haven't we? We treat it with hormones and antibiotics. So I don't eat as much of the red meats anymore; but I do eat some because we need the protein.

A Final Thought

Recent studies have shown that a healthy diet can keep the mind healthy as we grow older and ward off Alzheimer's. We are advised to increase our daily intake of colorful fruits and vegetables, as well as to eat more oily fish and nuts. We are supposed to steer clear of foods high in saturated fats. So let's make those healthy changes today for a healthy tomorrow.

Blessing

Lord, bless each woman reading this today. I thank You so much for them, for the wonderful bodies You have given them. I pray that You would help them keep their bodies as temples of the Holy Spirit so that You might work effectively through them. I pray that each of them might take these biblical principles to heart and incorporate them in their daily lives. I thank You for these wonderful women, Lord. I pray in Jesus' name, amen.

$\mathcal{H}$OW TO HAVE A "BODY BY GOD"

SHERI LERNER

Why are you interested in learning more about a health and wellness regimen? Maybe you want to have a better body. Maybe you just want to feel better. Some of you may just want to make sure you're around longer for your families. Those are all really great reasons, but there's a bigger reason that we all need to look at our health and our wellness: God has called all of you women as leaders, and you've got a group of followers behind you, people who look up to you and follow you. So if you're not taking care of your health and wellness, guess what? Neither are they.

No one questions the fact that we need to honor God with our bodies (see 1 Cor. 6:20). But in order to do that, we must first have a plan. Job 42:2 says, "No plan of yours can be thwarted." If we search out God's plan for our health and prayerfully seek Him, we will succeed. Once we have a plan, we need to be committed to the plan. Proverbs 16:3 tells us, "Commit to the LORD whatever you do, and your plans will succeed."

Today we're going to take a look at how planning—and then committing to—an exercise and healthy eating program can help you fulfill God's call on your life.

Exercise

The first thing you need to understand about exercise is why you should do it and how it can help. If you understand the great benefits of exercise, it's going to be a lot easier to motivate yourself. And just in case you're wondering, I have to force myself to exercise probably four out of six times a week. Of course, once I'm exercising, I love it. Plus, I know that if I get my tush out of bed and do the exercise, I'll have way more energy than if I had had the extra hour of sleep.

Why Exercise?

Exercising at a very minimal level will immediately improve many medical conditions, including arthritis, diabetes and heart problems; total lack of exercise will lead to an early death. Extreme levels of fitness are not even good for you: Athletes who train at a very extreme level actually suffer detrimental side effects, So the key here is to focus on moderate exercise: 20-30 minutes, 3 to 4 times a week. Those who exercise moderately can expect significant health benefits.

- Exercise increases your life expectancy.
- Exercise speeds up your body's ability to detoxify, lowering the risk of cancer.
- Exercise increases the amount of oxygen carried to your body's cells (lack of exercise literally chokes your cells).
- Exercise burns fat; therefore it won't go to your heart and clog your arteries (and it won't go to your thighs).
- Exercise strengthens your bones and muscles.
- Exercise decreases your resting heart rate.
- Exercise increases your immunity.
- Exercise allows your body to handle stress more effectively.
- Exercise gives you time alone with the Lord.

How to Get Started

Starting an exercise program does not mean you have to join a gym. It doesn't mean you have to buy spandex. It doesn't mean you have to leave your home. You can start right in your living room with some basic cardio exercise. Cardio exercise is the first part of an exercise program and includes any kind of bodily movement, such as walking, jogging, biking, dancing. It doesn't have to be any kind of fancy movement. You just need to start moving.

The second part of the exercise program is what we call resistance training. This type of exercise helps you achieve maximum fat burning as you really tone your body. You will probably want to get a set of small weights, or dumbbells, and begin at home with simple biceps, triceps and chest presses. (More information on these exercises can be found in our book *Body by God*.) But remember before you get started with resistance training to learn how to exercise safely. When you're doing these exercises, you want to look at your posture. You want to make sure you're maintaining a healthy posture for your spine.

Nutrition

Now that we've covered the basics of exercise, let's move on to nutrition.

Seeing the Value of Good Nutrition

Consider this: If a pastor of a church were an alcoholic or a drug user, how often do you think he would really be hearing from God? And how effective do you think he would be in reaching his congregation? Not very effective. Well, when you are putting bad food in your body on a regular basis, the result is exactly the same. Those chemicals and addictive ingredients interfere with the way that God is able to reach you and the way that God is able to speak to you. So that's part of the reason that we need to take our nutrition more seriously: God wants us to hear Him, and He wants us to hear Him as well as we can.

Body by God

Our Body by God plan is our view of how God wants us to eat. The neat thing about it is that it's not a diet. We have certain rules for Body by God, and one of my favorite rules is the vacation rule, which allows you to occasionally eat your favorite foods. Having vacation days, knowing that you're going to get to eat the things you really like, makes it a lot easier to be more disciplined during the rest of the month.

The Body by God plan features food by God, the food that God made and intended for us to eat. It also features food by man, food products that are far removed from their natural state and potentially harmful to the body. Let me give you a couple of examples so you can clearly see the difference between the two. First, let's consider an apple. God made it; you pick it off the tree. Now you've got to wash it because a lot of pesticides have probably been sprayed on it. But you eat the apple and your body knows exactly what to do with it. Your body can digest the apple and get all the good stuff out of it in order to nourish your cells. Now let's consider a snack cake. You eat all that gooey, yummy pink cake with fluffy frosting, and your body asks, "What the heck is this?" It has no idea what to do with it. It goes into panic mode, throwing your whole system out of balance.

The overall goal of the Body by God program is to eat as much food by God as you can and as little food by man as you can. Did you notice I didn't tell you that you couldn't eat any food by man? That's because when we totally deprive ourselves, we're never satisfied—and we fail. If you've really struggled with your eating habits, I encourage you to pray about it. If you really struggle in getting good stuff in and not eating the bad stuff, then that's something you need to pray about. Ask Him to bless your plans, and they'll succeed.

Food by Man List

Let's take a look at the nine most harmful things on the food by man list.

Number 1 on the food by man list is *pork products*.

Number 2 is *shellfish*. (Please don't close the book!) I mean, I love shrimp and lobster just as much as the next person. So just limit the amount of shellfish you eat.

Number 3 is *sugar substitutes*. They are man-made products. Sugar substitutes are not supposed to be ingested into your body, and your body will react to them as it would to any other foreign object. I also want to point out that a packet of sugar has only 15 calories—so if you really want a sweetener, just eat the sugar.

Number 4 is probably the hardest one to eliminate: *hydrogenated oils*. The reason that it's so hard to eliminate is because it's in just about everything that's in a package. But you can find a good health-food store that sells packaged projects that do not use hydrogenated oil. It's an extra trip and it might cost a few more dollars, but it's not worth getting cancer over.

Number 5 is *fast, refined and fried foods.* They're chemically altered and, again, your body doesn't know what to do with these processed foods. A lot of people, when we start talking about getting on a healthier diet and buying things from the health-food store, say that it's just way too expensive. Well, the other day I asked someone how much money she spends when she takes her family to McDonalds. She told me that it costs $25 to feed her family of five at McDonalds. With that $25, you can buy a lot of stuff from the health-food store.

Number 6 is the *regular use of animal products.* A lot of the protein that we recommend in the Body by God plan is an animal product: chicken, eggs, moderate amounts of red meat. But the problem is that the stuff you buy at the grocery store has been injected with hormones, antibiotics and steroids. So it's really important for you to find an organic source of protein and animal products. If you go on the Internet, you'll find a number of different companies that will actually ship directly to your house. It is a little bit more expensive, but it's well worth it.

Number 7 is *dairy products.* Again, dairy products are filled with all sorts of chemicals. If you are concerned about calcium, you can easily get all you need by eating a balanced diet.

Number 8 is *caffeine.* (It hurts for me to put this on the list). It's obviously very, very addictive. Caffeine is also hard on your stomach and harmful to your heart. (All of us coffee drinkers can lift each other up in prayer about getting off this bad stuff.)

Number 9 is, you guessed it, *sugar.* It is very, very addictive, as we all know. And that is why a lot of people just can't eat sugar in moderation. After you've eaten tons of sugar for years on end, your pancreas wears out—it doesn't work anymore. The result? Diabetes. So if you really have a lot of trouble with sugar, your best bet is just to go cold turkey with it. Otherwise, your body will develop an addiction, and you'll always want more.

A Final Thought

I do the best I can to live a "body by God" life, But I'm not perfect. I eat cookies three times a week (though I usually choose to eat healthy cookies). And, yes, I drink coffee every single day. And I do often eat a handful of Wintergreen Lifesavers. Yet these things are balanced by a whole lot of really good things that I do both nutritionally and exercise-wise. I feel great—I'm at a place now that I wasn't 10 years ago. So I do understand the challenges you face as you seek to live a healthy lifestyle.

The point I want to make is that all you are called to do is your best. So if you haven't been exercising much or if you haven't been eating a healthy diet, don't beat yourself up. Just start somewhere—and take little steps. Try adding a 10-minute walk to your daily routine. Try substituting a healthy snack for that afternoon candy bar. You *can* honor God with your body. Resolve to get started today!

Blessing

Dear Lord, please bless the woman who is seeking to make healthy
changes in her life. You see her heart, Lord; You know that she desires
to honor You with her body and her soul. Give her the strength
she needs to commit to a plan for making moderate exercise and
good nutrition a part of her life. Bless Your daughter's efforts,
Lord. I ask this in Jesus' precious name, amen.

$\mathcal{H}$EALTH AND WHOLENESS MADE EASY

JULIE MEEK

Have you ever wondered why it is so difficult for us to be successful in caring for ourselves? I mean, we know that we should eat nutritional food and exercise regularly, but often we don't. Or if we do, our grand scheme for staying fit and healthy is short-lived. And it's not because we lack willpower that we fail; rather, it's because we lack a plan. Most of us plunge headlong into a new diet or new exercise routine. We make up our minds, and then we run out and get started without really thinking it through. That's a recipe for failure.

Developing an Action Plan

So what do we need to do as we seek to live a healthy lifestyle? We need to have an action plan. Let's take the first step.

Identifying the Problem

Think of a time in your life when you were not doing your best because you were not feeling your best. Perhaps that time is right now and it has begun to affect what you are able to accomplish on any given day. You find it increasingly difficult to just power through your day. What contributes most to your not feeling well?

Well, I promise you that your answer is one or more of the five following things: physical symptoms that are bothering you (such as headaches); chronic conditions (such as diabetes); stress or stress-related emotions (such as anxiety); negative lifestyle behaviors (such as alcohol addiction); and basic need issues (such as lack of adequate food or shelter). Now, if you aren't feeling well, you are probably experiencing at least two of these. But if you could only change one of the things you identified—the one that would have the greatest impact on helping you feel better and function better in your everyday life—which would it be? Write it down on a piece of paper.

Identify the Benefits

You will only make successful behavior changes when the benefits of changing to that new behavior exceed the benefits of your current behavior. So that's why it's really important to think about how changing this aspect of your life would improve how you are feeling and what you are able to do. And write down everything you can think of that would be a benefit of really focusing on this aspect of your health. Perhaps you're thinking, *If I could just get off 10 more pounds, I could wear those 6 outfits that have been hanging in the closet. They are just a little too tight, but I can't throw them away because I spent too much money on them.* Whatever your benefits are, the important thing is that they are real to you and they mean something to you.

The other thing to think through is whether changing would be a benefit to someone in your life who is important to you: your husband, your children, a close friend. I don't know if you're like me, but I think a lot of pastors' wives are like nurses—we are more motivated to change something in our lives to help someone else than we are to help ourselves.

Identifying Barriers

Now here's the tricky part and the one that is really important. The next thing you need to do is write down all the things that could get in the way of your being successful. So I want you to start writing down the barriers. What could get in your way of being successful? Perhaps it's lack of time or money. Maybe it's lack of convenience. Maybe you don't have the support you need.

Overcoming the Barriers

The next step is to think about how you can overcome each barrier in a way that will work for you. Not in a way that works for Pastor Joe's wife, because her life is not like your life. No, find a way that works for you.

Let me give you an example from my own life. I travel a great deal; my schedule is crazy. So the hectic nature of my life is a barrier to my getting regular exercise. How do I plan each day to overcome that? I look for little ways to fit in all the exercise I need. If my husband, Ted, and I want to go to the theater and it's only seven blocks away, we don't get in our car; we walk there and back. So now my pretty inactive and pretty hectic life starts looking like a life that has fitness built in. Of course, I don't have an exercise program in the traditional sense, but I'm getting an adequate amount of exercise. What's more, I'm strong and I'm agile and I feel good. And why? Because I've got a plan—and I'm making the most of my life by overcoming barriers.

Finding Support

One of the most important factors in determining whether or not people are successful in making some change in their lives is not only that they have a plan but also that they have some support. For example, you may want to change your diet, but your family doesn't want you to quit cooking what you've been cooking for years because the status quo menu tastes good. And so you're faced with having to cook two meals or to challenge your family's eating habits, which is a very difficult thing. In this case, you have to recognize that you'll need to have a conversation with your family about the importance of healthy eating. Ask them what would be some initial changes to your menu—in the way you cook and in the way you shop—that would be acceptable to them. That way they can support you as you try to make a change in your life.

The bottom line is that you need social support. It may be a family member, a coworker or a neighbor. Actually most of us profit best from having support from people we don't know all that well—they are somewhat outside of the realm of our daily life. This allows them to be more objective and to give us perspective.

Putting It All Together

This is when you bring everything together and really get to work. Set a couple of short-term goals and announce your decision to your family, friends and other members of your social support network. This way you will have built-in accountability as you set your plan in motion.

Keep your "overcome the barriers" plan handy and revise it as needed, because new barriers will pop up that you hadn't considered. Develop a tangible, explicit strategy for dealing with each new barrier.

Reward yourself. This is very important. Plan some special treat for yourself when you reach a short-term goal. Your reward could be anything: a hot bath, an outing with a friend, a trip to the mall.

Remind yourself of your commitment. The way you do that is to write out your plan: your strategy, your benefits, your barriers, your short-term goals, whom you are going to ask for support, your reward. Then sign your plan. Hang it on your bathroom mirror or above the kitchen sink.

Yes, there will be days when you think you can't change things, when you think that you are doomed to not feel well. But take heart. You can make the changes that you need to. God assures you that you can do all things in Him (see Phil. 4:13). So commit your plan to Him and He will ensure its success (see Prov. 16:3).

A Final Thought

The final thing I want to share with you is that relapse is not the aberration. Relapse is the norm. Relapse means that you're a normal human being. So when you relapse, stop and ask yourself, *What did I learn from this?* rather than feel guilty about it. You know, it doesn't do any good to feel guilty. But it does do you good to get up and try again!

Prayer

Dear Lord, help me to devise a plan that will allow me to feel better. Right now I feel tired and sick. I feel like I am not able to do all that I should for myself, my family, the church. I need Your help, Lord, to feel better. I need Your guidance as I set my goals and seek to overcome barriers. I need You, Lord, to be beside me each day. I thank You, Lord, that You are faithful and that You work in all things for my good [see Rom. 8:28]. I pray in Jesus' name, amen.

PART THREE

FREE TO SOAR THROUGH NURTURING MARRIAGE, FAMILY AND RELATIONSHIPS

How to Raise Well-Rounded Children in an Odd-Shaped World

LISA CLAY

Every career has its struggles, including full-time pastoral ministry. It is imperative for parents in the ministry to plan their parenting, just as they plan important events and outline church-growth strategies. Parenting on purpose is an exceptional success model; children who have parents with a plan will prosper, grow and excel!

Remember the story of David and Goliath? Young David took on combat with the Philistine giant Goliath and won. In a similar way, our children face cultural giants: sexual immoralities; addictions; integrity issues such as dishonesty, cheating, stealing and corrupting behaviors, to name just a few enemies. At times these giants will seem invincible and overwhelming until we remember that David slew Goliath with a fistful of rocks and a heart full of God. In the same way, our children, armed with their own five smooth stones, can triumph over the giants that threaten them.

Let's look at four of these smooth stone strategies for raising well-prepared, well-armed children who will grow into godly men and women prepared to take on their culture and win.

SMOOTH STONE #1:
Teach Your Children How to Handle Conflict

Train your children how to handle the conflicts that arise in life. I can't speak for you, but we have had our share of conflict in the pastoral ministry. Personally, I wish I had been better equipped to handle difficult conflict; life would have been much easier! We can prepare our children for the challenges of conflict in the following ways:

We begin by helping our children take personal responsibility for their reactions in conflict. They must do more than deal with the obvious conflict at hand; they must look deeper into their own attitudes and reactions. Each of your children will handle conflict differently. For instance, the strong-willed leader type is decisive but can also be overbearing in conflict, often becoming forceful, bossy and mean. Help that child to think before speaking, to pursue self-control, to back away from an explosive situation and to seek peace.

Help your child to recognize how serious and important it is to practice forgiving others. When your child holds a grudge, he is setting himself up to be disciplined and punished by God. Matthew 18:32-34 reads:

> The master called the servant in. "You wicked servant," he said. "I cancelled all that debt of yours because you begged me to. Shouldn't you have had mercy on your fellow servant just as I had on you?" In anger the master turned him over to the jailers ["tormentors" in the *King James* translation] . . . until he should pay back all he owed.

Your children are never too young to be taught to forgive. You must begin instilling this truth into their lives so they will be prepared to handle difficult people and explosive moments.

On a practical level, you can begin by noticing when your child takes offense. Notice when he or she is holding a grudge. Work with your child to understand the Father's mercy and his or her obligation as a Christian to be merciful to others.

Teach your children to respect, honor and obey authority. Rebellion and stubbornness toward those in authority will guarantee your child a very difficult life. First Samuel 15:22 reads, "To obey is better than sacrifice, and to heed is better than the fat of rams. For rebellion is as the sin of divination [witchcraft] and arrogance [stubbornness] like the evil of idolatry." You would never tolerate your children bringing a graven image into your home and building an altar at which to worship it. But that is exactly what you are doing when you do not deal with your children's rebellions, both large and small. You can't allow the spirits of rebellion and witchcraft to prosper in your home.

Are you concerned that your child might be rebellious? Some symptoms that will clue you in to a rebellious spirit are partial obedience, a pattern of stubbornness toward people or situations, good intentions without follow-through, justification of self and blame of others, and resistance to correction from anyone in authority.

SMOOTH STONE #2:
Teach Your Children God's Purpose for Their Lives

Ephesians 1:11 says that it's in Christ we found out what we are living for. Your precious children have divine assignments from the Holy Spirit and a specific purpose for being alive. Share this amazing truth with your children, whether they are small or teens. Train your children to be conscious of their purpose, and let them know that the Creator has a very important reason for their existence. Did God speak to you when you were pregnant with your child? What did He say? Share that beautiful promise with your child.

Here are suggestions for making an impact on your children in this area.

• Teach your children that their destiny can only be fulfilled through Christ. Every other road is a dead end.

- Ask God to give you a Scripture promise for your child, and then pray that promise over your child. Remember the words of Jeremiah 29:11, "For I know the plans I have for you . . . plans to prosper you and not to harm you, plans to give you hope and a future."
- Teach your children to expect opposition and to overcome it. Satan will use every tool available in his evil tool belt to thwart God's purpose for your child's life. Daniel 11:32 says, "The people who know their God will firmly resist him."
- Help your children shed other people's expectations. Encourage them to stand up for what God has gifted them to be. Even well-meaning people can confuse your children as to their purpose in life. Continually steer your children back to God for His definition of their life's purpose.
- Teach your children to have the spirit of a finisher. Train your children to handle opposition to their dreams and purpose by having the spirit of a finisher. "I have fought the good fight, I have finished the race, I have kept the faith" (2 Tim. 4:7). As you try to encourage your children to be finishers, focus on helping them finish in small ways: school projects, soccer commitments, babysitting schedules. It's in the day-to-day obligations that you will train them to be finishers and to persevere. By planting the seeds when they are young, you help ensure that they will not give in and give up when the devil discourages them from discovering their destiny.

SMOOTH STONE #3:
Teach Your Children to Manage Their Thought Life

Teach your children to manage their thought lives, for as they think in their hearts, so are they (see Prov. 23:7). Satan will introduce "junk food" thoughts to your children and then attempt to get them to buy into those thoughts, ingest them and feed their souls with those nasty thoughts. Teach your children to recognize "junk food" thoughts and to toss them out as they would a bag of spoiled, moldy, rotten potato chips.

How do you know what your children are thinking about? Listen carefully to what is coming out of their mouths! Is it negative? Is it critical? Is it corrupt or immoral?

Take note of what your children are always talking about, because that is what they are thinking about. Train them from the time they are young to manage their thought life, because their thoughts determine how they behave and who they will become.

SMOOTH STONE #4: Teach Your Children to Fail Forward

We know from experience that failure is more a part of life than success. Train your children to understand that failure is not the end but only the beginning of other, perhaps greater, opportunities. Your children will learn from their failures that life isn't fair and wasn't designed to be fair. With that understanding comes humility, patience and enduring perseverance. Failing forward means failing without losing confidence in God or self, believing that all things (especially hard things) are designed to mold and perfect us for our divine assignment.

There is a poem, written by an unknown author, that aptly describes the power of enduring through failure. I hope you read it to your children when they have experienced the sting of failure.

You Mustn't Quit

When things go wrong as they sometimes will,
when the road you are trudging seems all up hill,
when funds are low and the debts are high,
and you want to smile but you have to sigh,
when care is pressing you down a bit,
rest if you must, but never quit.

Life is strange with its twists and turns,
as every one of us sometimes learns.
And many a failure turns about
he might have won if he'd stuck it out.
Stick to your task though the pace seems slow,
you may succeed with one more blow.
Success is failure turned inside out,
the silver tint of the clouds of doubt.
And you can never tell how close you are,
it may be near when it seems afar.
So stick to the fight when your heart is hit,
it's when things seem worse that you mustn't quit!

Blessing

*Jesus, I love the pastor's wives who are reading this book, and I ask
You to bless and anoint them and their children. Rescue any prodigals
who have strayed from the truth. Bring about Your purposes for each
and every pastor's wife and every one of their children. I pray that the
children of these women will be servants of the living God for as long
as they live. I thank you for the protective covering of the blood of Jesus
upon the lives of these pastors' wives and their children. I pray for
power, authority, wisdom and joy to rise up and conquer fear, doubt,
anger and pain. Pour out Your love upon them right now, in the name
of Jesus Christ of Nazareth, the resurrected One. So be it!*

SIMPLE STEPS TO INTIMATE RELATIONSHIPS

LYNNE DUGAN

What makes people happy? Is it wealth or success? No. The winner is relationships. It's that bonding together that we need. And there's only one real problem in life here on Earth—loneliness. In 1989, we conducted a national survey of pastors' wives. What was the deepest need that the wives said they had? Can you guess? Relationships, a friend, someone they could pray with. But back then we didn't share our own needs with other pastors' wives.

Why is it that relationships are our greatest need? Because we've been made in the image of a relational God: God the Father, God the Son and God the Holy Spirit have relationship with each other. And we have been made in His image. That's why the deepest need that we have is for loving relationships.

What is the Great Commandment? Simply this, that I love the Lord my God with all my heart, strength, body, soul, and my neighbor as myself (see Mark 12:30-31). Our closest neighbor is our husband. When we love God passionately, we are able to love our husbands and ourselves. Can you take out your mirror and look at yourself and say, "I like me; I love me"?

Do you love yourself? Do you know that God loves you more than you can ever ask or think?

Before Intimacy Comes Identity

We cannot have a truly intimate relationship with anyone, especially our husbands, unless we have a deep sense of identity. Otherwise, we would want our husbands to complete us. For me, I thought my identity was my voice—after all, I was a soloist. But when I lost my voice, I lost my identity. Performing had been my identity. And when I lost my voice, I thought, *Who am I?* And so I went to the Scriptures and found out that I was a child of God. That's what mattered. If Jesus loved me, then I did have an identity. If Jesus Christ died on the cross for my sins, then I had a new life.

Dealing with Emotional Pain

Nothing keeps us from having intimate relationships more than emotional pain does. In my own experience, I found that harboring animosity and bitterness robbed me of my joy in the Lord—and my usefulness to Him. Once I finally forgave those who had sinned against me, I found new joy in the Lord's forgiveness. I found healing and was free to soar. Not coincidentally, after my healing, God opened up to me the opportunity to minister to women. God is so blessed. He does restore us and heal our hearts.

Perhaps you are wondering what to do with your pain. Are you supposed to forget your past, your hurts? No, you have to work through your pain. What we are to forget is our anger and bitterness—and we are to forgive.

But what about the pain that comes to us when we remember our own sinfulness? Jesus was sinless, so He was the only One who had the authority to pound her with stones, but He loved her and had compassion on her. He forgave her; and then out of her great love she anointed Him (see Luke 7:46-47). Think of it. She loved much because she had been forgiven much.

Women, do you love Jesus so much? Do you know that you've been really truly forgiven? Oh, He loves us so much. And He wants to take our pain away, and He does.

Recognizing Diverse Needs

Once we have undergone our own healing, we need to be aware that in our marriage relationship we have needs that are different from those of our husbands. Our first need as a wife is for affection; our husbands' is for physical/sexual fulfillment. We want conversation; our husbands want companionship. We want relationship; our husbands want an attractive wife—and the most attractive woman is a woman who can smile. We want trust and honesty; men want domestic support. We want the support of the family in practical ways; men need admiration and respect. Once we are able to recognize that we have these different needs, we can more easily prioritize and meet the needs of our husbands—and we can more effectively communicate our needs to them.

The Secret to Staying in Love

What's the secret to staying in love with your husband? It's dialogue—communication. Through dialogue you give the key to your heart to your husband, and your husband gives the key to his heart to you. Dialoguing is not just discussing where you might go for vacation; it's feeling empathy for each other and listening without interrupting.

I wonder if you have monologue with your husband rather than dialogue. You're talking a lot and you think he's not listening. You know what I found out? Men consider one thing at a time. But you can handle five different topics in the same sentence. The problem is that he's still back at the first thing you said. He's not following you. So alert him: "Honey, I'm changing the subject now." He'll follow—I promise.

Besides covering just one topic at a time, we need to remember that our husbands can't read our minds. Often we get angry and resentful with our husbands. We think they intuitively know how we feel; but that's not how they are made (that's how we're made). So if you are hurt or disappointed or angry, you need to communicate that to him.

A Final Thought

As you seek to renew the intimacy of your relationship with your husband, I encourage, even challenge you, to dialogue with your husband over the space of a few months to see what has been holding you back in your marriage relationship and what needs to be healed, restored and renewed. Some questions that you can discuss include: What did your parents tell you about your worth when you were a child? Did you feel worthy? Did you feel accepted and loved? Did you feel rejected?

What has God shown you that you need to change in your own life with your husband? We're not talking about what he needs to change, but what you need to change.

Blessing

Lord, I do pray that these pastors' wives can put away past hurts and
come alive through Your love and forgiveness. Father, I pray that
You will make the way straight for them. Take away any stumbling
stones that they might have in their own lives. And the only stone
that they need in their lives is the Rock, Jesus Christ. I thank You,
Father, that these women will share these truths with their husbands.
And I thank You for revealing to us what You want us to change.
I thank You that we have been made in Your image. I thank You,
Father, that Your Son is our Bridegroom, our husband,
and that we are Your bride. Amen.

$\mathcal{L}$OVING YOUR COMPANION

BECKY HUNTER

Freedom to soar in any aspect of life, including our relationship with our husband, comes only from a personal relationship with Jesus Christ. Christianity is so upside down from the world's ways. When you give, you get; when you surrender, you win; when you lay down your life, Jesus picks you up with His. In *THE MESSAGE*, Luke 6:38 puts it this way, "Give away your life; you'll find life given back, but not merely given back—given back with bonus and blessing." Being good to your husband is possible when you do it for God. Your husband will be so blessed when he is the recipient of the overflow of what you're doing for Jesus Christ.

Women in general, but wives in particular, are bombarded with the concept "Be all you can be." But the emphasis is all wrong. It needs to be, "Be all you were meant to be." What did God mean for you to be? How does a Christian wife, let alone a pastor's wife, find out what she was meant to be? We can discover it in traditional ways, reading the Bible and talking to women who've gone before us, but God often shows us biblical principles through very ordinary daily activities.

Staying on the Home Keys

Early in my marriage, God brought to mind a typing class that I had taken in high school, and He had hidden biblical principles of marriage in those mundane typing lessons. Let me take you there to show you what I learned. During the first week of typing class (for those of you who are younger, this would be called keyboarding), the teacher was trying to train us not to look at our hands. One day during that first week, I was typing along, thinking that I was doing pretty well. When our time for the assignment was up, I looked down at my typed sheet and was taken aback: It was obvious that I had set my hands on the wrong home keys. What I had spent all that energy on had produced nothing but a mess. It wasn't useful to me or to anybody else. But I had thought I was doing just fine. What was the problem? I had forgotten to check to be sure that my hands were positioned properly to accomplish the goal.

There is a lesson in that—a biblical lesson for marriage: We have to have our hands on the home keys. What are those? They are the priorities God has given to us from which we have the potential to reach any other place that requires our personal touch. I found the priorities in Proverbs 31. We all have mixed emotions about the woman described in this chapter. Yes, she is a godly and wise woman, but we have such a difficult time living in her shadow! Even so, let's take a close look at how she is characterized. She is devoted to God, but Proverbs 31 also talks about her husband (see v. 11); her family (see v. 15), and then her servant girls; and in a later verse the poor and the needy (see v. 20).

These are also the home keys for us: first, God; second, our husbands; third, our children and the people who are in our home; and fourth, the community. Your rejection or acceptance of these priorities greatly affects your life. Let me explain what I mean. Do you see yourself as a great mom, married to a guy and, "Oh yeah, I'm a Christian"? If your answer is yes, then you have rearranged God's priorities. You won't get the long-term result from your efforts that you desire. If, on the other hand, you see yourself as a woman who loves Jesus, is married to a wonderful man with whom you're raising your children, then your priorities are biblical. The difference between those ways of thinking may seem like no big deal; but the truth is, your priority filter determines everything from your attitude to the clothes you wear. Every stage of life is unique, but God's home keys never change. His priority filter is always the one we should choose to use.

Making a Difference

We look at the world and we think, *How can I make a difference?* You make a difference by loving Jesus and walking with Him every day. You may not see the difference every day, but your faithfulness is going to make a difference. How do you know when you're doing life right? It's right when you see everything through Jesus Christ.

My husband, Joel, likes to tell the story of how when he was a young boy he would attend church with his grandmother. It was a dark but beautiful church with stained-glass windows. When the preacher would get ready to talk, Joel's grandma would pass a cellophane-wrapped butterscotch candy to Joel. He took great care to twist open the wrapper a little at a time because he didn't want to make noise while the preacher was talking. When he'd finally get it unwrapped, he'd pop the piece of candy in his mouth. But according to him, that wasn't the best part. The best part was taking that yellow cellophane, closing one eye and holding that wrapper up over the other eye—when he did that, the whole place looked different; it glowed.

When God looks at us, He looks at us through the raised-up cross; He looks at us through His Son Jesus Christ. We need to be able to see each other in that same way. Can you see your husband through Jesus Christ? I have a theory that the whole proverbial rose-colored glasses is just an earthly glimpse of what it means to see somebody in the very best light, the way God sees us. May I say to you, if you have lost those "glasses," find them and put them back on.

People appear very different when you look at them from God's perspective. A strong-willed child looks like a potential leader; a husband who forgets your birthday is a man who is willing to overlook the fact that you are aging. Seriously, let's reflect a bit on that last example—because many of us can relate to it. You could lose an evening, or more, grousing around about a card you didn't get from a man who, at the moment, you're not sure you even like; or you can be gracious and give him one more place to connect with you. Choose to be good to your husband on purpose. Good means reflecting the character of Jesus Christ.

First Corinthians 10:24 says, "Nobody should seek [her] own good, but the good of others." I love that verse. But it engages me at a new level when I put my husband's name in the place of "others" and I ask myself, *Am I doing that for Joel?* Amid all the stresses and demands of life, our true calling is to be a faithful helpmate. It's not an accident that we are pastors' wives; it's an awesome privilege!

Being a Helpmate

For our second typing test of the semester, our teacher told us we could have as much time as we needed to complete it. What was the catch? She didn't want our paper turned in until it was perfect. So we all got started. As I was typing along, I noticed that the girl next to me had a test that was different from mine. I thought, *Well, this is just great. One of us didn't get the right test.* The next day, the teacher returned our tests—most of us had As, including me and the girl who had been sitting next to me. Then our teacher said, "You know, class, I really think that all of you did an excellent job. I've been keeping track of all your paperwork, and I developed individual tests for each of you to improve on your weaknesses, the things you usually haven't done right."

I believe that God does the same thing in my marriage. Through my weaknesses, He's working to make me a better person as I seek to be a helpmate to my husband. That's my assignment, you know, to help the man that I married. And my assignment may not look like anyone else's—in fact, it's probably not like anyone else's. The same is true for you. Perhaps you could help your husband by talking more or, maybe, by talking less; maybe you should do more or perhaps you should do less. You get my point. These are the kinds of things you and God have to figure out. It's so weird that we think every marriage should look alike. We know that no two people are alike, so why would we think any two marriages would look anything alike?

Let's take a closer look at this call to be a helpmate: "Now the Lord God said, It is not good (sufficient, satisfactory) that the man should be alone; I will make him a helper meet (suitable, adapted, complementary) for him" (Gen. 2:18, *AMP*). The temptation for most of us when we start talking about being a helper, being submissive, being respectful is to cop an attitude and say, "Women should not have to do this for men." But this Scripture is referring to the man who is her partner, not to every man on the planet. Satan loves to take whatever God has called us to do and exaggerate it so we feel overwhelmed and are tempted to give up before we start. We may feel upset that God has called us to help. But, we'd likely be more upset if He had implied that *we* were the ones who needed help!

God, through Scripture, has given wives two very specific ways that we can be excellent helpers. The first way is to be respectful and the second is to be submissive. Ephesians 5:33 says, "However, each one of you also must love his wife as he loves himself, and the wife must respect her husband." Respect simply means to look at again. "Re" means "again," like if you redo something, you do it again. "Spect" means "to look," like spectators are watchers, and spectacles are vision aids. How long has it been since you really looked at your husband? Think about his situation from his perspective for a minute. Would you want to be married to you? Imagine that you're him and try to think what his daily routine must look like to him. It'll make you so much more sensitive to his needs, and you'll probably begin to pray for him more than you pray about him.

While you look at him again, notice that he is male. Remember that you are your husband's only holy option for sexual intimacy. Did you know that if your husband wants to make love to you and you want to go pray, that God would tell you to make love to your husband? It's true! First Corinthians 7:5 says, "Do not deprive each other except by mutual consent and for a time, so that you may devote yourselves to prayer. Then come together again so that Satan will not tempt you."

I want to talk briefly with you about submission. Do we really believe that God would put something in the recipe for life that wouldn't be as good for us as it is for our husbands? And even more important, do we not trust that God commands all things for our good, to accomplish His purposes in our lives? Think about the word "submission." "Sub" means "under," so essentially "submission" means that you "come under his mission." Doesn't sound like such a big, terrible thing to me.

But think how Satan has warped what it means to be a biblically submissive wife. When we say "Be submissive to Jesus Christ," do we mean "Go be a wimp for Jesus"? No, that never crosses our minds. Of course we want to submit our best selves to Jesus. We bring the best that we can when we serve Jesus. Why should being a submissive wife be any different? Bring your best to your marriage. And be assured that biblical submission prevents abuse. If your husband were to ever ask you to do something that was sinful, something that God does not approve of, you would have to say no. Your first priority is to God. But the reality is that most pastors' wives are married to incredible men who are giving their lives for Jesus. Be grateful for your husband and don't fear giving your best to him.

Persevering

Let's say you're not afraid to give your life, but you really feel like there is a little part of this that is driving you crazy because you're fairly respectful, you're fairly submissive, and actually, now that you think about it, you realize that you're kind of incredible. You've been doing wife-life right, and you think, *Hey, I've got this down. But don't you think maybe he should do some stuff, too? Shouldn't he be reading a book on being good to his wife or something like that?*

Let me take you back to typing class one last time. We had just started a timed test, and our teacher was at the door talking to the principal. I glanced at my typed sheet and noticed that every place there was supposed to be an *a* or an *e* there was a blank—the key was going up but nothing was showing up on the paper. But I decided to keep typing; I figured that if I quit I definitely wouldn't be able to get my grade adjusted. When the test was finished, I told the teacher about my dilemma. She said, "Oh, Becky, I am so sorry. I gave you the type-writer with the *a* and *e* that don't work. I tell you what, though, every-where there's a gap, I'll know you did the right thing on that word and so you'll get full credit."

This illustrates for us the consoling biblical truth that God knows what our part is. He knows what our husband's part is. You still get an

A if you do your part. It's okay if there are gaps. God can see that you did what you needed to do.

What is important is that you keep pouring out your life for Jesus' sake—because that's what He's called you to do. When Jesus said in Matthew 6:21, "Where your treasure is, there your heart will be also," He was talking about the principle of investment. If you invest your life and serve God by expending great energy in ministering to your husband, then your heart—your feelings for him—will grow. Remember, the grass isn't greener on the other side of the fence. The grass is greener where you water it. So pray for the living water of Jesus, Himself, to fill you to overflowing.

A Final Thought

Do you ever get creative with a recipe, substituting ingredients or ignoring directions? Yes, we all do sometimes. And what happens? We end up with something we didn't expect and don't like the taste of. The same thing happens in our lives and in our marriages. Sometimes we think we know better than God does, so we throw in "a little something" or deviate from His directions. But the results we get will produce something we never intended.

God's recipe for a fulfilled life and a happy marriage is difficult to follow because we like to do things our own way. But His directions are actually quite simple. Always look to His Word, not to the world or your own ideas, and the results will be "much more than we ask or think through His power working in us" (Eph, 3:20a, *NLV*).

Prayer

Dear Lord, change my vision of myself. Help me to see that I am first Your daughter, a follower of Jesus, a member of Your Church. Then let that realization of who I am in Christ bring grace and beauty to my role as a pastor's wife. Enable me, through Your Spirit, to be a faithful helpmate to my husband. Teach me, Lord, how to serve him with joy. Thank You, Lord, for the blessing my husband is in my life. Amen.

*H*OW TO ADD VALUE TO YOUR HUSBAND

RUTH TOWNS

When I was a little girl, I wanted to be a preacher's wife. I don't quite know why I thought that was going to be something wonderful, but I knew it was a way of life that would allow me to serve the Lord. Even as a child I knew that if I did what the Lord wanted me to do, I'd be happy. If I didn't do the Lord's will, I would suffer, either from guilt or depression or some other negative emotion.

It works the same with our husbands: When we're helping them and doing what they need done, we'll be happy. After all, that's what we've been made to do. Remember that in Genesis God declared each of His creations good: the birds, the fish, the animals, the day and night. Then He made a man and said, "It is not good for the man to be alone. I will make a helper suitable for him" (Gen. 2:18). So God created a woman to be man's companion and helpmate.

But where do we begin when it comes to our role as helper to our husbands who are spouses to us and shepherds to our churches. I believe it begins with prayer. For me, I began praying for Elmer many years before we even met!

Praying for a Preacher

As I've said, when I was a little girl, I *did* want to marry a preacher; and so from the time that I was saved, at age five, my mother would tell me, "Now, I want you to start praying for your husband, because if you want to marry a preacher, you start praying for him now." So when I would pray, I would say, "Now I lay me down to sleep and bless the man I'm going to marry." Or sometimes I would add, "and make him cute." And sometimes I would say, "and make him very, very handsome." And a lot of times I would say, "and give him lots and lots of muscles." But most of the time I would say, "and help him love You."

When I was getting ready to go to college, my mother asked me, "Do you still want to marry a preacher?" I said, "Yes." Then she said, "If you want to marry a preacher, you have to go where they make them." So I went to a Bible college. I went to find a preacher, and I did. I did not pick him first. I looked around and saw a wonderful football-player-type with red hair and muscles and I said, "He's the one." He had a best friend, a scrawny lookin' little kid with big ears—his name was Elmer. Well, I figured out if I wanted to attract my chosen spouse, I should become friends with his friend. And so Elmer and I became good friends.

As it happened, Elmer wanted to date a girlfriend of mine. Well, things worked out well for both us—we got dates with our respective "dreamboats." Before that big date night, Elmer and I went out and practiced our manners. I would go down the steps and say, "Thank you, Duane." And he'd say, "You're welcome, Mary Faith." And then we'd go around the corner and down the curb, and I'd take his hand and say, "Oh, thank you, Duane." And he'd say, "You're welcome, Mary Faith." And you know, it was weird and uncomfortable.

The next week, after we had gone out with our dates, we decided to go out together and compare notes. (Just an excuse, I guess, now that I look back on it.) Anyway, we compared notes and decided that our dates had been OK, but we agreed that we had more fun together. You know why? We didn't put on any kind of outward appearance. I mean it was just normal, everyday Ruth and Elmer—that's it. And we began to have such good times together!

I guess it's no mystery that Elmer and I started dating each other! And you know what really got to me? He would pray with me. No one that I had dated before had ever prayed with me. When I went home for the summer, I remember thinking, *I don't know if I love him or not, but I sure don't want anybody else to.* When we came back to school in the fall, he proposed. I had realized that I did truly love him. How did it all begin? With prayer. That's where we need to start. We need to make a habit of praying for and with our spouses every day. They need our support and love, but they also need us to intercede for them at the Throne.

Now that we've laid the foundation, let's take a look at the practical steps we can take to assist our husbands, to make their work more effective.

Adding Value

Let's talk about "value" for a few moments. We hear this word used all the time these days, but what does it mean to give value to someone? Elmer tells me that it means "to bless." So if we add value to something, we have blessed it. And we all want to bless our husbands, don't we?

But how can we bless our husbands—add value to their lives—if our own homes—our hearts—are cluttered? We can begin by cleaning our windows! If we make the windows of our life clean and shiny, those looking in will see that there is order, peace and harmony in our lives.

Making Good Friends

The second step is to live in a good neighborhood and establish uplifting friendships. Good friends bless your family, and a good marriage can show a neighbor or a friend how to live. Over the years, Elmer and I have always tried to establish a good friendship with some other couples in the church. You probably know that if you take two couples in which the husbands like each other but the wives don't, there won't be a real, lasting friendship. But if the women like each other, the men can get along with each other. So you need to "shop around" a bit. But you know all that. You deal with churches and church ladies all the time—you know that friends will show themselves friendly.

A word of caution here: Be mindful of "needy" friends. There are some people who are great friends and who will do anything for you, but they pull you down. Let me give you an example. I have a friend who often wants me to be with her for every doctor's appointment and shopping trip. She wants me to pick her up to take her places. She wants me to go through her closet with her and tell her what clothes are "in" this year. Yes, she prays for me, and she's a sweet, wonderful Christian; but she doesn't have the grown-up personality that she needs. As a result, she pulls down the people around her. So be mindful of friends who bring you down.

Being Beautiful: Start with the Inside

Beauty comes from within (see 1 Pet. 3:4). Elmer always says that what's in the bucket comes up from the well. We know that what's on the inside shows on the outside. We can look at a person's outward appearance and tell what's inside. If we see someone with rumpled hair and wrinkled clothes, we'd probably be right in thinking that this person is relaxed and laid-back—and not terribly attached to externals. And maybe we can learn a lesson from such a person: It's what's on the inside that really matters.

So when you decide to make yourself over, don't start with a new hairstyle or new makeup. Do the inward makeover first. The holy women of old made themselves beautiful from within: "Your beauty . . . should be that of your inner self, the unfading beauty of a gentle and quiet spirit, which is of great worth in God's sight. For this is the way the holy women of the past who put their hope in God used to make themselves beautiful" (1 Pet. 3:3-5). And if we want to be godly women who can influence the men in our lives, we have to work on the inside first. Then our inner beauty will transform us.

Avoiding Being Critical

Once we've started down the path of seeking inner beauty, we are less likely to do ugly things, especially to our spouses. About the worst thing we can do to our spouses is to criticize them. As pastors' wives, we have to be careful not to tear down our husbands. For example, if your husband asks your opinion of his not-so-great sermon, how do you respond? You don't want to devastate him—you don't want to say, "Well, you said this and you didn't say that; and you meant to say this and you said the wrong words." It's better to wait until later to say,

"You know what? Next time you preach that sermon it would be great if you would include the story about this or that." There's a way to suggest something without killing his spirit.

Being on Guard for Your Husband's Sake

We must not only be the encouragers but we must also be our pastor-husbands' protectors. You know that there will be a woman in your church who may be the critical termite or the gossip or maybe she just loves your husband. The latter is the most dangerous. And please know: A female member of the congregation will love your husband. So we have to be careful; we have to be the eyes for our husbands. Watch out, not in a condemning way, not in a jealous way, but you have to be careful because conversations and interactions can be misunderstood.

Becoming a Trustworthy Wife

I think the greatest value that you can give your husband is to be a trustworthy wife. I want him to be trustworthy, and I want to be trustworthy myself. My husband could not travel the way he does almost every weekend if it weren't for the fact that he could trust me at home with the children when they were young and that I could trust him to be faithful. He teaches in a college with 5,000 gorgeous girls, and I trust him. He's come home for 52 years; I expect him to come home for the next 52 years. That doesn't mean that I don't have to be careful and that I don't have to pray for him.

Staying Healthy

Stay healthy! This is such an important point for pastors' wives to reflect on. It's hard for a man to leave his sick wife in order to go to work. You know, we just have to carry on. And I know it's difficult to be sick and to still carry on and do the work you're supposed to do; but you know moms can't get sick and pastors' wives shouldn't. The best way to prevent illness is to stay healthy in the first place. Plan time for exercise. Take your vitamins. Take care of yourself, and you'll be able to add value by taking care of your husband and your family.

Learning to Listen

Don't underestimate the value of listening. Let's learn to listen to our husbands because they're telling us things that are important. When my son died, my husband reacted to things in an entirely different way from the way I did. He got really busy with everything. I learned that that was his way of dealing with grief. But by giving him time and space and listening to him when he was ready to talk, I came to see what I could do to help him. Little by little he shared his thoughts and needs with me.

Appreciating the Role of Children

But what are some things that gain interest value? How about antiques? I love antiques because they bring back wonderful memories. One time we went in an antique store and saw a highchair. Well, I looked at it and passed it by; then Elmer looked at it and he said, "This looks just like the one we had for the kids when they were little." And I said, "Uh hum." It was. But it brought back some memories of the kids, memories that teach us again what we learned through our experience of raising children.

We had three children. When our oldest was born, my husband was in seminary and I was teaching school. Debbie was my vivacious, inventive, creative, impulsive firstborn. And she could do everything, even as a child. Now as an adult, she paints fine china and digs wells. She goes deer hunting and she will tan the hides. She even made her own wedding dress—an Indian leather dress and moccasins! Yes, she's the vivacious energizer bunny that her daddy is.

Then our son came along 13 months later. From the very beginning the doctors told us there was something wrong with him. He was floppy like a rag doll—and he didn't seem to ever improve. Finally, after a year of wondering, *What's wrong here?* we were told by doctors that Sam had muscular dystrophy and that he would die, probably within a year. My husband said, "If he's going live a year, he's going to live a good year." So we made him learn to get up on a little stool and then pull himself up into bed. He would flop over into bed and laugh and giggle—he was a happy child—and go to sleep.

As it turned out, Sam lived to be 45—and he led a wonderful, full life. He always said he was going to be smarter than his dad was and do more for the Lord than his daddy had done. He was killed three years ago in a truck accident. Somebody once said that the pain of losing a child lessens over the years, but I don't think so—at least not when they've lived 45 years. But we thank the Lord for the 45 years that he had. And we were amazed at what *his* children had to teach us about his death—they added value to our lives, even in our sufferings.

When Sam died, his little girl, Collyn, was six at the time, and his little boy, Brad, was five. The morning after Sam's death, Collyn told her mom, "I did something I shouldn't have done."

And Karen said, "What is it that you did?"

"I went downstairs to see Daddy's picture."

And Karen said, "Okay, did you talk to him?"

"No."

"Did he talk to you?"

"No, but God did."

"Oh!" Karen exclaimed. "What did God say?"

"Daddy's with Me, Collyn, and he's doing just fine."

Collyn later drew a picture of Sam, and Karen said, "What's in the picture?"

"That's Daddy."

"Well who's the man with the crown?"

"Mom, that's Jesus."

"Well what's Daddy got in his arms?"

"That's a baby."

"Why is Daddy holding a baby?"

"Because God needed him in heaven. He needed the best daddy on Earth to take care of all the babies in heaven." You tell me little children can't understand God's love? They most certainly do—perhaps better than we do.

Children understand what you teach them. Children can pray. You teach them, and they will bless your lives. Children can bless their daddies, so encourage them to do so.

Being United as a Couple

"Together" is a word that's important to God, and I think it's important to married couples. Yet togetherness is something we neglect.
We can be together and yet be far, far apart. We can be in the same
room and have no conversations. So we should make a point to be
present to our husbands, to find out what's on their minds, what
concerns they have, what their needs are. We need to remember that
the times we spend together should be times when we enrich our
spouses' lives.

A Final Thought

The best gift You can give your husband, the best way to add value to
his life, is to be a helpmate who's fit spiritually, mentally, emotionally
and physically. How do you go about doing that? Well, just start with
the ABCs.

A

You need to be affordable—don't be so high maintenance that nobody
can ever get to you. Be affectionate—your children need affection from
you. Teach your children to climb up on daddy's lap, to love him, to
hug him, to say thank you, to welcome him when he comes through
the door. Be an assistant, a helper. I use "assistant" because it starts
with *a*, and because you have to be attentive and have a little ambition
in order to be someone's assistant. Be alluring—in a modest way. Be
active. Be accountable. You have to be accountable, first to the Lord
and then to your spouse. Do not hide things from your spouse. Be
accurate. Don't stretch the truth. And be appropriate—that's Elmer's
favorite for describing me. (I tell him it's not flattering, but he says it's
a good description, so I'll take his word for it.)

B

Be benevolent and generous. Be balanced. You are already blessed. Be
believable, so tell the truth. Be brave and blameless—carry burdens
without letting them weigh you down. Be well behaved. There is a

beauty in a woman who knows how to conduct herself, both in public and in private.

C

Be congenial, considerate, a worthy companion, Christlike, consistent, careful, confident, compassionate. Remember, you have to have character, and you need to be able to give and to take constructive criticism. Don't forget your role as your husband's counselor. Learn how to keep a confidence. Don't tell everything you know! If your husband has told you something that is not supposed to be known to the congregation, for goodness sake, don't even tell your best girlfriend. It'll get around.

Prayer

Father, thank You for this lesson on adding value. I thank You for the husband that You've given me. I pray that rather being destructive, I might add value to him and that others would see Christ in my life. Help me to be a good example. I ask all this in Your precious name. Amen.

HOW TO BUILD A GREAT CHURCH WITHOUT LOSING YOUR FAMILY

BOSE ADELAJA

We all know that God loves marriages. God is the wellspring of the desire that joins a man together to a woman, because the Bible says that one can defeat 1,000 but when they get together and these two become one, then they can defeat 10,000 (see Deut. 32:30a). God brings a man and a woman together because He wants them to accomplish something greater than either of them could accomplish alone.

Laying a Sound Foundation for Your Church and Family

For those of us who are pastors' wives, we, together with our husbands, are meant to nourish our churches and our families. But that seems like a lot. Often we feel as if our family comes second to our church. I am here to tell you that it doesn't have to be that way. You can have a flourishing church and a wonderful family life. But how do you go about leading the church without losing your family?

See Divorce as the Non-Option

In your mind and your thoughts, never allow yourself to think that you could lose your family. Don't have that as an option. In the world, people consider divorce to be acceptable, but for those of us who are Christians, divorce is not an option. Why? Because our great God desires to keep unified each man and woman whom He has brought together through marriage. God is strong to fulfill His will and His purpose in our lives. So let's just agree at the outset to leave divorce out of the equation. Instead, let's consider how to keep our families intact in today's world.

Remember God's Great Love for Us

Jeremiah 31:3 says that God loves us with an everlasting love. The love He has given to us in the family, the love He has given to you and your spouse, is an everlasting love. The kind of love we have in our families is the kind of love we get from God. Everything about God is everlasting. So, our calling is everlasting. The love and joy He gives us is everlasting, as are the peace and the great things He is doing in our lives. All of this is everlasting.

Keep in Mind Your Calling

In Numbers 3:12, the Lord tells us, "I have taken the Levites from among the Israelites in place of the first male offspring of every Israelite woman. The Levites are mine." If your husband is a pastor (or you are one yourself), you are a Levite either by marriage or by calling. As pastors' wives, we are special people. As pastors' wives, we are the new Levites. We have been set aside as a royal priesthood, a special nation, a kingdom of priests and kings. Out of the all the Christians in the world, the Lord has called us.

Perhaps at times we don't feel worthy of this special calling. But whatever our feelings of inadequacy, this doesn't change the fact that *He has chosen us.* We always have to know and realize this. This is not a game; this is about destiny. This is something serious—God, Himself, puts you in the place where you are today. What a joy to be chosen by God to be the wife of a man of God, to be the wife of a Levite, to be the wife of God's choice. What a joy, what a grace, what an anointing to serve God in the ministry and in the family! That is the hand of God in our lives. So, when I reflect upon the fact that I am a pastor's wife, I tell God how blessed I am among all women.

If you are a pastor's wife, begin to strengthen your marriage by believing this amazing truth: You are blessed. You have been uniquely chosen, and God's blessings flow through your life.

Living a Healthy Balance

A real relationship with the Lord will help us to balance the needs of the ministry with the needs of our family. Have confidence in God's Word and in what you are doing. He has called you to ministry and He has called you to family life. He will give you the grace you need to love your ministry *and* your family because He is working through you.

I see this reality borne out in my own experience. I love my church, and I love my family. I am full of life because of my ministry. I am full of life because I love my husband and I love my children. I am happy to have them. I am dedicated, I am focused, I am courageous. Find your focus in the Lord, and He will give you the courage to embrace your calling to both the church and to your family.

But beyond seeking Him in prayer and asking for His help, what else can you do, practically speaking, to safeguard your family? The demands of ministry can sometimes seem overwhelming. So how do you make sure your family's needs don't get overlooked? Below are some practical steps you can take to keep the church and your family healthy.

Having Right Balance Between God and Family

We as pastors' wives need to have a right balance between the family and the church. Yes, the church is very important, but so is the family. You are probably familiar with the popular priority list for pastors: God first, then the family, and then ministry. You know, though, that things don't usually work out that way. Why? Because everything is about God. You and your spouse pray together in the morning, you hear about God in the church, you speak about God with your children and spouse, you prepare Bible study topics. Then you come home and it is still about church because you and your spouse are receiving phone calls and requests for prayer and home visits.

So how do we keep the balance when ministry always seems to be encroaching more and more on family life? It is so simple. First Corinthians says that our body consists of many parts. We have the big parts, the large parts, and we have those unseen parts, the small, hidden parts. It is written in the Bible that those hidden parts are more important, and we need to pay attention to them (see 1 Cor. 12:22-24). If we are to compare the ministry to the family, the ministry is the part that you see all of the time: the anointing, the noise, the shouting, the "pastor this," the "pastor that." The family is like the hidden part of the body. And God's wisdom is teaching us that we have to pay more attention and have more love for the family, because attending to the hidden parts requires more motivation.

As a pastor's wife, I have to make an effort to pay more attention to the family, because their needs can be taken care of by someone other than me. It is so easy to get a babysitter. It is so easy to get somebody to cook for your husband, somebody to fix the house. But don't give in to the easy solutions for your family. Decide to pay attention to the family, to pay attention to your spouse—invest in your family.

It is not so easy to neglect the ministry. You have to be in the church. That is why many pastors and many pastors' wives do well in the ministry. They have to be there—they have nowhere to hide. So, this wisdom goes on to teach us, for the weak parts, the parts that can be easily neglected, provide more care, bestow more attention. As for the other parts—your public roles in ministry—you will naturally do well in those. When you work for this balance, God will bless both your ministry and your family.

Getting the Family Involved

The second point is this: Get your family members involved in your church. Numbers 18:1 reads, "The LORD said to Aaron, 'You, your sons and your father's family are to bear the responsibility for offenses against the sanctuary, and you and your sons alone are to bear the responsibility for offenses against the priesthood.'" Here we see that we need to get our family involved in what we do in the ministry. In your family, you no doubt have a few natural leaders. You don't need to ask them to be involved—they are already there and that is good. You just need to train them and teach them not to misuse their position or provide a poor witness. Let them know that they are representing you and that they have more responsibility because they are the pastor's family members.

For those who are not natural leaders and those who are not actively involved, we have to pray. We have to put in some effort to get them involved in the ministry. Why? The family members that are not involved in your ministry will not get to enjoy the grace and the blessing of God on you and on the ministry. You cannot reap where you didn't sow. Being around doesn't really mean anything. You have to plant and to sow—and they have to get involved.

This why we have some pastors that are doing well but their wives are not doing well, because they are just around. They are hanging around, but they are not baptized, they are not involved. They cannot substitute for their husband when he is not there.

Are any of you pastors' wives not involved in your husband's ministry? You should be! The Bible says the two shall become one. If you are not involved in something, the resulting grace cannot be released upon you. You have to be involved. For those of you who are shy or who feel that you have not been specially gifted for ministry, realize that it takes time and wisdom in order to get involved in a meaningful way. In the early days of my marriage, I myself was not interested in being part of my husband's ministry. But I thank God for my husband's wisdom for the way he worked with me, motivated me, and wooed me into the ministry. Now, I am very happy to be involved in the ministry.

Celebrating Ministry Success with the Family

The third point is that to bring this balance to the ministry and the family, you as a pastor's wife or as a pastor have to celebrate the success of your ministry with your family. As ministers, there will be times when people will celebrate us. They will say wonderful things about us!

When they say these things over and over again, you have to be wise to share and celebrate the success with your family. Make them a part of it by sharing with them how they have been a part of your successful ministry—let them know they are appreciated! In particular, always remember to thank God for your husband.

Appreciating the Role of the Church in the Family's Well-Being

The fourth point I want to make is this: Appreciate the role the church plays in fostering the well-being of your family. Always let those in the church know that you appreciate their prayers for you, your husband and your children. Always let them know that you covet their prayers. If anything good is happening to you, always let them know that they have a share in what is happening to you; they have a part in it because of their support for you and for your family. Show the church that you respect them and that you appreciate any effort on their part in helping you to continue being a good family person. Let them know that they have a part to play in your becoming successful, both in the ministry and in the family.

Recognizing the Need to Protect the Family

My fifth point is an important one: Protect your family as much as possible from the burdens and challenges of the ministry. As the ministry grows, so do the challenges and the burdens. You, as a woman of God, have to be very careful. You have to protect your family from the burden and the challenges of the ministry. You must already have overcome the shock and the weight of a particular challenge before breaking the "good" news to your family in a good way. If your family perceives that the burden you are undertaking seems too great in your eyes, they will start doubting if you are really in the right place. They will want to save you from the stress, and they might even attempt to get you to leave the ministry, because they fear losing you.

If God has called you, He has enough grace for you to pass the test and overcome the challenges and burdens of the ministry. So whenever there is a trial in the ministry, make sure you overcome it and relate it to your family in a constructive way. Let your spouse and your children know that you are more than an overcomer. Explain to them why this is happening to you. Always show your family the best part of the ministry until they are assured enough to go through the hard times with you, giving you good advice and not judging carnally. Not all of your family members will share your spiritual maturity, especially the children. You have to be prudent so that you don't break their spirits, so they don't get discouraged about your ministry. By protecting your family members as much as possible from the burden of the ministry, you ensure their support for you and for your ministry. And perhaps more importantly, you ensure that they don't see the church or the leaders as enemies.

Seeing a Need to Protect the Church

Next, guard your church as much as possible from your family challenges. You have to be careful when you are dealing with some problematic issues in your family, or before you know it, the church will be filled with rumors: "the Pastor's son is this" or "the pastor's daughter is doing that." You have to keep the church informed as much as possible—that is one way that you guide the church. If you have any challenges with a teenager or something similar, rumors can easily result. If those rumors are not addressed, they can destabilize the church. So don't be afraid; have fewer secrets. Always keep the people in the church informed as much as possible and they will be honored. They will feel like part of the family and won't feel the need to guess things for themselves.

Having a Good Attitude

The final point that I would like to make relates to your attitude as a pastor's spouse. Having a good spirit is very important—much more important than how you present yourself physically. Your husband might be doing everything right, but if you do not really understand your husband's ministry or if you see every female church leader as a potential threat, that could cause a problem in the church. If jealously isn't an issue, what about being too authoritative? You know what I am talking about. So if you really want to keep the church and family in good health, you need to be in one spirit with your pastor-husband.

A Final Thought

Remember that you, the pastor's wife, are the greatest testimony a pastor can have. As a helpmate, companion and cheerleader, you will help him to pastor without tears. Balancing your family and the ministry is really all about pastoring without tears.

Blessing

I just bless Your people, Lord, especially the wives of Your shepherds. I pray that You increase their knowledge and that it will later develop into wisdom. I pray that by the spirit of faith they will be successful in the ministry and will not have problems in their families. Thank You, Father, for You have done this. I thank You because You are very much interested in their marriages and in their ministries. Thank You, Father, because You want to teach these beautiful women that family and ministry can coexist peacefully and fruitfully. In the mighty name of Jesus I pray, amen.

$\mathcal{A}$ GOD-GIVEN CALL

H. B. LONDON, JR.

Beverley and I were married when she was barely 19 and I was barely 20. I had been kicked out of college and didn't have a lot else to do—so I asked her if she would marry me and she said yes, because she didn't want to go home to this little town in central California. And then, two of the most unlikely people in the world were called into ministry. She had always said the last thing she ever wanted to be was a pastor's wife, and I'd always said the last thing I wanted to be was a pastor.

Jim Dobson talks about our family—that our granddad prayed and claimed four generations of our family for the Lord. In those four generations, every offspring was either a minister or was married to one, and I thought that was overkill. But then the Lord got hold of me (and Beverley got hold of me), and suddenly we found ourselves back in seminary. Now, we were a very unlikely pair to be in seminary—I didn't even own a briefcase. I didn't know Matthew from Malachi, to be honest with you.

China and Doilies

I was walking down the hallway one day in seminary and I saw a pink slip of paper on the bulletin board that said, "Parsonettes to meet Thursday night at 7:30." I didn't know what the Parsonettes were, but I knew that they were sponsored by the seminary professors' wives. So I went home to Beverley—we had a baby by that time—and I said, "Beverley, I'll keep the baby—I'll do anything—if you'll just go to the Parsonettes meeting."

So, Beverley went to the Parsonettes meeting, and when she came home, her eyes were all glazed over. "What in the world went on there?" I asked.

"Well," she said, "they taught us that if we are going to be good pastors' wives and good pastors, we need to have people over for dinner every Sunday after church. They taught us how to set the table—using our best china and our best crystal and our best silver."

"We don't have any of that," I said.

"I know," she replied, "that's part of the problem." I asked what else was said at the meeting, and she said, "Well, they taught us how to place doilies around, in appropriate places."

I've always hated doilies. Doilies reminded me of my grandmother's house—she had doilies everywhere. You couldn't even find the toilet in the bathroom because of all the doilies. I know that I'm stepping on some toes here, but doilies make no sense. They have holes in them, and when you wash them they shrink up like little amoebas, turn brown and turn up on the corners. When I would stand up after sitting on a chair in my grandmother's house, I'd have one doily hanging from my arm and one from my neck. I hated doilies.

Snowball in Hell

I finished seminary when I was 23, and we received an opportunity to pastor a church out in southern California. When I got out there, I discovered that they really didn't have a church building; they had a house. They had knocked some walls down and put in some mismatched pews, and one of the deacons—feeling very religious—had gone down to the junkyard and bought an old fiberglass steeple to make the church look less like a house. The deacon had put that baby up on the roof but didn't attach it correctly; so when it rained, we had a baptismal service right there in the front room.

My office at the church was really a big closet—it was so small that you couldn't do anything in it. But it was there, within the first two days of our arrival, that the Lord came to me and said, "H. B., you're living out here by Disneyland, and I want you and Beverley to win all of this area for Me." He gave me an idea how we were going to evangelize the whole area out there, and I felt pretty good about it.

I went home to tell Beverley, who was still unpacking from our move. We had two kids at that time, and they were crying, and Beverley was perspiring and the boxes were everywhere. I said, "Beverley, I've been up at the half office, and the Lord's really been speaking to me. I was just wondering how you would feel about using our gifts together to move forward into this vast uncharted land of sin and degradation, how you and I could use our gifts—you with me and me with you—to touch this world that desperately needs to know Jesus Christ." Now, she was wiping sweat away and I don't remember everything that she said, but I do remember that in one sentence there were the words "snowball in hell." I remember those words very clearly.

Lessons Learned from My Wife

As I look back on the life that Beverley and I have spent together and the churches that we have pastored these last several years, I realize that she's taught me a lot. She has taught me lessons that I needed to know; because to be honest with you, I didn't have the best model growing up. As a result, I made a lot of mistakes.

Beverley was from a layperson's home, and I was—as I said—from all those generations of pastors. I grew up in a home with folks who were overseers and district superintendents. They would go out and hold big tent meetings and then organize the church—they were always going and going. The only example that I ever had of a pastor's wife was my mom, who was a kind of super pastor's wife who did it all. She would go to the tenement houses and the bus routes and make a hundred personal visits a week. She was there all the time, and I thought that Beverley would want to be just like my mom. But then I found out she didn't even like my mom, so that was a problem!

Find Your Own Place

One day, Beverley said to me, "Why don't you just let me find my place? If you let me do what I do best, I promise that you'll be better served and so will the church and our family." I thought that my ministry was going to be validated by how people saw Beverley and how they responded to her. I had no right to put those great expectations on her, but I did so because I thought it would make me look better if I did. The reality is that our congregations will take from us whatever we can give. Few ever say, "You need a few more days off" or "If you don't want to come to church on Sunday, that's okay."

When my wife and I had been in ministry for quite a while, we were offered a great big church in southern California. Beverley's predecessor had been a prolific writer and speaker. At a tea to welcome Beverley, people began telling her about the women's Bible studies that 200 women attended every Tuesday morning. "We know that you would want to follow in the steps of your predecessor," they said, pushing papers toward her, "and this is the curriculum for the next . . . "

Well, Beverley just turned white. "You know, I don't even like women's Bible studies very much," she said. "I might come and take roll or something, but I don't teach Bible studies." Beverley was a musician, and she could play an offertory, after which 3,000 people would stand up and applaud for her. That's what her gift was—it wasn't teaching junior high kids or staying all night with a bunch of girls to have a sleep over. Her gift was music.

Love Your Family More Than the Church

I made some huge mistakes in those early years. Not only did I think that my ministry would be validated by what Beverley did, but for some reason, somebody had patted me on the head one day and said, "H. B., you just get out and build the church and God will take care of your family." Well, I know that's not true. Every day, I see pastors' families, marriages and careers jettisoned because of commitments made to excellence or to their own success, or because their commitment to prestige and position has become more important than the ministry. Some of the saddest letters I read and phone calls I receive are from pastors' kids—age 20, 30, 40—who, to this day, are bitter at the church and have unresolved issues with their parents simply because their parents were never there for them.

Another important lesson that Beverley taught me was this: she said, "I love the church, but I love you and the kids more." One Sunday, we had a lady sing for our church who had never hit a song's high note in her life—and I knew she wouldn't this time without Beverley's help on the piano. Our son, Bryan, was sick, but I said, "Beverley, if you would just go play the piano, I promise you that I will get a good babysitter out of the high school department and she will watch the kids."

Beverley did it, but when she got home, Brian had the croup, and both he and the babysitter were scared half to death. When I walked in the room after church, my wife had that look on her face. It's a look that defies words; one that says, "If you think I'm ever going to do this again, you're mistaken." I didn't understand—I just thought that you're supposed to be on the front row looking pretty and have the kids right beside you. But Beverley didn't see it that way.

When you come home and take off your ecclesiastical trappings and sit around the dinner table, you need to root for each other. You need to say to your husband, "That was a great sermon," and your husband needs to say to you, "I don't know what I would do here without you." We need to say to our kids, "You're the most important children in this church." You need to tell each other these things, because if you don't, all of a sudden you begin to take each other for granted—you become ships in the night. The focus of your lives shifts to the church and the congregation, rather than your God-given responsibilities as husbands, wives, fathers, mothers—and sons and daughters.

Be Heard

Often, I will get a phone call from a pastor's wife—we'll just call her Mary—who will say, "Pastor H. B., my husband seems distant. He's coming in late, he's not home for dinner, he's irritable with the kids, and we don't seem to talk anymore." And I will say, "Mary, what do you think is going on?"

"Well, it's probably nothing, but it may be some kind of emotional attraction to one of the ladies at church."

"Mary, have you talked to him about it? Have you asked him?"

"Well, no—you know, the church is going so good and it's growing fast and he's got so much on his mind—I just don't want to bother him."

"Mary, you need to understand that the most important thing in the world is for you to resolve these issues that you're facing. You have to promise me that you will talk to him." She will be quiet for a moment before she says, "Well, Pastor London, thanks. Thanks for your time." I know what that means—she's going to put the phone down and wipe away a tear. She doesn't want to address it, because she doesn't really want to know the truth. One day down the line, there will be a collision. It may not be tomorrow or the next day, but it will occur. The ministry will be wrecked, the marriage will be dissolved, and the pastor and his influence will be tarnished forever.

I think that if you ladies are having a hard time getting your husbands' attention—for any reason—you need to stand up on the roof and get two garbage can lids and just slam them together. Or you need to impale yourself on your husband's office door—just hang there. In some way, you have to be heard. And you and your husband have to ask each other from time to time, "How are you doing? Are you making it okay? Are people treating you okay? Are you comfortable with the way things are? What can I do to make it better?"

Be Part of the Solution

Another thing Beverley taught me was this: she said, "I want to be a part of the solution, not a part of the problem." I can't tell you how important this is. You can't extricate yourself from your husband's world—you must help him find the solutions. Beverley didn't have an unrealistic need for recognition. She was real and she was content to accept where God had called me. She said, "If this is where God has called you, we're going to make a home here." She was not too demanding on my schedule if she knew it was for ministry. But if it wasn't, she was like a warden.

The best thing Beverley ever did for me was to help me choose my battles. One day she came in and said, "You got blood all over this place." Other times, she would say, "Why don't you just pick two hills that you're willing to die on. At least then if something happens to you,

I'll know where to go look." You can't let your husband fight every battle and climb every hill. Sometimes it just doesn't matter.

A Final Thought

My dad was a prolific speaker and spoke in the largest pulpits in America. But I chased my dad's love all of my life. He was a great dad but not a very good father. He gave me everything I wanted, except he never gave me of himself. When I had grown up and God had blessed my ministry, it was almost as if there was competition between us. I remember when I wrote my first book, *Pastors at Risk*. I sent him a copy, and he hadn't even looked at it yet, but he said, "Junior, let me tell you where I'm going next week to speak." When I put the phone down, Beverley stood there and said, "You know, he's just going to keep breaking your heart. Why don't you just let it go?" And I remember saying, "Beverley, I can't. His love is more important to me than his ministry."

When my father got older, I wanted to bring him to Colorado Springs, and for five months we moved him from one care facility to another. Then one morning, he just died. I stood in the hospital room, looking at my dead father; they hadn't even covered him yet. I remember speaking to him as if I were eight years old again, saying, "Dad, we never threw a ball. You only came to see me play football one time. Why couldn't it have been different? Why did the church, the ministry and what you were doing supercede all the things that I wanted you to do?" And there was no answer.

As Beverley and I were driving back from the funeral, I just started crying. I said, "I didn't say everything that I wanted to say and we didn't get to do all the things we wanted to do." She reached over and touched my hand and said, "I know you loved him and I know you miss him. But I promise that I'm not going to let you be like him."

A few months ago, I was in Oklahoma City and drove out to the cemetery where we buried my dad. As I stood by the grave, I realized that I had forgotten that day when the funeral director had called and said, "We have to put something on your dad's gravestone. What do you want it to be?" I remember that I couldn't say that he was a great father or that he was a loving husband. About the only thing I could say was that he was a great preacher. I heard that Billy Graham had said that my dad could "draw the net" better than anybody he ever saw.

I remember getting down on my knees and pushing away the dirt and the leaves that were on top of that gravestone. Little by little the writing appeared: "Holland B. London—he was a great preacher." Kneeling there at the gravestone, I said the very same words that I had said to him in that hospital room: "Dad, why couldn't it have been different? It should have been different. It could've been different. I love you, Dad. I miss you more than I can say. But to be honest, I don't want to be like you."

Let me say to you pastors' wives and your husbands that I love and appreciate you—you're my heroes. But let me also say to you, as clearly as I can, what Billy Graham said one time: If we had it to do all over again, we would read more and pray more; we would travel less and spend much more time with our families. I don't know where you're going to find that time, and I don't know where you're going to dig it out. All I'm saying is that the relationships you have as husband and wife, as mom and dad, as son and daughter—are the most significant relationships in the world. They are yours to preserve, they are yours to protect, and they are yours to prosper.

Prayer

Lord, I thank You for all the pastors' wives and their husbands. I pray that You will help them to use their unique gifts to find their place in ministry; to love their families more than their duties at church; and to always be open, honest and supportive of each other in the work that You have called them to do. Let them never have to look back on their lives and say, "If only I had done it differently." Thank you, Lord. Amen.

LIVING IN A STABLE FAMILY

GARY SMALLEY

I've never been this excited about a new message in my entire life. Listen to this truth: It is not what happens to you today or yesterday or tomorrow. It's not what people say or do to you that determines how you feel or what you say or what you do. Rather, Proverbs 23:7 tells us, "as he [or she] thinks within himself [or herself], so he [or she] is" (*NASB*). As you think in your heart, in your mind, that's who you become. It's the same message in Galatians: Whatever you sow in your mind, you're going to reap (see 6:7). Whatever you say, you're going to reap. Whatever you do, you're going to reap.

Expectations—Disappointments Waiting to Happen

You and I are responsible for all of our thoughts, words and actions. Our emotions are only a mere reflection of what we've been thinking. When I accepted this and surrendered to these two little, simple verses a year ago, I realized that I could no longer blame people for how I was feeling. I could no longer blame traffic. I could no longer blame my neighbor's barking dog. I could no longer blame my wife for anything she was doing or saying—or not doing and saying. And I could no longer blame American Airlines, which I did all the time. If things went wrong on my trips around the country, I would blame the delay or the airline's schedule. I was full of malice all the time, which is really a kind of general hostility.

So, I was stressed out, because disappointment is nothing more than unfulfilled expectations. But I decide what my expectations are. Nobody forces me to have expectations.

You, too, will only be as stressed as the number of expectations you have and the size of the gap between those expectations and what's actually happening. You decide all of that—it's totally in your power. When I made that decision, I realized that I no longer could point the finger at anyone and say, "Please change so I'll be happy." Now, I say, "Thank you for revealing my own core fear, my own level of maturity, my own lack or whatever amount of love I have. Thank you for opening up my heart to me."

Guess who you can change in this world? Yourself! Nobody else. You'll never change your husband. I've never changed my wife. Of course, I've tried over the years. I tried creative things, like trying to buy her off. Did it ever work? No, because God designed me to change myself with His help. I'm only working on me.

This past year, after my kidney transplant, I memorized Colossians 3. It was totally life changing. "Set your minds on things above, not on earthly things" (v. 2). Now I take my affections off the things of this earth. I don't have any expectations on the things of this earth. And Jesus has freed me from earthly expectations. Now I want my affections to be on the things above!

Perhaps the greatest freedom I have found is in my thought life. Second Corinthians 10:5 tells us, "We demolish arguments and every pretension that sets itself up against the knowledge of God, and we take captive every thought to make it obedient to Christ." You, too, can do that—today. Take your thoughts off the things of the earth, off sinful things, and focus them on "whatever is true, whatever is noble, whatever is right, whatever is pure, whatever is lovely, whatever is admirable—if anything is excellent or praiseworthy—think about such things" (Phil. 4:8).

It is amazing to me. For over a year I have not had a lustful thought. You know why? Because it doesn't fit with that teaching in Philippians. When I'm on the beach and see a beautiful person, now I might say, "God, you did a great job with that person over there." But if the thoughts go further, I just think, *Is this consistent with Philippians 4:8-9?* And if it isn't, I don't think it. I have the power from Christ not to think lustful thoughts or any other thought that doesn't match Philippians. That is freedom.

How Your Weakness Is Strength in the Lord

You have the same power inside of you. Paul tells us in 2 Corinthians 12:9 that he "will boast all the more gladly about [his] weaknesses." Why? Because in his weaknesses Christ's power rests on him. In my own life, I know that with every flaw and weakness that I have, Jesus' power in me grows stronger. The power of the Holy Spirit grows within me with every difficulty I have. Can you believe it? I have a four-page list of my weaknesses and flaws and I get blessed by knowing that He is growing each day within me through these "flaws."

Let me tell you, I have a lot of weaknesses and shortcomings. I'm ADHD and dyslexic. I can't spell anything. I can hardly remember anybody's name. I'll barely remember this experience a week from now. That's who God has made me to be. Yes, such shortcomings cause me to get discouraged once in a while. But then I lift that up and pray, "Oh, yes, that's right. You're made perfect in my weaknesses. Thank You, Lord." I see the truth of this because God uses my poor academic skills to help me keep His truths simple and easy to read. That could be one of the reasons why my books sell all over the world.

Trials are similar to weaknesses. When you're in the middle of pain, what do you do with that pain? You know what I do? Exactly what it says in Romans 5:3-5—I rejoice in it. I lift up the pain and I say, "God, thank You for this pain because You're producing endurance inside of me. That's producing Your character inside of me. That's producing hope, and hope never disappoints, because You're pouring love into my heart right now. Your power is growing inside of me today, this very day. I wish the pain was not here today, but since it is, thank You for what You are doing within me right now."

Your weaknesses and trials are your greatest strengths. Jesus is going to take you and use you. He has called you to feed His flock in your role as pastors' wives. But perhaps you only have two fish and four loaves. Don't worry. Just do your part. Jesus is going to multiply what you have—it's His problem, not yours.

A Final Thought

Resolve right now that you will no longer worry about what people say about you, that you won't worry tonight about a critical remark a friend makes, that you won't be overcome emotionally by an unkind member of the congregation. Don't worry about what hits you. Start thinking about what God wants you to think after it hits you. You alone control your thoughts.

I love Romans 12 in which Paul encourages us to renew our minds through Christ Jesus (see v. 2). Let Jesus give your mind the ultimate makeover. Have the mind of Jesus. Determine today to know the thoughts of Jesus and to desire those thoughts. What are His thoughts? Read His Word: It is a "lamp to [your] feet and a light for [your] path" (Ps. 119:105). He will guard your heart and your mind—your thoughts—and bring you true peace (see Phil. 4:7). And I testify to that. So move forward in faith and hope and love!

Prayer
Lord, thank You that You're filling this special wife today
with your love and power. Bless her today in ways that
she'll know it could only come from You.

PART FOUR:

FREE TO SOAR THROUGH FOSTERING YOUR LEADERSHIP SKILLS

WHEN TWO LEADERS LIVE TOGETHER

DEVI TITUS

Often when a pastor and his wife are both leaders, there is conflict in the ministry and in the home. One key to two leaders living in peace is in understanding "headship" versus "leadership." Usually leadership and headship are used interchangeably, as synonyms. But I want to spell out the very important difference between these two terms. When you, as the wife of a church leader, understand the difference between leadership and headship, you will be free—and so will your pastor-husband.

Headship and Leadership

Headship is assigned authority. It is a seat of authority, like the head of a government or the head of an institution. Headship is the source of direction for an organization. Leadership is not assigned. A leader, unlike a head, is able to implement how to get to where the headship wants to go. There are two parts of leadership: innate leadership (by virtue of personality) and developed leadership. In other words, that is why we have leadership seminars. You can train leaders to be better leaders.

It's important to understand that not all leaders have a natural, innate ability to lead. For instance, your husband might be the pastor of the local congregation. He is in a position of authority (headship) because a board voted him in or a denomination appointed him. The fact that he has authority doesn't mean that he has innate ability to enact a vision. That's where the frustration comes when you live with a leader, particularly if your leadership gift is innate.

Perhaps you often think to yourself, *I am a natural leader, so why can't I lead the family?* The reason is because marriage teaching says, "For the husband is the head of the wife as Christ is the head of the church, his body" (Eph. 5:23). Your husband is your head, and if you forget that he is your head at home, you will lose the release and the anointing God has for you in your role as a leader in ministry. However, because your husband is your head, when you honor and respect his role assigned by God in your marriage, he can then release your leadership skills to be used in partnership with him in your home. This kind of unity will be empowering for both of you.

Having two leaders in the same house only works peaceably when you recognize that each of you has different strengths as a leader as well as a different style of leadership. I mobilize the people in the crowd quickly, but they stay in contact with my husband for years. His leadership style is very mellow, a strong authority that makes you feel safe. I am much more extroverted and outspoken. But my husband and I both honor our differing styles. So my respect for him allows me to submit to his headship and prevents us from being in conflict and competition.

An important note here, too, before I move on to the next topic: It may look like I'm the head of my husband. I'm not his head, but he relinquishes the implementation of project-oriented tasks to me because that's what I'm good at—and it's not what he's good at. He is then free to do what he's good at—talk to people on the phone, pray with them, search the Word, and pray.

What Do Leaders Share in Common?

What I want to address now are some common characteristics of leaders. It doesn't matter if you're male or female, or if you're a forceful and extroverted leader or a quiet leader who is more relational. These characteristics are shared by all leaders, regardless of leadership style.

Leaders Have Followers

This is a very important issue when leaders live together: Leaders have followers, but his followers may not be yours, and vice versa. My people are not Larry's people. The fact that I've connected with you doesn't necessarily mean that your husband is going to connect with my husband. Sometimes it happens, but sometimes it doesn't.

You have a choice as to what you can do once you discover that your husband has a following that you do not share. You can resent his people, be jealous of the time his people take, or be angry with whatever else he gets himself involved in that is not your passion, your interest or your burden. You can complain about it. You can become possessive of his time and make him feel guilty every time he walks out of the house. You can choose to isolate yourself from his people, choosing not to attend his meetings, lectures and so on. And so your husband goes alone to minister. These are some choices, but they are very dangerous choices for you to make.

But perhaps the greatest danger is finding fulfillment in ministry apart from your spouse. What happens when each of you is happy with your own ministry? The time you spend apart from each other will take a toll on your marriage. You begin to grow apart because each of you is so fulfilled in what you're doing—on your own. So you must concentrate on keeping your lives blended by embracing each others' friends and followers.

Leaders Have Demands

Leaders have time demands. Schedules and deadlines are all part of leadership. So we must learn how to manage them. It's really important to keep accurate calendars and get together often. Talk at night before you go to bed about what the next day will bring. Managing the day-to-day demands will enable you to preserve peace and love in your marriage.

What happens when you don't honor each other's commitments? The result is often conversations that go something like this: "Oh, you have that? How could you have that? I have this, so I won't be home either. What are we going to do with the kids, and what about dinner?"

The tension grows daily, and soon you're wondering, *Where's the fatigue coming from?* and eventually, *Where did the love go?* So schedule your calendars together. Be flexible and prioritize.

Often, when you're focused, your mind is preoccupied. When you're preoccupied in your mind, your sensitivity is dulled. You don't mean for it to be; it just is. It's dulled to the needs of your children, and it's dulled to the needs of your spouse. You will speak sharply because you're not focused on what they are saying. You will be irritated when they interrupt you. So just be aware of your behavior toward your family when you're focused on your leadership and ministry duties.

Let's turn it the other way. When your husband's mind is focused and you're speaking to him but it doesn't seem like he hears you, you feel rejected, even though you have no reason to feel that way. You're a leader too, and you often don't hear your husband or your kids because your mind is preoccupied. So don't take it personally when your husband's mind is preoccupied. Expect nothing from him on Saturday, the day before his big day, and Wednesday, the day he has Bible class. And he's not much good on Sundays until after the service. So reconcile yourself to the fact that you have four and a half days with him—and make the most of them. That is the truth; don't be irritated by it. Allow him more space on those days and be more understanding.

Leaders Deal with Stress

Leaders carry stress, so it is important to understand what stress does in your husband's life—and in your own life. You may enjoy unloading your stress, but your husband doesn't. He probably is not ready to open up about it. When we press men to "just talk about it," they shut down. So give your husband some space to carry that stress and be the subordinate in order to relieve the stress. When my husband is preparing his Sunday sermon, I do what I can to ease his burden. I lay aside whatever I am doing in order to meet his needs.

Likewise, when I'm getting ready for an event and am consumed with preparations, my husband comes alongside me and just supports me in the stress. If he needs to throw a load of laundry in, he does. I don't ask him to and I don't expect him to. But he does.

Leaders Need Affection

Our pastor-husbands often tend to be task-oriented leaders. They get so focused on their vision or on what they are doing that they isolate their emotions in a lot of ways. If you're married to a task-oriented leader, you want to be sure he is not emotionally disconnecting. This means you need to be the affectionate initiator. He needs to be touched. When you enter and leave each other's presence, always greet each other with a look, a touch, a kiss.

And we ourselves need affection. But I guarantee that if you give affection, it'll come back to you. Don't tell him, "I need you to be more affectionate to me." You just get things started. He'll be affectionate to you in return—I don't know a man who won't.

Leaders Need to Walk with Jesus

Matthew 11:28 tells us, "Come to me, all you who are weary and burdened, and I will give you rest." Leaders get tired. We need to remember to give our yoke to Jesus, to walk side by side with Him. He invites us to give Him our anxiety and to accept a yoking of tenderness. We need to reflect His tender power.

Please remember, you don't have to assert yourself to be effective. The more tender and soft you become, the more empowered you are. Tender power empowers others. Assertive power defrauds others. You might say, "Now, Devi, nobody will take me seriously if I lead in that way." But I assure you, power transformed by tenderness is sensitive strength, empathetic leadership, caring leadership, loving influence, gentle pressure. Do you see how empowering that is?

So I call you pastors' wives to empower the leader with whom you live. Empower your husband with tenderness, and empower your own leadership with tenderness. It will transform your home and your ministry, and it will ensure that you never have to sacrifice peace and love in your life for the sake of leading your ministry.

A Final Thought

One final piece of advice to those of you women who lead: Take the boss's hat off when you get home and become the servant. Philippians 2:1-6 tells us:

Therefore if there is any encouragement in Christ, if there is any consolation of love, if there is any fellowship of the Spirit, if any affection and compassion, make my joy complete by being of the same mind, maintaining the same love, united in spirit, intent on one purpose. Do nothing from selfishness or empty conceit, but with humility of mind regard one another as more important than yourselves; do not merely look out for your own personal interests, but also for the interests of others. Have this attitude in yourselves which was also in Christ Jesus, who, although He existed in the form of God, did not regard equality with God a thing to be grasped (*NASB*).

Jesus knew that He was a member of the Trinity, but His role on Earth was as a Servant-Redeemer. What does this tell us about what our attitude should be? That regardless of whether your husband is good at being your head, regardless of the fact that you're a better leader, regardless of the fact that you're more sensitive to the Spirit, you are to honor and respect him, to love and to serve him.

Prayer

Dear Lord, please help me to live in peace with my partner in leadership, my husband. Help me to honor his gifts and his commitments, even as I seek to honor my own. Enable me to recognize his headship in our marriage and home, even as I work alongside him in ministry. Lord, grant me the grace to always honor, respect, love and serve the amazing pastor-husband You have given me. I love You, Lord. I pray all this in the precious name of Jesus, amen.

LEADING IN CHANGING TIMES

TOGETTA ULMER

I have been a pastor's wife for 25 years, and the Lord has blessed my husband and me tremendously. I would not change my life experience for the world—but, oh, what a journey I have had! It is that journey that I want to share with you. Let me start at the beginning.

It was in January 1977 on a Sunday morning, a month before my husband and I were supposed to be married. The pastor of the church we attended asked if God was speaking to anybody's heart about coming into ministry. The pastor was relentless—the choir continued to sing and then he would ask again. Nobody moved. Then the pastor said, "Someone here has been called to the ministry, but that person is running from the call." Little did I know that it was my fiancé. He was sitting at the organ, playing the music. Eventually he came down the center aisle—and of course I almost fainted. While I rejoiced that day in his call—I was happy for him—in the back of my mind I thought, *What in the world have I gotten myself into?* You see, I didn't have a problem with *his* being called to the ministry—I had a problem with *my* being called into ministry with him.

His Calling Is Yours Too

It didn't take long for me to figure out that since I was his wife and his helpmate, I, too, had been called into the ministry. Believe me, this really rocked my world. You see, I thought I had it all figured out: God had called him to preach, but I was already singing in the choir, so I thought I was covered. He could preach; I could sing. But then, the inevitable happened: My husband was called to pastor. I really questioned God about that. I complained to Him, *Lord, you not only called him to preach but now he's also got to be a pastor?* Wasn't his being a preacher enough?

In my heart of hearts I felt that I was not cut out for the role of a pastor's wife. This was not in my job description. In my mind, I was constantly bargaining with the Lord to try to get out of this pastoring business. And my fear of the unknown didn't stop there.

A few years later, after the Lord called us to Faithful Central, I didn't know what to expect. I thought I had to be perfect—all these eyes were going to be on me all the time—and that didn't sit well with me, because I'm really an introvert. I can't begin to tell you how frightened I was. I may have been smiling on the outside, but believe me, on the inside there was a war going on. Unfortunately, nothing in the Scriptures gave me a description for a pastor's wife per se, so I had another question for the Lord. *Lord, what is happening now? You said that anything I needed to know was already in Your Word.* Then I found out that there is no distinction between what is required of a pastor's wife and what is required of a Christian woman.

First Timothy 3:11 says to all wives, "Be women worthy of respect, not malicious talkers but temperate and trustworthy in everything." I said, *OK, God, that's a good start. But what else am I expected to do? Do I have to attend every service? Do I have to love everybody in spite of the fact that they don't love my husband sometimes and are often critical of my children? Do I have to be transparent and seek to model what a godly woman should be? You see, Lord, I can't do that. I have a self-esteem problem. I first have to learn to love myself. I don't want these people to know about all of my inadequacies and all my problems.* Now let's be honest. How many of you ladies reading this have had those same questions for the Lord and voiced those same fears? I know I'm not alone.

The good thing for those of you who are new to the ministry is that the path has now been trodden by many feet. Unfortunately, when I became a pastor's wife, I didn't have the benefit of others' experience. I got to make my own mistakes and experience many heartaches. When I became a pastor's wife, it wasn't really acceptable (and definitely not encouraged) to seek advice from another pastor's wife or another sister at the church. But what a transformation we've made in this area. I praise God every day that I can now call up some other pastor's wife, some other sister in the faith, and tell her what I am going through—she will be more than happy to speak with me, to console me, to pray for me.

Learning Lessons from Elizabeth, the Pastor's Wife

Now that we've established that we are part of this pastoring business whether we like it or not and whether we feel adequate or not, let's find encouragement from the story of a very famous pastor's wife, Elizabeth. Elizabeth was the mother of John the Baptist and a descendant of Aaron—and she was married to a pastor, Zechariah. She had many of the same struggles that you and I do—we can relate to her story. Through Elizabeth, the Lord showed me three important truths that have helped me in my role as the pastor's wife: what I wanted, how I felt, and what He could do for me.

First, God showed me that He knew what I wanted. When I got married, my husband had two daughters, and I loved them like they were my own. I called them "my daughters." But I wanted a baby of my own. I wanted bone of my bone, flesh of my flesh—I didn't think this was too much to ask God. But we tried everything and still could not conceive. I felt unworthy, frustrated and disappointed. I felt like something was missing in my life and that it was all my fault.

Now, Elizabeth and I share an emptiness and a loneliness. Do you remember that Elizabeth was barren? Notice it doesn't say that Zechariah had no children; the verse puts emphasis on Elizabeth (see Luke 1:7). She watched Zechariah go to the Temple every day to bless other women and their children, but they had no child. I could relate.

But in the end what happened? God blessed Elizabeth with a child (see Luke 1:57). In the end, what happened to me? God gave me the desires of my heart. God taught me that what I really wanted more than having a baby was to be a mother. In my head I wanted to physically have a baby—to gain weight (well, not too much), shop for maternity clothes, and be able to talk to other women about what was going on in my pregnancy.

God showed me that He doesn't give me the desires of my head, but He gives me the desires of my heart. In my heart I wanted something more than having a baby—I wanted to be a mother. I know many women who have babies, but they are not mothers. So what did the Lord do for me? He gave me a son through adoption. My son's name is Kendan; we adopted him when he was seven months old. Kendan is now 18 and in chef school—and he is still the answer to the desire of my heart.

What else did God do for me? He gave me a friend. Again, let's look at the parallel in the story of Elizabeth. Luke 1:39 tells us that Mary greeted Elizabeth. Both women were walking the same path for carrying miracles, and they both were testimonies of the power and the mercy of God. In the same way, I have a friend named Connie who is a blessing to me and a gift from God. She thinks God put me in her life for her, but I believe God put her in my life to both encourage me and rebuke me. We have been friends since junior high school and she has always been there for me. She sees me at my best and at my worse. She still walks with me, not because I'm the pastor's wife, but because she loves me—flaws and all. As a matter of fact, there has never been a major event in my life that Connie hasn't been a part of.

My prayer for you, dear pastors' wives, is that God will send you a friend to walk with you, someone whom you can trust. She should be someone you can tell your deepest troubles to, someone who will listen. You know, even though we have wonderful husbands, they don't understand certain things the way a girlfriend does. So I encourage you to find someone like my Connie.

Let's look at the end of Elizabeth's story: "Her neighbors and relatives heard that the Lord had shown her great mercy, and they shared her joy" (Luke 1:58). What's the message here for us? Keep your true friends near, but stay away from the backstabbers, the naysayers, the jealous people, the so-called friends. God will always send someone to you who can not only weep with you but also rejoice with you. God will always send someone who can encourage you when you're down and rejoice with you when you're up. God will always find someone who will not only go through the valleys with you but also cheer you on when you are on the mountain top. When David said, "I will bless the LORD at all times" (Ps. 34:1, *NASB*), he wasn't satisfied to do it alone. He said, "O magnify the LORD with me, and let us *exalt His name together*" (v. 2, *NASB*, emphasis added).

Free to Soar

Pastors' wives, now is your time. It is your time to be delivered from low self-esteem, from jealousy, from insecurities. You are free to soar. You are free to lead in changing times. God has already given you the gifts you need to do what He has called you to do. God has given you the task to lead in these last days. I can assure you that even though it seems bleak sometimes and even though you may want to give up on God, your life and even the ministry, God assures you that He will give you the strength that you need—He will give you the peace that you need. He will make a way out of no way: "He who began a good work in you will carry it on to completion until the day of Christ Jesus" (Phil. 1:6).

A Final Thought

I thank God that He knows us better than we do. It has been proven to me again and again that God is sovereign. God had a call on Elizabeth's life, a call for her that no one else could fulfill—to birth John the Baptist. And you, pastors' wives, be assured that there is a special call on your lives. God wants to use you in a unique way in the lives of other women. In spite of your disappointments, your struggles, your inadequacies, He can use you. So I encourage you to answer His call to lead and to bless women in your church.

Blessing

Dear pastors' wives, rejoice, because the Lord has given you the desires of your heart. Rejoice, because weeping may endure for a night but joy comes in the morning [see Ps. 30:5]. Rejoice, because He loves you too much to leave you where you are. Rejoice, because He has gifted you to lead and to minister in these last days.

I pray, dear Father, that You would bless these women exceedingly, abundantly, above anything that they can imagine. I pray this in the precious name of Jesus, amen.

TOGETTA ULMER

$\mathcal{H}$OW TO WORK WITH STAFF IN YOUR CHURCH

JELLY VALIMONT

The issue of staffing can often be a tricky one. At our church, we have made the process of staffing much easier by outlining three basic requirements for any staff member: passion for God, a strong work ethic, and teachability. If you do not have those three things, you might as well not pursue being on staff with us, because at our church you are going to work hard, pray hard and love Jesus with all of your heart. So I encourage those of you who are pastors' wives to consider these qualities as essentials as you provide input for the staffing of ministries at your own church.

Keys to Leadership for Pastors' Wives

Pastors' wives often ask me how they can inspire their staff to be faithful followers—how they can be good leaders.

Be Approachable

The first key to good leadership for a pastor's wife is be approachable. Let staff members know that if they come to you with a problem, you are not going to knock them down in the dirt. You are not going to castigate them. You are not going to say, "Well, why aren't you more spiritual than that?" From the beginning, you must be approachable.

Be Willing to Take the Time

The second key is to take time with individual staff members' wives. I try to take individual time with each staff wife whenever possible. This does not mean that I take one hour every week or one hour every month or any particular allotment of time, but I do take time with these ladies when I can. One particular staff wife at our church is very shy. So we try to meet for lunch once a week; we talk and I tell her different ways that she might improve on her relationship skills. She benefits from our times together, and so do I.

Have Clear Expectations

Another must when it comes to staff interactions is to provide clear expectations. Yes, the staff members probably have a workplace manual filled with your church's policies and procedures, but what do you expect of your staff wives? Do you expect them to have their own jobs outside of the church? Do you expect them to be in church? Do you expect them to come to prayer meetings? Do you expect them to head up every committee that flows from the ministries of the church? What is it exactly that you want your staff wives to do and your staff members to do and to be? If you do not have clear expectations, confusion is sure to follow. Who is the author of confusion? Satan. You do not want to give him any opportunity to work mischief in your church, so have clear expectations.

Allow Them to Flow in Their Own Personality and Gifts

Staff members need to be allowed to bring their own personality and gifts to ministry. Don't think that just because there is a job that needs to be filled, the first person who comes along should have it. God has put clear giftings in each one of us, and He has put a clear calling on the lives of each staff member. Honor their individual gifts and calling, just as you do your own.

Catch Their Backs

This is a Southern saying, but it means that you need to protect and support your staff members. As a leader, it is your job to protect them. Catch their backs. Nothing will win and keep the respect of the staff like leadership that stands up for them and their needs. On the other hand, nothing will dishearten staff like leadership without a backbone.

Do Not Foster or Allow Competition

You must never encourage, foster or allow ministry or personal competition among the staff members. One of the ways that you probably will have to work on this is by not playing favorites among your staff members. Don't allow them to feel that they have to compete with each other for your affection or for their place on the totem pole, because that is not healthy.

Never Pretend to Be Omniscient

Be sure that your staff members know that you don't have all of the answers. I mean, let's be honest here: You *don't* have all the answers. Some situation will arise for which you won't have a workable solution—you just won't have it. And that's OK—nobody's perfect. Most staff members will feel more comfortable working for an imperfect but honest pastor's wife than they will for a Mrs. Know-It-All.

How to Connect with Staff and Their Families

If you as a leader want to have strong relationships, you must connect with your staff and their families. How do you connect with other people?

Get Acquainted

The first thing that we do in our church is to get acquainted with each staff member and his or her family. But just learning their names doesn't mean you are acquainted with your staff. You have to spend time with them. Remember, you don't do this ministry thing alone. It takes good people loving Jesus and loving each other before they can make a success of the ministry that God has given them. So get acquainted.

Be a Nurturing Family

Most churches consist of every type of family you can imagine. But we are called to be one family—to have unity as the family of God. How do we create a godly family? By nurturing one another. Philippians 2:2 says,

"Make my joy complete by being like-minded, having the same love, being one in spirit and purpose." Our one purpose as leaders is to be relational—and to not just be relational with each other but also to signify the relationship that our church families need to have as part of the larger Body. If we are in confusion with each other and in competition with each other, our church families are going to feel that same confusion and that same competition. And soon they will be imitating us.

Have a Defined Prayer Time and Play Time

The third point I'd like to emphasize is the need to be intentional about prayer time *and* play time. Don't just pray together, don't just go to church together, and don't just go to conferences together. Being intentional about your prayer time while neglecting play time will send an unhealthy message to your staff. So be sure to set aside time for play.

Find a Confidant

Fourth, find a confidant or a connection—someone who will aid your walk with Christ. Choose a friend who is also in ministry. This person need not belong to your denomination—she only needs to be a born-again believer who is also working in the vineyard.

A word of caution here: Although church members love, honor and respect you, you should not choose your confidant from among them. Don't do it. That would be an unequal yoke. You have been called to ministry with the Lord, and as a result of that, you are going to have to carry the cross as a bondservant to Jesus Christ. If, as a bondservant to Jesus Christ, you complain to your congregation about how much you have to do, they are going to become resentful for your sake. So don't find a confidant or a connection among the church members.

The Next Step: The First Wives Club

If you really want to build a support group for the wives on your staff, you might consider forming what we jokingly refer to as the First Wives Club. It might sound like a sorority, a gathering of women who are seeking friendship and affection. Certainly it is that—I love my girls and they love me—but the First Wives Club also serves some very important, ministry-related purposes.

Fulfilling Administrative Needs

I don't know how your husband is, but my husband thinks I can read his mind. I can't. If I don't take an active role in finding out what his day-to-day activities are, I will never know. So I have trained my husband's personal assistant to call me anytime there is a change in his schedule. We do our calendar a year in advance. She prints out everything she has on her computer for my husband's commitments and gives it to me. I cross-reference it with my calendar. I then cross-reference it with the calendars of my staff wives, and in turn we make sure that nothing conflicts with church community events. It is important that we know what is going on, or we will get caught with our pants down.

Enhancing Information Sharing

By sharing information, I do not mean that you say, "Did you hear what has happened with so and so? He is having an affair and their marriage is on the rocks. Do you know who he is having an affair with? Oh, let me tell you." That is not the kind of information I need—that is called gossip. God hates gossip, and I for one want to be loved by God. No, I'm talking about sharing information. If there is some news that is important for our staff to know, we share it with them. You don't want to walk up to somebody and congratulate her on her pregnancy if she's just had a miscarriage, do you?

When you are sharing this information, it is critically important that you maintain a very high level of confidentiality. Some information you can share as a group, and some information you are going to need to share with a particular individual.

Providing Accountability

The First Wives Club provides a place where wives can feel safe and comfortable; they are then willing to be transparent and accountable. If you cop a bad attitude to me, I will gently confront you about it: "Are you having a hard time at home? Are you having a hard time dealing with your family? Please share with me what is at the root of this attitude, so I can help you." Such accountability is important for each of us, and the First Wives Club provides the needed structure to encourage it.

Following Rules, Staying Healthy

In order to keep the First Wives Club healthy and true to its purpose, we do have rules that are enforced.

The first rule is to remember that we are family. We don't talk about each other. We don't talk against each other. I am not going to tell any other member of the church that I've got a problem with my sister if my sister doesn't know it.

The second rule is that we don't discuss staff issues with church people. End of discussion.

The third rule is that problems at the office remain at the office. We strive to not let them interfere with our relationships.

The fourth rule is that if my spouse has a problem with another staff member, he and that staff member work it out—I don't. If my husband has a problem with your husband, we let them handle it.

The fifth rule is that we don't receive accusations against each other. If someone has a problem with another staff member, he or she needs to address that problem with that individual. I don't receive an accusation against any of our staff members.

The sixth rule is that we don't answer an offense for another staff member. If somebody tells me that you have offended him or her, I will call you and say, "Hey, so-and-so called me and said this happened. I want you to call so-and-so and work this out." You then handle it immediately.

The seventh rule is that we work together as a team. We strive to be in unity with one another. Not only are we a family, we are also a team.

A Final Thought

Let me add a final note about letting go. Staffs change. We can't keep everyone on staff indefinitely, nor is it healthy to do so. Change brings sharpening and stretching. Change helps you to grow as a staff and as a church. When a staff member resigns, you need to remember that this is what you have nurtured them for—so they can be independent and go forward to make new disciples.

We are not in the process of building our own kingdom. Our ministry is not our own—it belongs to God. Just as you are making disciples for the kingdom of God, you are training others for leadership. Some ministers are destined to be in a support role, while other ministers are destined by God to lead the charge. Only God makes the final call.

Blessing

Dear Lord, grant this precious pastor's wife Your guidance as she seeks to interact with staff and staff wives in a healthy way. Help her to see the role that she plays in creating a family out of the diverse staff members in her church. Help her to be approachable and hospitable. Keep her always mindful that she is working to build Your kingdom. Bless her, Lord, with every good thing. Bless her abundantly. I ask this in the name of Jesus, amen.

PART FIVE

FREE TO SOAR THROUGH BUILDING HEALTHY MINISTRY

$\mathcal{W}$HAT EVERY BEGINNING PASTOR'S WIFE NEEDS TO KNOW

JEANA FLOYD

The life of a pastor is the only life I've ever known. I grew up in a pastor's home, and now I'm married to a pastor. Of course, like many of you, I grew up saying that I'd never marry a preacher. And my dad use to laugh at that. But you know, regardless of what I said then, I would not change my life for anything. I love what I do. I love my job, and I love being the pastor's wife.

My husband has been a pastor since the day we got married—in fact he was a pastor six months before we got married—so it was no surprise to me. I realize that may not have been the case for many of you. You might have married your husband, and then he decided to go into the ministry. I understand that has its special challenges, but for me, this life is the only life that I've ever known.

Life Lessons

I would like to share with you some of the lessons that I have learned in the hopes that you might find them helpful as you learn to deal with the special challenges of being a pastor's wife.

Life Inside Your Home

First, let's look at the issues related to life inside your home.

Respect. I want to tell you something that was taught to me as a young pastor's wife: Honor your husband. Your husband needs to be your number one priority, so honor and revere him. He needs to be your very best friend; he must be a priority above your female friends and your family. Other relationships should never supersede your relationship with your husband.

There are going to be times when it seems like it's just you and him against the world. I want to challenge you not to live a separate life from your husband. It's so easy to do, because we get so caught up in things. And if you have children or a career or whatever, it's very easy to sleep in the same bed and not have your lives be joined together.

His physical needs. This brings us to another issue: Go to bed with your husband; *meet his needs physically.* If you don't, something else will. I say "something" because we no longer live in a world where a man has to go somewhere to have an affair. He can have it right in your home on his computer. If you are a married woman, you know that God designed men to have a great physical need, and we as wives have an opportunity to meet that need in their lives. We are doing a great disservice to ourselves by putting our husbands into a position of temptation and lust when we do not fill those needs. So fill your husband's physical needs.

Awe of his call. Never get over your awe of the call of God on your husband's life. How can you not be constantly amazed at what He has called your husband to do and to be? How can you ever take for granted the awesome role that you play in that calling? I want to tell you, I am constantly amazed at what God can do through us as vessels. I don't say that in a boastful way; I am more amazed than anyone else that God would choose me to accomplish His purpose in His kingdom.

When you are in awe of your husband's call, you reflect that in how you treat your husband—everything from ironing his shirts to speaking well of him in front of others. Your awe inspires you to free your husband up to accomplish the ministry God has called him to do. Let the world know that you serve him out of your passion for him and what he does, not out of your position as his wife.

Honor his commitments. Do you ever pressure your husband for time when you know others are pressing him so much and he doesn't have any more time left? Sometimes we are guilty of that, aren't we? I want to challenge you in this area. Give your husband room to grow. Many of us, myself included, have had to grow in the area of time and life management.

Teach your children to love your husband's boss. Another point I want to make is the need to teach your children to love the Lord and His church. Your children will really know if you love the church by the things you say at home when church members are not around. The greatest prayer that we can pray for our children is that they would love Jesus Christ and love His Church. When you think about it, if they love Jesus and they love His Church, all of their decisions will flow from that love.

Life in the Community

Let's talk about your life in the community.

Sharing your faith. What an awesome responsibility and opportunity you have as the pastor's wife: to share your testimony. Now perhaps some of you don't particularly enjoying sharing your faith with others, but that's part of your job description. Just accept it. Just realize it and seek to live your life above and beyond. For whom are we serving anyway? We're serving the Lord. You want your life to be without reproach because you're serving Him. Don't resent this, but just embrace it as part of the call of God on your life. It's a small price to pay compared to what Jesus has done for you, isn't it?

Witnessing to the world. The world, especially the lost world, is watching to see how you react to life's challenges. What are you going to show them? If we live out Christ's teachings in our lives, the world will be attracted to His truth and love in us. Jesus said in John 12:32, "And I, if I be lifted up from the earth, will draw men unto me" (*KJV*).

Relationship with Your Staff

Okay, let's move on to your relationship with your staff. Here's where it gets really easy!

Letting the men be the men. Your role as a pastor's wife is to be a support to your husband, not to be in charge of the staff. For you to attempt to solve staff problems and staff issues that your husband should be dealing with is a rebuke to your husband. That's not the message that you want to send to your congregation. God called you to be your husband's helpmate—He didn't call you to be the pastor, and He didn't call you to be in charge of the staff. Your role should be to minister to your husband and to staff wives.

Fellowshipping with staff wives. I've been very blessed in every church that we've ever been in to have good relationships with other staff wives. And you know what? It's normal to be closer to some women than to others. You don't need to be stressed out about the fact that you are not all best friends, but you can be each other's best supporters.

At our church, we have a monthly luncheon for the staff wives. This has been a great fellowship builder. We get together and we just visit. Occasionally we have a program and have a devotional, but that time is devoted to fellowship, not to Bible study. It provides a wonderful way to fellowship, and it helps resolve problems among the women. You know, it's rather difficult to stay angry at a woman who is sitting next to you at lunch. You begin to sense her heart and come to understand that she's going through a difficult time. So this monthly meeting is a great way to foster forgiveness as well as fellowship.

Relationship with Church Members

Let's talk about your relationship with church members. This boils down to one important principal: Watch your tongue. Don't share your personal problems with church members. If you do, you lessen your husband's influence and disqualify his leadership with some folks. Now that may or may not be fair, but that's what will happen, because the average church member cannot handle the humanity of the pastor and his wife. For some reason or another, all of our church members put us up on a pedestal and think we have it together in every way. So don't share your personal problems with them. Instead, when difficult times come in your marriage, seek godly counsel from another church leader or a Christian professional.

Friendships in the Ministry

Let's talk about friendships in the ministry—yes, I said you can have friends in the ministry!

Having boundaries. Just remember that there are boundaries with every relationship. You are smart enough and know what those boundaries are, so go ahead and have relationships. Although there will be those friends who will disappoint you, there will be friends who will faithfully walk alongside of you. The greatest joys and the greatest hurts will come from relationships with church people. But don't let the pain of some keep you from the joy of most. After serving as a pastor's wife for over 28 years now, I have found that most people are a joy to serve.

Learning to be an overlooker. I learned this when I had cancer. As the pastor's wife, I knew I couldn't hide my illness from the congregation, yet I still felt so exposed. But it was a wonderful time for our church. When we look back on it, we see that God did a great work in our church during that time. I learned that when people want to say the right thing, they will say the stupidest things. So look past the words and see the loving intentions in their hearts—and say "thanks," even though your own heart might be hurting. Try to be an overlooker. Just love them and get on with things.

A Final Thought

In closing, I would just say that you have got to determine whom you are going to serve. Will you serve your husband? Your children? Your community? Your congregation? Your Lord? I believe that we would all say it's a combination of all of these things, but ultimately, you should be serving the Lord. For when you serve the Lord, you serve others. One of our young staff wives said it well: "Don't be too hard on yourself or others. Be willing to stand for issues that are important to God. Be willing to bend on issues that are not that important. Keep your walk with God strong, and problems won't look so big. He has a way of bringing it all into perspective." For a young woman, she's got a good grip on what ministry is all about.

Blessing

*Dear Lord, right now there is a pastor's wife reading this book,
seeking Your guidance. Perhaps she is new to her role as a pastor's
wife, or perhaps she has been in the trenches for many years.
Whatever her story, please bless her, Lord. Give her Your strength
and Your wisdom as she seeks to serve You, her husband and her
family. Bless her, Lord. We love You. Amen.*

*L*OVING YOUR CHURCH

JEANNIE McCULLOUGH

We are so blessed that the New Testament is filled with stories that emphasize Jesus' humanity. These stories help us to visualize the oneness we have with our Lord in our moments of pain, discouragement and hurt in ministry. I find my sweetest encounters with Christ have taken place when my burdens outweighed my strength and everybody and everything had left except Him. This realization taught me the importance of embracing the difficult instead of trying to escape it. When I embraced the difficult times, God really taught me how to love my church with the same love that He has for His Church.

How to Love Your Church

If I asked what are the three most important things to remember when we're shopping for real estate, we would say "location, location, location." But what about the three most important things to remember when we are searching for how to love our church? Simple—just remember three things: love Christ, walk with Him; love Christ, work with Him; love Christ, watch Him.

Walk with Him

Colossians 2 reminds us that we can grow up healthy in God only as He nourishes us. And how easy it is for those of us who care for the souls of others to discover that we ourselves are malnourished, running on fumes instead of fuel. Satan would love to make us believe that

Sundays will sustain us, when in truth they could sink us if the Sunday service is our only means of caring for our souls.

How does nourishment come? I believe it comes in three main ways. First, it comes through confrontation—when the Holy Spirit reveals to you the condition of your soul. Second, it comes through confession, when you respond by acknowledging the sin that God has revealed by His blessed Holy Spirit. If you do not call sin by its right name, you will not change your behavior. Third, nourishment comes through commitment, when you devote time to learning God's Word and being radically obedient to it. Matthew 5:1 tells us, "When Jesus saw his ministry drawing huge crowds, he climbed a hillside. Those who were apprenticed to him, the committed, climbed with him" (*THE MESSAGE*).

Work with Him

The second thing that we need to remember in loving our church is to love Christ by working with Him. In Colossians, Paul tells us, "[I'm] asking God to give you wise minds and spirits attuned to His will, and so acquire a thorough understanding of the ways in which God works. We pray that you'll live well for the Master, making him proud of you as you work hard in his orchard" (1:9-10, *THE MESSAGE*). As you learn more and more about how God works, you will learn how to do your work.

I have spent much of my life working for God, and I have learned that there is a big difference between working *for* God and working *with* God. Working for God is either other-directed, meaning that you're working where other people think you should be working, or it's self-directed, meaning you're working where you're comfortable and confident and you're commended. But working with God is Spirit-directed. God showed me that when I worked for God, my gifts were useful, but that when I worked with God, even my weaknesses were usable. And when I became open to working with God, His blessed Holy Spirit began to speak to me. As a result, I embraced a life of radical obedience that sent me on the incredible adventure of a lifetime: working with God.

When I began that journey, the Holy Spirit searched my heart. You see, I discovered that I had been lost at church, doing all the right things for all the wrong reasons. So God spoke to my heart—He asked for all of me. He said, "I want everything—including your disabilities." I couldn't believe what I was hearing—I had tried to hide my dyslexia and poor memory for years. So I gave God my disabilities, wondering what on Earth He would do with them. Then He told me, "Do not fear the reproach of man, for I have put My words in your mouth and covered you with the shadow of My hand. *Work with Me*." At that moment, I could imagine what Paul felt like when He heard Christ say, "My grace is sufficient for you" (2 Cor. 12:9). God's power is made manifest in our weaknesses. So the weaker I was, the stronger I became in Christ Jesus. God is an amazing coworker—He steps right in and does the job!

Watch Him

Third, love Christ through watching Him. Watch Him in the pages of Scripture, especially the Gospels. Saturate your lives with the events from His life, and watch fears fade, faith flourish and trust triumph. But also watch for the Lord in your own soul. When you're crushed, you'll discover He's carrying you. When you're hopeless, you'll discover He's helping you. When you're empty, you'll discover that He'll empower you.

When I began to watch God, I noticed that He often had quite a bit to show me. I remember that when my daughter, Ginger, was in college, she was seeing a young man who wasn't quite my cup of tea. He had long hair and wore a leather jacket—and earrings. The first day he came to the house and asked for Ginger, I didn't know what to do. So I shut the door in his face. God said, "Tacky, tacky, tacky," and since I had begun to *watch Him*, I knew He wouldn't believe that I hadn't heard Him. So I opened the door and invited the young man to come in. What would I have done had I not been watching Him and listening to His voice? I probably would have left that door closed—ignoring my Christian call to charity and hospitality.

A Final Thought

One night, God placed a burden on my heart to pray for my daughter. She was a grown woman, yet she had not been saved. Suddenly, I thought of Christ's words in Philippians: "He who began a good work in you will carry it on to completion" (Phil. 1:6). So I began to praise God and to thank Him for His faithfulness. That night my daughter accepted Christ. It was the most amazing thing. The next night she came home, gave me a kiss and went upstairs. Then I heard her begin to sing, "He who began a good work in you, He'll be faithful to complete it in you." Beautiful.

Blessing

Father, bless the women reading this book—they are seeking
You with sincere hearts. Help these dear pastors' wives to love You and
to love their church. Help them to love You and walk with You.
Help them to love you and work with You. Help them to love You
and watch You. And out of these experiences, may there spring up
in their hearts expressions of genuine love for the Church.
I ask this in Your strong name, amen.

$\mathcal{H}$OW TO MOBILIZE WOMEN IN THE CHURCH

LYNN MATHISON

I want to share with you the story of how God broke my heart for the women of the Church. My husband and I were in New Orleans on vacation. On a trolley ride, we met a woman with a little boy. As I normally do, I just started talking, asking where they were from and what her husband did for a living. She replied, "Well, my husband is a Methodist preacher here in New Orleans." I said, "Oh really, my husband is a Methodist preacher." She looked at me and she said, "You don't look like a preacher's wife." I thought, *Oh, what does a preacher's wife look like?*

I forgot about the incident until a couple of weeks later when we traveled to Kentucky—my husband was going to speak to a group of pastors' wives. During the women's program at the conference, I could see the hurt and the pain on the faces of the pastors' wives. I wept for the pain and the hurt that I saw. I said, "God, I have a message for these women. Please, Lord, open doors." That was my prayer, that God would open doors to help me share with others how to mobilize women in the Church, how to free them to be the women they were meant to be.

So, with that prayer in my heart, I began to wonder, *What does a pastor's wife look like?* I went back and sat at the feet of Jesus. I said, "God, You have birthed this message in me, and You have put me in a position of being a pastor's wife." This is why I knew I needed to share an amazing message with you, a message of love from the heart of God, a message that will indeed give you wings to soar.

Finding Freedom

About eight years ago, God birthed this passion in my heart for women. I realized that there was no model for a pastor's wife—that the pastor's wife is a gifted individual, created by God to be unique and to be free to serve wherever she is called to be. In my eagerness to share my vision, I set out with several other women to start a women's ministry in our church. In doing so, I found that we were struggling. We prayed a lot and we struggled. As I sat back, I said, "Lord, this is just what I saw before. These women hurt. They are not freed up to minister to the other women because they are themselves hurting."

God taught me in a dark time in my life. He birthed in me the message of love and gifted me so that today I can share out of a free heart. He freed me from the pain of my past. He freed me from the things that had bound me, enabling me to soar so I could spread a message of love. I truly believe that we cannot mobilize women in our churches until we are mobilized ourselves. But how do we go about doing that? Very simply: through our message to our people, through the ministry that God would have for us wherever we have been placed, and through the purity of our motives.

The Need to Be Loved

This is the message that God gave me and I want to pass it to you: You are His beloved daughter, and if you know who you are as a child of God, you have the power within you to mobilize other women—the women in the church whom we are privileged to serve. If we are giving from an overflow, if we are relating to the women in our churches out of what God has done in us, they catch it. They don't catch us; they catch the glory of Jesus. They catch the very essence of God, Himself. So know that you are a daughter of a King. He has called you by name and has chosen you for this time and for this place. For the church you serve, you are the Esther for this time. He wants to tell you that you are loved beyond all measure.

I just get so excited when I begin to understand the power of God's love. God loves me just because I am His daughter. He loves you just because you are His daughter. As a pastor's wife, as a leader in the church, I know that if we are going to mobilize women, we need to be firmly grounded in the truth that we are His beloved daughters.

How many of us don't have a clue as to who we are? God says, "I love you, Lynn. I love you just because you are you. It doesn't matter what you did in the past. I want to forgive you for your sin. I want to wipe your sin away. I want to take your mess, and I want to make a message out of it." Do any of you have troubles in your life? God says, "I want to take them and use them for My glory. I want to use them to your good and My glory. Give your troubles to Me. I want you to mobilize other women in the position in which I have placed you, and I want you to do it with freedom. I want to free you up so that you are free to soar" (see Ps. 27).

Ladies, I want to suggest that you step up and move into the position that God has called you to. You can do that with the precious anointing and power of the Holy Spirit, because He has gifted you. He has called you and put you in such a place. He wants to live His life through you.

The Need to Belong

I don't know anyone who doesn't struggle with the need to belong. When we first started our women's ministry, it didn't thrive, even after we prayed a great deal. So we went back to the feet of Jesus. We soon realized that the women trying to do the leadership were hurting, so I decided to spend a lot of time with those particular women. We talked, we prayed, we struggled. We talked over issues in our lives. What we found, just within our core group, was the need to belong. We each needed a place to belong, to be a part of something.

You, too, have at some time or another felt that need to belong. Be assured: You belong. You belong to the family of God. You have been chosen; you have been called.

The Need to Make a Difference

One of the other needs that we have is to be significant—to matter, to make a difference. Why do most of us want to make a difference? Why do most of us need that attention? Well, maybe because we didn't get that attention from our parents. So we have been looking for it in what we do. We say, "I just want someone to notice me. I wish the members of our church would think I am doing a good job. I wish they would really value my contribution."

Do any of you have those struggles? We all do. I want to tell you today that you are significant to the Father, to Jesus Christ and to the precious Holy Spirit. If we please the Father, that is all that matters. If He can do the work in us, we can sit at His feet and say, "Lord, this is where I am today; this is the ministry we have today; this is the church we have today." If we are not happy in that place but will surrender it to Jesus Christ, He can mobilize us—and thus mobilize the women in our churches. Because we are free, they are free. Once we understand that our significance comes from Almighty God, He tells us, "You are the most valuable thing I have. You are My daughter and you are valuable. I have paid the price for you—I gave My only Son, Jesus Christ, for you. Your very being is significant."

The Need to Feel Adequate

We look to everybody else and everything else and all the other ministries and wonder if we're adequate. We often feel as though we're not doing a good enough job. We often struggle with feelings of inadequacy, thinking, *I don't measure up.* But God is doing the work in us; therefore, it is He who is the adequacy within us. He is our strength.

I do believe that the reason we found success in mobilizing women in our local church is because we took time as a leadership group to pull back and look at the issues and struggles in our lives, and became free inside. We became free to be the women that God called us to be so that in turn we could free up others. Oswald Chambers, the writer of *My Utmost for His Highest*, says it this way: "There is no way that the ministry can free up another person until it has first been worked in you."[1]

These four key principles are your message to the women in your church. It will mobilize them. The message is first to you and then to the women you lead. These basic needs can be met by women who have been empowered by God, women who understand that it is God and

God alone who can meet these needs. They will come to understand that it is not about other people—it's about God's wanting to live His life in them and through them. Jesus gave His life for us so that He could give life to us, to live life through us. That is very simple to say, but it is a process that takes time and effort to work out.

Working the Process

I want to share a little bit about what God has done in my life. Because of the pain and the hurt that I have suffered in my life, God birthed a ministry that we call From Pain to Purpose. It is the one thing that I do in our church that enables me to give back to God: sharing the message that He has worked in me. In my ministry, I start by talking about our identity in Christ. This brings freedom to many women, allowing them to find healing from their past, particularly from their anger and their pain.

Anger

Let me expand a bit on anger, because it's important to talk about the reality of our anger and what it is that causes us to be angry. Perhaps we are angry at the members in the church who are not quite pleased with us. They like to tell us how to do things. A lot of times, they won't take charge or take responsibility because they expect us to take charge. We need to learn not to take on the expectations of others. Once we learn how to leave behind those expectations, we'll find ourselves free from anger.

Pain

Once we deal with anger and get emotionally honest with ourselves, we are able to really take steps forward. How many of us wear the mask? How many of us try to pretend to be something that we are not? How many of us try to look like the "good pastor's wife"—calm, cheerful, energetic? How often do we deny our very selves, our emotions and, most importantly, our pain? Most of the time, Christian churches and Christian people will just tell us to forgive and forget and move on. We do that, but we go on with a reservoir of pain. We try to live life with that reservoir of pain, but it weighs us down. God tells us, "I want to free you up."

I would like to suggest that if you, as a pastor's wife, are not free to soar, it is because you have not addressed these issues that need to be dealt with. God wants to free you up—today. I believe He wants to free you up so that you can free up others in your church. If you are not empowered and if you are not freed up, you can't free up anybody else—and bringing freedom is our ministry. If you are so busy trying to put together the women's ministry in your church and you are struggling, step back and say, "God, I want to deal with me." Draw a circle. Be willing to step in it and say, "Lord, heal me. Lord, mobilize me. Empower me, Lord, with Your precious Holy Spirit."

As a pastor's wife, you need to not only learn to grieve your own losses but also to learn how to help other women through their grieving process. Grieving is a good thing, so be a gracious presence as these women tell their stories and weep with you. They need their feelings validated, so be quick to listen and slow to speak. Once they have grieved, they can then come to accept the pain in their lives. Whatever the loss, whatever the pain, grieving needs to take place.

Forgiveness

When we uncover the loss in our lives and we learn to grieve and come to acceptance, there is always forgiveness. Forgiveness, I find, is the most important key. What is keeping you from being free to be that woman that God created you to be? To walk alongside your husband, free to partner with him in ministry, free to share the privileges and the joy of your calling, free to take the opportunities that God has given you? Is there an unforgiving spirit present in your life? Do you have bitterness in your life? Is there resentment in your heart? God says, "I want you to give it to Me." When we forgive others, we choose to let go and not hold on to the resentment, but to give it to God and to allow Him to work in the situation. Why can I do that? Because God has told me that I am His daughter and that He just wants to live His life through me. If I have been forgiven and if I have the empowerment of the Holy Spirit every day, why wouldn't I want to forgive? Inasmuch as He has forgiven me, I can forgive others.

Love

When others speak wrongly of us, we need to uncover the lies that we believe about ourselves. We need to learn to interact with difficult people, and we need to learn to respond to criticism. We can learn to respond in a godly way, instead of just reacting, by having a motive that is based solely on love. What I saw in my own life is that I thought I was loving other people, but the Lord challenged me: "Lynn, it is easy to love those who can love you back. What I want to really teach you is *love*, My love, *agape* love." To have His love is to embrace an unconditional love. It is a love that loves even if you are not loved back. It is a love that is looking for nothing in return.

I would like to suggest that we, as pastors' wives, need to love the women in our churches with just such a love. If we can't, I truly believe that we have failed to embrace the love that God has for us and the position that God has for us. At a recent conference called Every Member in Ministry, I was privileged to watch a group of pastors' wives become free. During a time set aside for personal interaction and discussion, we shared our struggles and our faith and discovered the pain and hurt in our lives that had kept us from enjoying the position that God had given us. So I would like to encourage you who are also pastors' wives to set aside time for such interaction with the staff members at your church—empower them. Free your staff members, and then let them reach out to the women of the church.

What I pray and what I feel is that God wants to empower you with this love so that you can be that sweet fragrance of encouragement to the women around you. Without His love, all of our efforts are worthless.

> If I [can] speak in the tongues of men and [even] of angels, but have not love (that reasoning, intentional, spiritual devotion such as is inspired by God's love for and in us), I am only a noisy gong or a clanging cymbal. And if I have prophetic powers (the gift of interpreting the divine will and purpose), and understand all the secret truths and mysteries and possess all knowledge, and if I have [sufficient] faith so that I can remove mountains, but have not love (God's love in me) I am nothing

(a useless nobody). Even if I dole out all that I have [to the poor in providing] food, and if I surrender my body to be burned or in order that I may glory, but have not love (God's love in me), I gain nothing (1 Cor. 13:1-3, *AMP*).

With that, God says, "If you know My love, it's My love within you that is the power."

Doing Things God's Way

Once we learn to deal with our anger and pain, forgive as Jesus forgives and live in His love, we can really begin to grow. We move beyond the baby steps and begin to blossom. But how do we go about our daily tasks? How do we bring a little bit of heaven to Earth?

God's Timing

First, we have to learn to wait on God's timing. We are so impatient, aren't we? It's not that we aren't working for worthy goals—we are—but sometimes we forget that Someone Else sets the agenda. I find that in waiting long and in enduring long, sometimes God says, "It is not in your timetable, Lynn." Our women's ministry in particular took time to grow and flourish. We waited and prayed, but things weren't turning out the way we thought they would, and we had to die to it. We had to let it go and regroup and do it God's way. We had well-equipped and qualified people, yet we still had to wait on God's timing to bring our desires to fruition.

God's Leading

I would like to suggest that if you are in a dark time in your life, instead of saying, "Why is this happening to me?" and being angry about it, just say, "God, thank You. Thank You for what is going on in my life. Thank You for the church we serve. Thank You for the women who are critical." Through those dark times, He is trying to grow us and mature us. When we are broken and at the end of ourselves, it is then that we are open to God's leading in our lives.

When He brings you to the end of yourself, to the place where you say, "God, I can't," He says, "Hallelujah, that is just where I want you. I want you to start right here. I am going to take over for you, and I want you to know that I love you." As a result, we come to a place of understanding of His love and of the hurts of others. We do not judge other people, then, because we also have been in a place of hurt, a place of need, a place where we needed to be recognized and understood, a place where we just wanted to be loved and accepted. Once we understand that love and acceptance come from God Almighty, we can love others on this side and help bring them up, help mobilize them, and help them come to that place of peace.

God's Call on Your Life

We always look over the fence and think that the grass looks greener on the other side. Yet God says, "Be thankful and be content with the lot that I have given you." For me, I find that when I get the focus off everyone else's lives, everything in my own life falls into place. Know this: God meets your needs. If He has called you to be a pastor's wife and has called you to mobilize women in your church, His promise is that He will give you everything that you need in order to carry it out (see Phil. 1:6). If He has called you, He will give you what you need in order to do that ministry.

Are you wondering, *What is He waiting on*? Let me suggest that perhaps He is waiting on you. He wants you first to be free. He wants you to come back to your first love—the Lord—and to understand that it is His love that will empower you to do the ministry that He has called you to do. Have we forgotten that this love does not wear a sign that reads "Look at me"? There is no pride in real love.

Yet we do struggle with pride, don't we, in our role as pastors' wives? What is it about pride? I think a lot of times we just say, "Well, you know I can do this by myself. I can figure this out." But it's OK to say, "Lord, as a pastor's wife, I want to know where I fit in. What should I be doing? How do I approach women's ministry?" God wants to free you of undue responsibility. He wants you to remember that He has called you. He is saying, "It's OK—ask Me."

God's Perfect Work

God is at work in us, energizing us to will and to work for His pleasure and for His glory. We are never perfect, but He is always growing us and progressively moving us. He is conquering the things in us that would hinder our ability to mobilize those around us. How? By teaching us, a little more each day, how to love as He loves. His love in us does not insist on its own right or its own way.

But how do we as pastors' wives implement this principle in our daily lives? If you are like me, you like to make lists! I don't let myself go to bed until I have checked off everything on my to-do list. I like a lot of order, yet in my desire for order, I run up against the fact that love does not insist on its own way. So, though I still like lists, I have learned to let go. If I leave the house and there are dirty dishes in the sink, that's OK.

We have to realize that the perfectionist tendency in all of us can trip us up. Our desire for order and organization has to be kept under control—it cannot be allowed to control us. If it does, what happens? We stop inviting people over unless our house is perfectly clean. We stop wanting people to see us, to see how we live, to really get to know us.

So we should balance our desire for order with our desire to be hospitable. For myself, I like to have people in my home. My husband and I often invite over study groups so they can come into our home and see what we are all about. This is a wonderful way to mobilize people, because this way church members can get to know us on a personal level. We are not just the pastor and his wife—we are fellow believers. As "real" people, we can build relationships with others and learn from them.

I believe that when I open my home, I open my heart to others. So, I want to encourage you, if that is something that you like to do (not everyone is comfortable doing this), to practice hospitality. Have groups from your church over to your home. Let them see who you are and what you are all about. Whatever it takes for you to allow that to happen, do it. That is loving others, and you'll find that it's a wonderful way to mobilize women.

God's Definition of Humility

Inevitably, someone in the church will say a critical word about you, your husband or your church. Criticism is something that pastors' wives deal with all the time. But too often they react, making things worse. Here are some ideas for dealing with critical comments.

First, instead of trying to defend or explain the situation, sit down with God the Father, because He loves you and said He would work all of this for your good (see Rom. 8:28). Second—and this is not easy to do—ask yourself, *Could there be any truth in what is being said?* Third, ask yourself, *Lord, what do I need to change here? What is it that You are trying to get at in me? What is it that You would like for me to do? What are You trying to heal? What are You trying to do with me, God?*

If you are open and vulnerable to the leading of the Holy Spirit, He will free you from the pain inside. He will free you from the hurt and pain of what other people think. He will give you the right responses to the people in your church. If you know who you are, your response to them ought to be, "Well, I am sorry that you see me that way." Or, "I wish things could be different." There is no need to explain or defend. The Bible says that after we have done all else, we are to simply stand (see Eph. 6:13).

So at the end of the day, know your position and step into it. To serve as a pastor's wife means that you are going to suffer criticism. There is a statement that I use that really helps me: "Not everybody liked Jesus, so what makes me think that everybody is going to like me?" Not everyone is going to always agree with every program that we try to do. With the leading of the Holy Spirit, we do the best we can. There is always going to be criticism and there is always going to be someone out there who wants to stir the pot. That is just the way it is.

Don't fail to see that criticism often springs from the unhappiness of the one doing the criticizing. When other people are critical and difficult, it is usually because of the struggles in their own lives. I find that what these individuals really want is for you to come up and put your arms around them, love them, accept them and give them a place to belong. Everybody cries out in different ways for love. The women in your church are hurting and they need someone who can reach out to them and understand them. If they are critical and if they say negative things, reach out and love them. Reach out and touch them, hold them, love them and try to give them a place.

A Final Thought

"Love never fails" (1 Cor. 13:8). The empowerment of love will help mobilize you and then allow you to mobilize other women.

Love bears up under anything and everything that comes its way (see 1 Cor. 13:7). Its hope endures in all circumstances, and it will never weaken. Love is always ready to believe the best of everybody. God wants us to believe the best of everybody. He wants us to start with our family first, and then the people in the church. I don't look at the people in their hurt and pain. I try to press through to see the people that God created them to be.

Most people cry out to be loved, to be accepted, to belong, to know that they have value. Dear readers, I believe that God has put us in that position, to tell the women of the world that they are beloved daughters of the King. What an amazing calling we have. What an honor and what a privilege!

Blessing

Dear pastors' wives, I pray that you would follow the example of the Lord and walk in love, esteeming and delighting in one another. I pray that you would give up trying to live up to everybody else's expectations, trying to please other people, trying to pretend that you are something you are not. God wants you to be real. He wants to mobilize you. So I pray that today you will find the courage to be free in Him, free to be the person that God created you to be, free to soar. I pray that the power and the love of Almighty God will be your strength as you minister to women. May God richly bless you.

Note
1. Oswald Chambers, *My Utmost for His Highest* (Ulrichsville, OH: Barbour Publishing, 2004), n.p.

$\mathcal{M}$AXIMIZING YOUR WOMANHOOD IN MINISTRY

TERESA MERRITT

Maybe you looked at the title of this chapter and thought, *What does she mean by "maximizing your womanhood in ministry"?* Well, I mean exactly that: You can use your womanhood to make the most of your ministry.

At the start, I want you to get this thought into your mind: God wants His best for you, and He wants you to do your best for Him. Romans 8:37 says, "In all these things we are more than conquerors through him who loved us."

In today's society, everything is being maximized, especially womanhood. Yet I still sense that there are a lot of women who are unfulfilled. You may be one of those women. You may be unfulfilled in your life. You may be unfulfilled in your ministry, in your home or in your role as a wife or mother. You need to realize that God has amazing things He wants to do for you, if you just let Him.

Many of you are not maximizing your womanhood. Many of you are wasting your days. I hope that the following story gives you pause for thought.

Shortly after Paul "Bear" Bryant, the college football coach, died, his family found a crumpled, yellowed piece of paper in his wallet. From its condition, it appeared as though he had carried this piece of paper with him for years and had unfolded it and read it many times. This is what was written on that piece of paper:

This is the beginning of a new day. God has given me this day to use, as I will; I can waste it, or use it for good. What I do today is very important because I'm exchanging a day of my life for it. When tomorrow comes, this day will be gone forever leaving something in its place that I've traded for it. I want it to be a gain, not a loss; good, not evil; success, not failure, in order that I shall not regret the price that I paid for it.[1]

Have you been paying a price of a wasteful day? I think this is so powerful because there are so many times that we put things ahead of what's really important in our lives. Once we have allowed a day to pass, we can't ever relive that day. We need to maximize our lives every single day.

Right Priorities

If you doubt your value to the Kingdom, the ministry, your church, or your home or family, I want you to begin to focus on the right priorities. These are priorities that God has given to every woman. These priorities might not make you Wonder Woman, but they can make you a wonderful woman in the eyes of God. But in order to have these right priorities, you're going to have to focus on four things.

Faith

First, you need to focus on your faith, just like Eunice and Lois did. Second Timothy 1:5 tells us, "For I am mindful of the sincere faith within you, which first dwelt in your grandmother Lois, and your mother Eunice, and I am sure that it is in you as well" (*NASB*). These women had genuine faith. You may be wondering, *Well, what is genuine faith?* It is faith that seeks intimacy with God. Every day you must make a point to communicate with God. You must make a point to pray and to spend time in His Word.

I challenge you, dear pastors' wives, to get serious about the Bible. Start meeting with God on a regular basis. I know I'm meddling here, but don't ever sacrifice time in the Word for hours—and I do mean

TERESA MERRITT

hours—spent on reading magazines or novels, or watching daytime TV, or talking on the telephone. What about e-mail? How many of you have said, "Well, now I'm just going to check my e-mail," and two hours later you're still sitting there at the computer? Do you realize that the Bible, the Word, is God's e-mail to you? He has a daily e-mail for you—a personal message just for you.

Staying in the Word will activate your conscience. It will help you stay on the right track. I want you to think about this. When your schedule's tight, your discipline must be tighter. We're all busy as moms, busy as wives, busy in the ministry. But you can't be too busy for God. When pressure begins to mount, you've got to set your priorities. If you don't plan your day, somebody or something else will. So schedule time alone with God—you need it!

Family

The second thing you need to focus on is your family, just like Priscilla did (see Acts 18:26). Priscilla was a partner to her husband. And there's no better way that you can maximize your womanhood or your ministry than to partner with your husband and focus on your family.

The greatest support that I gave my husband was taking the burden of rearing my boys and making a godly, happy and stable home for my family, which freed him up to do God's ministry. This role of loving wife and homemaker (I hear that "domestic goddess" is what we now call a homemaker) is missing from today's society.

The greatest movement of the second half of the nineteenth century was the movement of men from the farm to the factory. The greatest movement of the second half of the twentieth century has been the movement of women from the home to the office. This movement has separated parents from their children and wives from their husbands.

Now, I realize that there are some women who need to work, especially if your husband pastors a small church. But I wouldn't trade anything for the amazing joy of having been a stay-at-home mom. And my husband has always said that my homemaking was just as much a part of his ministry as his preaching. The same is true for you.

Of course, there are times when the house, the kids and the husband can seem like a burden that's too large to bear. So what's the solution? Give your burdens to Jesus. When you get on your knees, God gives you a solution to your problems. Matthew 11:28-30 tells us, "Come to me, all you who are weary and burdened, and I will give you rest. Take my yoke upon you and learn from me, for I am gentle and humble in heart, and you will find rest for your souls. For my yoke is easy and my burden is light." Women, never forget this. The one who kneels to God can stand up to anything. And I do mean anything!

The Church

The third thing you need to focus on is your fellowship, or what I call the church—just like Phoebe did. In Romans 16:1-2, we are told, "I commend to you our sister Phoebe, a *servant* of the church in Cenchrea. I ask you to receive her in the Lord in a way worthy of the saints and to give her any help she may need from you, for she has been a great help to many people, including me" (emphasis added). Now, the word "servant" in this verse means "minister." Every woman should be involved in the local church and in a meaningful ministry.

The ministry is not a bed of roses. It's very rewarding, but it's difficult, and you need to be your husband's number one partner.

Do you want to serve in the church? Do you want to fit in? If you do, there are two things you need to remember. First, you need to remember to be yourself. Some surveys—and I think this is so true—show that many women in the ministry have completely given up trying to be themselves. They've given up trying to do any of the things that they enjoy. They've even given up on God's will for their lives. Why? They fear they will hurt their husband's ministry. They've completely conformed to the demands of the church members.

Ladies, you cannot please everybody. Jesus couldn't please everybody, and neither can you. This gives the answer to the often-asked question of why so many ministers' wives are unhappy. They're resentful, they're frustrated, and they're even sick and depressed. For many of them, sickness is like a retreat; it provides respite from the pressures of ministry.

You need to remember, ladies, that there will always be someone out there who is prettier or smarter. There will be somebody who will have a bigger home or drive a better car or have raised smarter kids who do better in school. She may have a husband who fixes things around the house while you have a husband who just sits on the couch. But you've got to let it go. You've got to love yourself and your circumstances—whatever they are.

Friendships

The fourth point that you need to focus on is your friendships, or on what I call our girlfriends. Here we look to Mary and Martha, who were friends of Jesus, as our models (see Luke 10:38-39).

The longer I live, the more I realize how important friendships are. Life is all about relationships. You're going to make a lot of acquaintances in this life, but you're going to make very few friends. So choose your friends carefully, especially if you're in the ministry. Choose a friend who can be trusted—someone who loves you because of you, not because of who you are, what you do in life or who you're married to.

No matter how much you love your husband, no matter how much you love the children, you're going to need girlfriends. Remember to go places with them now and then. Do things with them. Remember, girlfriends are not only your friends but also your sisters.

Girlfriends bring you casseroles and scrub your bathroom when you're sick. Girlfriends keep your children and they keep your secrets, too. Girlfriends give advice when you ask for it (and sometimes when you don't). Girlfriends still love you even when they don't agree with you. Really, how could we live without them?

A Final Thought

You have a choice. You can close this book and go on with your life as usual. You can continue just being another woman, or you can be a wonderful woman in the eyes of God. You can decide today to be a focused woman. You can decide today to live according to the God-given priorities in your life. Do you desire this? Then go to God in prayer today and tell Him, "I want to be all that I am meant to be. Maximize my life, Lord. Maximize my womanhood. Maximize my womanhood in my ministry."

Prayer

Dear Lord, please help me to be the woman that You made me to be. Guide me as I seek to make Your priorities my own. Grant me wisdom and strength as I answer Your call to ministry. Maximize my womanhood in ministry, Lord. I ask this in the mighty name of Jesus, amen.

Note

1. Pat Williams, *Secrets from the Mountain: Ten Lessons for Success in Life* (Grand Rapids, MI: Fleming Revell Publishing Company, 2001), n.p.

PART SIX

FREE TO SOAR
THROUGH EXTENDING
YOUR MISSION

$\mathcal{A}$ SAINTLY COMPASSION

DONNA MULLINS

Did it ever occur to you that God may want to birth a vision of compassion to reach the lost and brokenhearted through you? You may be thinking, *Oh, I'm not a visionary; that is my husband.* Well, my husband's a visionary, too, and he has a huge vision. But I have learned that through prayer and waiting on the Lord, God may want to birth a vision through you, just as He even did in me, a pastor's wife.

I want you to know that I have never viewed myself as having any special gifts for ministry. I'm not an exhorter. I've lost my singing voice. I'm not a great pianist. And even though I enjoy teaching, I don't consider myself a great teacher. But the Lord has placed deep in my heart a compassion and a love for people. We all share in His love and compassion, because as born-again believers, we have Jesus in our heart. There is a passion for the lost that He has put inside every one of us. I just want you to stop and think about the compassion that's been placed in your heart.

Seeing the Plight of the Little Ones

In 1993, Tom and I traveled to Russia and Romania. It was in Romania that we visited a church-run orphanage. My heart was so completely overwhelmed with joy as I saw the hope in the eyes of those little children. They had been rescued from a state-run orphanage and were in that wonderful, loving home. At one house in particular, a beautiful little five-year-old girl ran across the floor and jumped into her house father's arms. As he held her, he told us her story.

She had only been with him for six months. When she had first arrived, she couldn't walk and she couldn't talk. She had more or less lived in a little crib for the first four and a half years of her life. With his love and the support of his family, she was able to enjoy some of the little things that a child should enjoy. Ladies, that's the power of God's love. That's the power of a life that's being transformed.

Well, when my husband and I got back to the States, we had a Saturday night prayer meeting. It was during that prayer meeting that God spoke to my heart from Isaiah 1:17: "Defend the cause of the fatherless." He placed a deep longing in my heart, and it was as if I could hear the cries of the children. It was as if I could sense their pain. As I was weeping and crying, Tom came over to comfort me and I said, "Honey, we've got to do something." So that night at church, Tom stood before our people and declared that we were going to start a children's home for our community. Applause suddenly burst forth from our congregation, because God's call had been birthed in their hearts too. We rejoiced and prayed, and the Place of Hope was born! We gave it that name because it has always been our goal and desire to bring hope back to the little hearts that have been so broken and bruised.

We then researched the physical need for children's homes, and I was shocked at the facts that we came across. There are currently over a half million children in the foster-care system in the United States. That is 20,000 more than last year. There are only 144,000 foster-care homes.

Child abuse is a national tragedy, taking the lives of three children every day and affecting children and families everywhere. Survivors of child abuse and neglect are at greater risk for problems later in life, such as low academic achievement, drug use, teen pregnancy and criminal behavior. And, as we all know, this doesn't just affect the child and his or her family; it affects society as a whole.

Seventy-five percent of siblings are separated when they enter the foster-care system. When a brother-sister connection is broken, they lose hope because they've been disconnected from the people they love.

Now, I am not trying to attack the foster-care system. There are many wonderful families that have opened up their homes and their hearts and are taking care of these needy children. However, if you read the paper or listen to the news, you know that the foster-care model is suffering. We wanted to provide a model that would honor God and give hope to the children by providing an environment in which they could be physically safe and spiritual healed.

Meeting the Need

Our goal was to start small, establishing community homes with full-time house parents and on-site staff. We also wanted to reunite siblings who had been separated in the foster-care system. Place of Hope seemed like such a huge task (and it was), but we knew that when God is in something, He will provide. Jesus assured us of this promise in Matthew 7 when He said, "Ask and it will be given to you; seek and you will find; knock and the door will be opened to you. For everyone who asks receives; he who seeks finds; and to him who knocks, the door will be opened" (vv. 7-8).

We began by forming a team that researched and then visited the best national models available. We wrote manuals that were in line with state and national policies and guidelines. We selected and trained staff. Then we purchased our property. This preparation time was not easy, but God always went before us. In fact, we started this ministry right in the middle of a huge campaign to build a second sanctuary for our church. Many people thought we were crazy to take on both of these projects at the same time, but we knew the children were waiting and we wanted to be faithful for their sakes.

God provided one miracle after another. One particular miracle was when God allowed us to meet with a couple who wanted to know more about the vision and how they could help. After we finished sharing with them, they committed themselves to assuming some of the financial planning for the project. We were so thankful because we didn't know how God would provide for our plan, but He did through people like this generous and compassionate couple.

Today, we have six homes at the Place of Hope. Many of our children carry physical and emotional scars from physical and sexual abuse, but we are now seeing these children find healing through the grace of God.

One family in particular had been separated in four different foster-care homes before coming to the Place of Hope, where they were reunited. Not long ago, one of the teenaged girls in the family said, "If it wasn't for Place of Hope, I'd be with my friends out on the street and pregnant." Her brother added, "I'd probably be in a gang somewhere." Place of Hope is making a difference and we are seeing lives changed.

It has been three short years and Place of Hope is already being recognized nationally as a successful model for childcare. Since then, we have also opened Place of Hope International. We now have homes in India, Mexico and Peru. Place of Hope is a beacon of light not only in our community but also to our world. It has allowed us to step out and to share the message of Jesus Christ with our community and the world.

A Final Thought

I want to encourage you to think about what plans God might have in mind for you. How does He want you to extend His compassion to those in need? In Jeremiah 29:11 the Lord tells us, "I know the plans I have for you. . . . plans to give you hope and a future." Dear pastors' wives, God wants to birth His compassion in your hearts, and He wants you to take His vision back to your churches.

You may have heard it said that "people don't care how much you know, until they know how much you care." Perhaps it is time to let your community know how much you care, because we live in a desperate world. We live in a world where people desperately need a touch from Jesus Christ. He has given us so much that our cups are running over, and as a result, we are called to give to others out of that overflow of His love and mercy. I pray that God will birth His compassion in your heart and that when He does, you will step out in faith and see how great God's compassion is for His world.

Prayer

*I know, God, that You have planted Your compassion in me,
and I praise You because You are a great God. You love every
child and every adult in this world, and I know that You want
them to know Your love and Your saving grace. I am Your hands
and Your feet, and I purpose today to reach the lost and the
desperate for You. I thank You and I praise You for all that
You are going to do through me in Jesus' name. Amen.*

*L*OVING YOUR COMMUNITY

SHARON DAUGHERTY

We know that we are in a battle right now in regard to the darkness against the light. Jesus told us that we are the light of the world (see Matt. 5:14). However, some Christians have been putting their lights under a bushel and blending in with the world around them. Why? Because of fear or being self-focused. Fear paralyzes and selfishness simply keeps us focused on our own lives.

No matter what our occupation is as a Christian, we are called by God to be His witnesses. We as pastors' wives, like any other believer, have been called to reach out to others.

I grew up in a pastor's home. I was a faithful church member but was not truly saved. At the age of 16, I was in a meeting when I suddenly heard God's call on my life. That night I surrendered my life to Jesus Christ. Although I had grown up in the church, I knew it was at that moment that I was truly saved, and all I wanted to do was serve God. I heard the voice of God say within me, "I have called you into the ministry." That was 1970, and there were only a few women ministers in the denomination that I was in. I wasn't really sure what to do with my call. At first I kept it to myself. But my father recognized God's call on my life, and at age 17, he put me over the youth group in our church. I can truly say I began to be stretched. That was the beginning of following God's call on my life.

Keys to Living in Community

I believe every Christian is called by God to ministry (see 2 Tim. 1:9; 2 Cor. 5:18; Eph. 2:10). Pastor's wives are not just wives of pastors. We are ministers of reconciliation, called with a holy calling to do God's will here on Earth. The keys to fulfilling that calling are the same for all Christians.

Surrender

First, we must live in surrender. Surrendering to the will of God is essential. And it's not just a one-time experience. Surrender is a continual experience, because you are surrendering your will to the will of God on a daily basis. You are putting your flesh down and letting your spirit dominate—which is not easy. Jesus said in Luke 9:23, "If anyone would come after me, he must deny himself and take up his cross daily and follow me." Understand that the cross is doing the will of God. The cross for Jesus was that which caused him to die for our salvation. For us, we probably won't die on a wooden cross, but we will definitely be required to daily die to self. And in that surrender, we will find that we are able to more easily relate to others.

Compassion

If we're going to be like Jesus, we must be filled with compassion. In Mark 8:2, Jesus looked out on the crowd, and seeing that the people were hungry, He had compassion. He fed them. You see, Jesus is concerned about the natural needs of people. So many times we're thinking in spiritual terms, but Jesus is also thinking in the natural. Again, in Mark 6:34, Jesus, even in His own grief over the death of John the Baptist, was filled with compassion for the multitude. At that moment, He released His grief in order to minister to others and bring healing to their lives.

Love motivates you to help others as well as to give them God's Word and pray for them. Pity feels sorry for others but does nothing. Compassion does something. Compassion moves you to find a way to meet the need in others' lives.

Be Sensitive to the Spirit's Leading

Another important key to loving people is sensitivity. You have to be sensitive to the Holy Spirit and sensitive to those around you. I found that I must be aware of those I meet in the course of my day. The Holy Spirit wants us to stay in tune with what He wants to do in our lives.

I remember once when I was in Wal-Mart that I passed a woman who appeared to be depressed as I walked by her. I said "hi" and she replied with a quiet "hi" in return. When I got to the checkout, I felt the Lord say to me, "Go back and pray for her." So I went back and looked for her. When I found her, I said, "Excuse me, but I feel like the Lord asked me to come pray for you. I don't know what you are going through, but could I pray for you?" She looked at me and said, "Yeah, well, okay. I guess everybody needs prayer."

After asking if I could take her hand, I began to pray. Believe me, I didn't know what I was going to pray, but I pressed in to the voice of the Holy Spirit. Immediately, I sensed the Spirit of God praying through me. At the end of the prayer, I opened my eyes and saw tears coming down this woman's face. She said, "Well, you hit the nail on the head." "Well," I said, "praise God." (I still don't know what her problem was, but the Holy Spirit operated through me by a supernatural understanding, the gift of the Word of Knowledge in praying exactly what she needed.) Afterward I hugged her; I haven't seen her since that time.

So many times we shove the voice of God aside because we think, *Oh, this is not an appropriate place.* I've learned that any time you feel the prompting of God, it's appropriate. It may seem embarrassing and it may seem awkward and odd, but people will respond to your sincerity and to the move of the Holy Spirit through you. What we do one-on-one in our daily lives will create a platform for God if He chooses to use us to establish other community outreaches. Our daily lives will reveal our inner motives.

A Final Thought

I believe God wants us to bring heaven to Earth. But He needs you and me; He needs every one of us. In Esther 4:14, Mordecai tells Esther, "Who knows but that you have come to the kingdom for such a time as this" (*AMP*). I know that we have all been brought to the Kingdom for such a time as this. This is your time and your call to minister and

SHARON DAUGHERTY

to bring the Lord's love to your community.

Let me just close with this mandate from a missionary: "When you stand at the judgment seat of God one day, He won't ask you what your husband did for Him or about the truth you received on Earth. He's going to ask you what you did with the truth you received and the opportunities you either accepted or shoved aside. God wanted to flow through you to help someone else know Him and experience His power to change their lives. One small act of obedience and love can change a life."

Prayer

Father, in Jesus name, I thank You. I thank You that You have called me with a holy calling according to Your purpose. Lord, I don't take that lightly, and so I rise to the responsibility that You've called me to. I know it's not by my might but by Your Spirit that I can do anything, so I yield to Your Holy Spirit. Lord, I choose to give You my life. Lord, I love You more than anything. Please use my life to bring others to you. I choose to fight the good fight of faith so that in the end I can stand before You and hear You say, "Well done, good and faithful servant. Enter into the joy of the Lord" [see Matt. 25:21]. Amen.

HOW TO BECOME AN EFFECTIVE SOUL WINNER

BETTY FREIDZON

We are in a key moment in a strategic hour for the Church in this world. It's not just another day; these are days of urgency. God tells us in His Word that there's a generation that He's raising up to gather in the last and final harvest. We have the privilege to be that generation. And this is such a special hour for women. More than ever before we can see that God is raising up a great army of women in the nations of the earth. The Lord is raising up spiritual mothers of multitudes. That's where you come in, dear pastors' wives: I want to share with you what God is going to do in your lives. He has called you from your mother's womb, just like the Word of God says: "Listen to me, you islands; hear this, you distant nations: Before I was born, the LORD called me; from my birth he has made mention of my name. He said to me, 'You are my servant, Israel, in whom I will display my splendor'" (Isa. 49:1,3).

God is a God of purposes and plans, and that perfect plan of God will have to be fulfilled in your life. Once you become a servant in this great army that He is raising up, He wants you right there in the front lines. God is calling you today to rise up and take the place that He has called you to take. No one else can take the place that God has given you as a pastor's wife. You are not only child of God but also a woman who has a call—a call to ministry, a call to serve the Lord, a call to fulfill the works and the purposes of God. That is why God has called you by name.

Recognizing Our Spiritual Authority

I don't know how many difficulties you have had in your life, how many hard times you've lived through, or what troublesome situations have threatened to distract you from the very call that God has given you. But I know that even the devil cannot thwart God's purposes, because God has given you a position of spiritual authority. "He made my mouth like a sharpened sword, in the shadow of his hand he hid me; he made me into a polished arrow and concealed me in his quiver" (Isa. 49:2).

"We are more than conquerors" (Rom. 8:37). We have the power of God that backs us up. The Word of God is powerful. If we have planted the seed, the Word, in our hearts, we will be empowered to preach to all creation (see Mark 16:15).

But how often do we ask, "How am I going to do this? How can God use me as an instrument?" Here again, we need to only look to the Word to see women who were raised up by God for a time such as this (see Esther 4:14). Consider Deborah, a woman who was used by God in a time of chaos, in a time of darkness, in a time of oppression (see Judg. 4–5). So God raises up women in the dark times and puts them in strategic places, in high places. No one can stop what God wants to do with you if you obey the call of God. So why do we limit ourselves? Why do we think to ourselves, *Oh, I can't do this, because I am the pastor's wife.* God has given you His grace and favor. He will open doors for you in this season so that you might become an ambassador of the kingdom of God (see 2 Cor. 5:20).

We need to fill the streets of our city with the Word of God, with prayers, with the worship of God. The Bible says that the earth shall be filled with the glory of the Lord (see Isa. 6:3). Not just the Church, but the whole world will be covered with His glory. That's what God desires. So we need courage to go out and fill the streets of our cities with the Word of God.

Allowing God's Work

But in order to be used mightily by God, we have to allow Him to work in our hearts. We must die to our own thoughts, our own abilities, to really depend on Him. It's when we say yes to God that we are able to be used mightily by Him. It's when we say yes to God that we are able to bear fruit for the Kingdom. In John 15, Jesus tells us: "If you remain in me and my words remain in you, ask whatever you wish, and it will be given you. This is to my Father's glory, that you bear much fruit" (vv. 7-8).

But unless we first surrender our lives to God, there can't be fruit in our ministry and we won't be able to be mothers of multitudes. We give God all that we are so that it is not by our own abilities we will be glorified—nor for our own vanity. I've never asked God to allow me to travel around the world. I've never even wanted to preach in front of multitudes. Still, God has taken my husband and me to spread His Word throughout five continents. However, before God could work in our lives, we first had to be willing.

We also have to have faith in His dreams and to live less in our sadness and disappointment. This is what the Lord is saying to you: "Stop being sad. Stop being distracted. You will be effective in the place of where I have chosen for you. You will be mothers of multitudes. And my dreams shall be fulfilled in you, for I have placed my glory and favor upon you."

Healing Our Hearts

Though I usually found great joy in my life as a pastor's wife, one day I was feeling sad and alone. Then the devil stepped in, whispering lies, telling me my husband and kids didn't love me anymore. So I got up one morning and said, "God, I'm just tired. I have reached the limit. I am not going to get up from this place until you tell me what is going on and why. What is the problem?" That's when God unveiled my heart. He said, "Betty, there's something there in the middle." Yes, He was pointing out what was like a big stone in my heart—a stone that had been created by the wounds of circumstance and the routine of ministry. Without realizing it, my happy work had turned into routine, and that's when the devil had me sad, frustrated and without strength.

In that moment God told me He could not hear my prayers, because they were the prayers of an unforgiving heart. And in that time, God showed me people whom I had held grudges against—He showed me the bitter places of my heart. Imagine a pastor's wife with sin.

Dear sisters, that is the day I cried the most in my life, because I hadn't known that God counted all those things. Then God shared with me that He was about to release something big into our lives, but first I needed a change of heart—I needed His heart. He said, "I want to give you My heart; I want you to start feeling what I feel so that you will be able to see what I see." I started to see again—only this time with the eyes of the Lord.

You know what, sisters? It's very important for us to realize that we must first be healed and transformed—completely—before we can be used by God. It begins with repentance in the presence of God, asking for forgiveness for each person, name by name. Then you must renounce the "poor me" attitude. You are not "poor me." You are an anointed woman, a warrior of God. You are an overcomer. You are the one who conquers in the name and in the might of the Lord. Isaiah 52 tells us, "Awake, awake, O Zion, clothe yourself with strength. Put on your garments of splendor" (v. 1).

The day my life was changed, the Lord said, "Betty, I'm going to take that dirty and sinful dress, that clothing of self-righteousness, away from you. I'm going to clothe you with My righteousness." Since that day, I've never been the same. I now have an amazing love that I never had before—a love for my husband, my children, and those in the Church.

A Final Thought

God has a tremendous plan and you are meant to be part of it. Isaiah 54 says, "Sing, O barren woman, you who never bore a child; burst into song, shout for joy, you who were never in labor; because more are the children of the desolate woman than of her who has a husband . . . Enlarge the place of your tent, stretch your tent curtains wide, do not hold back; lengthen your cords, strengthen your stakes. For you will spread out to the right and to the left; your descendants [your children] will dispossess nations and settle in their desolate cities" (vv. 1-3).

God wants to work a tremendous multiplication through your life, but it all starts with a transformed and healed heart. So give God your heart full of worries, full of work, full of fears. Ask God to give you a new heart—one that is filled with His love.

Prayer

*God, right now I surrender my life to You, because I want to
be effective in Your kingdom. Lord, I know that this is the day when
You are going to raise me up as a true woman of God. Lord, I'm going
to position myself in that place You have given me. I'm going to extend
and multiply so that Your name will be glorified in my life. And I'm
going to be right there in the front lines with my husband, shoulder
to shoulder, heart to heart. Lord, I want to have that vision that
You have placed in my husband. I receive right now the same
vision, the same desires, the same dreams.*

*Lord, I desire a personal transformation. Grant me a spirit
of forgiveness. Right now, I renounce the spirit of self-pity. I renounce
bitterness and resentment. I renounce all those plans of the enemy.
Lord, give me a heart of compassion. And I ask You right now to put
Your love in my heart. I declare right now, Lord, that I'm going to be
a mother of multitudes. I declare that I will rise up as a woman of
God to be all that You've called me to be and to be a spiritual
mother to all those destined from eternity to be born again.
This I declare in the mighty name of Jesus, amen.*

𝒜 SOUL-WINNING COMMITMENT

BEVERLY LaHAYE

Perhaps you're reading this book because you are looking for a fresh touch from the Holy Spirit. Maybe you're tired and worn out. Maybe you're looking for a new fire to be ignited in your heart. I hope to provide this as I share with you about soul winning.

Personality Types

As a pastor's wife, I can relate to the joys and challenges of your life. From the day I married my husband, I wanted to win souls for Christ. But there was just one problem. I was a very shy person, and I didn't know how to lead somebody to Jesus Christ. Although necessity cured both my shyness and lack of experience very quickly, I would like to share with you some facts about personality types—facts that I hope will help you better understand who you are and what your role in ministry is.

Of the four personality types, we first of all have the *cholerics*. These are the strong natural leaders who can talk to anyone. And they are great at organizing! But they also tend to be a little bit bossy, as they try to organize everybody else.

Then we have the *sanguines*, the warm, friendly ones who are the life of the party. They are able to bring cheer to other people, but they don't like controversy, so they don't get involved in conflicts. Someone has said that the sanguine lady is the one who enters the room mouth first, and she's also often undisciplined.

Then we have the *melancholics,* who are often gifted artists and like things done with perfection. However, they are prone to having a very negative spirit, and they can be happy just being alone. It's hard for them to push themselves into the outside world, because they are happy on their own.

And finally we have the *phlegmatics,* who are the calm, easy-going types. They are peace loving and often very shy. They like to work behind the scenes. It's difficult for them to enter into new situations that they're not comfortable with. They also struggle with fear and anxieties and prefer to not get involved.

Why do I bring up the subject of temperaments? Because opposites attract. An outgoing pastor very often will marry a calm, easygoing wife. That certainly has been true in my marriage. And my temperament has been a challenge to me, because soul winning means going outside of our comfort zones.

To be a soul winner, you must be willing to give of yourself. You've got to be willing to take time—time that might sometimes conflict with your planned schedule. There have been times when I've encountered someone whom I knew needed to know the Lord, but I felt that I didn't have the time to witness to him or her. But you've got to take the time when the Holy Spirit nudges you.

Soul-Winning Essentials

Being a soul winner starts in your own heart. It starts with you. You have a desire to win people to Jesus, but you may be too shy or too timid. Or perhaps you lack the faith to do so.

Faith

The faith chapter in Hebrews lays the foundation when it says, "by faith Abel . . . by faith Enoch . . . by faith Noah . . . by faith Abraham . . . by faith Sara" (see Heb. 11). And right in the middle of that "by faith" chapter, we read, "Without faith it is impossible to please God" (v. 6). We need, individually, to have the faith to do what God wants us to do, or we will never please Him. I trust that all of you pastors' wives reading this would love to please God, seek Him and serve Him to the very best of your abilities. You please God best when you obediently walk by faith.

Let me make it clear here that we are talking about *your individual journey of faith*—tagging along on your husband's spiritual walk doesn't cut it. You have to nurture your own faith. That means being in the Word, having a prayer life, letting God speak to you. It's easy for a pastor's wife to let God speak to her husband and then just tag along behind him and his call. But that's not God's plan. God wants each of us to walk by faith so that we might please Him.

Thought Life

Secondly, your thoughts will affect what kind of soul winner you will be. Philippians 4:8 says, "Finally, [sisters], whatever things are true, whatever is noble, whatever is pure, whatever is lovely, whatever is admirable—if anything is excellent or praiseworthy—think about such things." Think positively. You've got a message to bring to the world. You've got a message of goodness to share, a message of hope, so think positively and step out by faith and share that hope with those around you.

Relationship with the Lord

Third, we have to have a right relationship with the Lord. Now, maybe this seems like a no-brainer, but I'd like to share a story from my own life that might give you pause for thought.

I went to hear a Christian psychologist talk about the abundant Christian life, explaining how we could have victory over our anxieties. I thought to myself, *This man has never been a pastor's wife.* When it was all over, I went up to him and I said, "Could I have just a minute with you?" and he said, "Why, of course." I then said to him, "You know, in our church the people are so demanding of me; they want me to do this and they want me to do that. I can't play the piano well, I can't sing well; but they want me to do all these things. I think they expect too much of me."

After I had laid open my heart to this Christian psychologist, he said, "Young lady, do you want to know what your problem really is?" I said, "Well, yes, I would like to know what's wrong." He said, "You sound like a very selfish woman." Wow. Now, no woman likes to be told that she's selfish, but then he repeated back the words that I had just said to him—and all the things I said to him were all about me, not about other people.

How could I win anybody to Jesus when I was so fixated on myself? In my heart I knew that it would be Jesus Christ, the hope of glory, who would be their salvation—not my talents, not me. So that night, I asked God to forgive me for my sin of selfishness. I wanted my life to be changed, so I opened my heart to the filling of the Holy Spirit. I said, "Holy Spirit, come in and do in my life what I cannot do myself." And He did!

But it didn't happen overnight. I didn't go back to church the next Sunday and walk in the door and say, "Well, ladies, here's your new Spirit-filled pastor's wife!" No, step by step as I began to walk by faith and obey what the Word taught me about my thoughts, my anxieties, my worry, my fear, God began to use me. And there would never have been a Concerned Women for America if I had not been willing to confess my sin and then invite the Holy Spirit to come in and change my heart.

So let me emphasize this point: To win souls for Jesus, you must be in right relationship with the Lord. You have to let your life so reflect the love of Christ in you that unbelievers will be drawn to you. They will want to know what you have that they don't have.

A Final Thought

As we consider what might be holding us back from being soul winners, it's important for each one of us to take an honest look in the mirror. What is in your life that might be considered a sin according to Romans 14:23? Identify the sin and then confess it. First John 1:9 says, "If we confess our sins, he is faithful and just and will forgive us our sins and cleanse us from all unrighteousness."

If your sins have become habits, ask the Lord for help in breaking them. He will answer your prayer for help and healing. First John 5:14-15 says, "This is the confidence we have in approaching God: that if we ask anything according to his will, he hears us. And if we know that He hears us—whatever we ask—we know that we have what we asked of him."

If you have been working in your own strength, ask now for the filling of the Holy Spirit in your life. Luke 11:13 says, "How much more will your Father in heaven give the Holy Spirit to those who ask him!" When you walk in the Spirit, you will not struggle with being fearful, worried, anxious, angry or sharp tongued. No, you will represent Jesus Christ living in you so that you can then share that hope and win souls to Jesus Christ.

Blessing

Ours is a hungry world, Lord, but You want to satisfy the spiritual hunger of the world. You want pastors' wives to be there for the lost, to lead them to You. Let these women seek You with renewed strength, let them have faith, let them remove whatever barriers are separating them from You, let them be filled with Your Spirit. Let Your light shine in them so that others will see You in their lives. Let them win souls for You, dear Jesus. Amen.

$\mathscr{F}$REE TO SOAR CONTRIBUTORS

Global Pastors Network
www.gpn.tv

Global Pastors Wives Network
P. O. Box 621206
Orlando, FL 32862-1206
www.gpwn.tv

Bose Adelaja
Kiev, Ukraine
Sunday and Bose Adelaja are the founders and senior pastors of the 20,000-plus member congregation of the Embassy of God Church in Kiev, Ukraine, which has planted many other churches in the Ukraine and in other countries. "A great church becomes reality when all the elements of the Kingdom are functioning in their proper order," Bose recently shared at the Free to Soar Pastors Wives Conference. "To build a great church, many sacrifices are required. However, God never intended the institution and value of the family to be one of those sacrifices. It is God's will for the family, as with the church, to be great, glorious, successful, secure and satisfied. It is God's better will to build a church, without losing one's family, through total reliance upon Him and by paying special notice to the needs of the family."

Arlene Allen
Springfield, Missouri
An ordained minister with the Assemblies of God, Arlene is the director for the national women's ministries department. She currently sits on the boards of the national Women in Ministry Task Force, the Religious Alliance Against Pornography, and the Global Pastors Wives Network. Arlene has an extensive speaking history that includes pulpit ministry and women's and ministers' wives retreats. Arlene has been married for 40 years to Dr. Gary R. Allen, who serves as the executive

coordinator of the Ministerial Enrichment office of the Assemblies of God. The Allens are the parents of two sons and the proud grandparents of two incredible grandsons, Grant and Jacob.

Kay Arthur
Chattanooga, Tennessee
Kay Arthur has touched literally thousands of lives through her writing and teaching ministry. Her authority comes from the Word of God, which she continues to study zealously; her compassion stems from a life that has been touched by deep tragedy as well as great triumph; and her practicality springs from an openness of character. A well-known conference speaker and author of more than 100 books and Bible studies, Kay has a unique ability to reach people in an exciting, effective way—challenging them to change and equipping them to be used in the furtherance of the kingdom of God.

Vonette Z. Bright
Orlando, Florida
Vonette Z. Bright is founder of the Global Pastors Wives Network and cofounder (with her husband, the late Dr. William R. Bright) of Campus Crusade for Christ International. For more than 50 years, Mrs. Bright labored alongside her husband to build Campus Crusade into one of the largest and most influential Christian ministries in the world. The author of many works, including the *My Heart in His Hands* devotional series, Mrs. Bright can be heard nationwide on the radio with Women Today International. She is the mother of two grown sons and has four grandchildren.

Lisa Clay
Adrian, Michigan
Rich and Lisa Clay are the senior pastors of Bethany Assembly of God in Adrian, Michigan. They have been in pastoral ministry since 1985 and have two teenage sons. Lisa is the president of MountainTop Ministries, a premier online ministry for Christians, leaders and seekers of Jesus Christ, and she also serves on the executive board of the

Global Pastors Wives Network. Lisa is a dynamic, creative and inspiring teacher and speaker with a focused call on serving, encouraging and building up Christian leaders and their families. Lisa recently wrote *Rescued from Darkness,* a book for new believers, with a foreword from Dr. Bill Bright (available at xulonpress.com and amazon.com).

Sharon Daugherty
Tulsa, Oklahoma

Sharon Daugherty and her husband, Billy Joe, are founders and pastors of Victory Christian Center in Tulsa, Oklahoma, where she currently serves as worship pastor. Sharon teaches in Victory Bible Institute and ministers along with her husband on a daily television program, *Victory in Jesus.* Sharon has authored three books: *Called by His Side, Walking in the Fruit of the Spirit* and *Avoiding Deception.* Her music tapes include *Healing Songs and Scriptures, Covered by His Love* (protection songs and Scripture), and several live recordings of Victory Christian Center's praise and worship, including *Lift Up Your Eyes to the Harvest, Finishing Strong* and *Songs from the Secret Place.* Sharon and Billy Joe have four children and two sons-in-law working alongside them in the ministry.

Lynne Dugan
Palm Desert, California

Lynne Dugan is founder and president of Ministry Wives Network International. Formed in 1989, Ministry Wives Network International exists as a Christ-centered resource to encourage, empower, edify and equip pastors' wives to meet their unique challenges and opportunities in life and ministry. Lynne served as a pastor's wife with her husband, Bob, for Conservative Baptist churches in New Jersey, New Hampshire, Illinois and Colorado for a total of 18 years. Bob later was vice president and director of the National Association of Evangelicals Office for Governmental Affairs in Washington, D.C., and Lynne served with him for his last 11 years until their retirement in 1997. Lynne enjoys counseling and advising pastors' wives, assisting in the formation of new groups, and working with her board to plan national conferences, retreats and regional events. She has spoken to pastors' wives in the United States and in Canada. Lynne and Bob have two children and four grandchildren.

Lois I. Evans

Dallas, Texas

Dr. Lois I. Evans is president of the Global Pastors Wives Network and is senior vice president of the Urban Alternative, where she works alongside her husband, Dr. Tony Evans. Lois has been employed by the Billy Graham Evangelistic Association, the Grand Old Gospel Fellowship Ministry and Dallas Federal Savings and Loan, and she has served in numerous other executive management positions. She was honored in 1995 with the Good Samaritan Award from Dallas Baptist University for outstanding Christian service to the community and recently received the Woman of the Year in Ministry award presented by Women of Influence. Dr. Evans has written three books and is the mother of four children. She has six grandchildren.

Jeana Floyd

Springdale, Arkansas

Jeana Floyd is the wife of Pastor Ronnie Floyd of the First Baptist Church in Springdale, Arkansas. At the Free to Soar Pastors Wives Conference, she asked, "Are you unsure of your new role as a pastor's wife? I had the privilege of growing up in the home of a pastor, and for the last 28 years have walked by my husband's side in ministry as a pastor's wife. Although we serve in a very large church under the scrutiny of thousands, it all began years ago in a town of only 300 people. The places and names have changed, but the challenges remain the same." The Floyds are the proud parents of two grown sons.

Betty Freidzon

Buenos Aires, Argentina

Betty Freidzon and her husband, Claudio Freidzon, founded the King of Kings Church in Buenos Aires, Argentina, which now numbers 7,000 people. She came to know Christ at a very young age and began serving the Lord in different areas of ministry. Betty graduated from the Rio de Plata Bible Institute, a seminary of the Assemblies of God in Buenos

Aires, in 1978. She and her husband have had opportunities for ministry in various countries and have a prominent television ministry that has brought spiritual refreshment and renewal to many. Although she has done important work in the areas of praise and worship and teaching in Bible schools, Betty has been particularly used of God for ministry among women, family training, evangelism and working with ministers and leaders' wives. Hundreds of suffering and destroyed homes have been restored as the powerful hand of God has worked through her ministry. She and her husband are the parents of three grown children.

Rhoda S. Gonzales
Dallas, Texas
Rhoda S. Gonzales was born in Fort Worth, Texas, and spent most of her formative years in Dallas and Corpus Christi. At the age of 12, she accepted Jesus Christ as her personal Savior at a Christian youth camp through the ministry of praise and worship. God revealed His leading for her to study and develop a ministry in praise and worship and Bible teaching to women. Today, she has five musical recordings and is involved with ministry to women. "Living the victorious Christian life never meant living a life without struggles, trials and sometimes depression," she says. "As a pastor's wife, loneliness and depression can sometimes set in and cause division within the marriage, family and the ministry. Through hard times, God calls us to Himself. He desires that we seek Him as our refuge so He can heal us, mold, restore and recreate us. It is time to confront depression, call out its roots, seek God's Word as a standard against the enemy, claim healing by the blood of Jesus Christ, and be set free!"

Diana Hagee
San Antonio, Texas
Diana Hagee is the wife of Dr. John Hagee, founder and senior pastor of Cornerstone Church in San Antonio, Texas. She is chief of staff for the John Hagee Ministries television ministry and is a special-events coordinator and leader of women's ministries at Cornerstone Church. Diana is the author of the best-selling book *The King's Daughter* and of

Not by Bread Alone, a cookbook encouraging creative ministry through food. She was presented with the prestigious Lion of Judah award by the Jewish Federation of Greater Houston. Diana and Pastor John have five children and three grandchildren.

Gayle Haggard
Colorado Springs, Colorado
Gayle Haggard is the author of *A Life Embraced, A Hopeful Guide for the Pastor's Wife*. She has been married for 27 years to Ted Haggard, president of the National Association of Evangelicals and pastor of New Life Church in Colorado Springs, Colorado. From the early days of meeting in their basement to its growth into a megachurch of 11,000 members, Gayle has worked alongside of her husband in building the ministry. Today she oversees New Life Women's Ministry, which includes weekly Bible teaching and over 100 small groups for women. Gayle and Ted have five children.

Anna Hayford
Van Nuys, California
Anna Hayford is the wife of Pastor Jack Hayford, president of International Foursquare Churches in Van Nuys, California, and chancellor of King's College and Seminary. A nationally and internationally recognized scholar and teacher, Dr. Hayford draws on a wealth of experience to mentor other leaders and today is recognized as a "pastor of pastors." Like any good man, behind him stands his wife, Anna, who has a quiet and genuine strength, supporting her husband with her joy, humor and peace in the midst of a demanding ministry. Married for 50 years, the Hayfords have 4 children and 11 grandchildren.

Jeri Hill
Dallas, Texas
Jeri Hill is the wife of Pastor Steve Hill of the Heartland Fellowship Church in Dallas, Texas. "The first 18 years of my life was void of the presence of God," she says. "I thought God only existed in heaven and watched us run around in confusion, turmoil and pain. Then a miracle

happened in my life that set me on a journey I never thought possible. The past 29 years of serving God have been an incredible adventure." Jeri and Steve were first youth pastors and then missionary church planters in Spain, Argentina, Colombia and Belarus. On Father's Day 1995, they began a crusade in Pensacola, Florida, that became known around the world as the Brownsville Revival. In 2000, the Lord led them to start Heartland Fellowship Church in Dallas, which is now known for its passionate praise and worship, prayer ministry and efforts to train disciples locally and around the world.

Bobbie Houston
Sydney, Australia

Bobbie Houston's warm personality, fresh vitality, down-to-earth good humor and genuine love for God and His Word have made her a popular speaker at leadership and women's conferences all over the world. She and her husband, Brian, are the senior pastors of Hillsong Church, which is renowned for its praise and worship music. Bobbie's all-consuming desire is to see value placed on womanhood worldwide, and this passion lies behind the annual Color Your World women's conference held each March in Sydney. Her teaching resources appeal to young and old, and her books *I'll Have What She's Having* and *Heaven Is in This House* have liberated many. As a wife, mother, friend, pastor, creative visionary, communicator, author, role model and mentor, Bobbie Houston reflects what she teaches—a woman of God reaching for her full potential.

Becky Hunter
Longwood, Florida

Becky is a board member of the Global Pastors Wives Network and the Alliance for the Distributed Church. A former biology teacher, she currently speaks at women's conferences and seminars in the United States and abroad, encouraging women to make their relationship with God their top priority. Becky is the author of *Being Good to Your Husband on Purpose*. She is the wife of Dr. Joel C. Hunter, senior pastor of Northland Community Church, located in Longwood, Florida. The Hunters have three sons: Joshua and Isaac, who are in full-time ministry, and Joel

David, who is a physician. They have two daughters-in-law and four grandchildren.

Serita Jakes
Dallas, Texas

Serita Ann Jakes, wife of T. D. Jakes, is the founder of the women's ministry at The Potter's House, a multiracial, nondenominational church that is now 28,000 members strong. Serita has become a role model for women across the country. Whether through her National Debutante Program with teenage girls, her work as a board member for Dallas Baptist University, or by way of her numerous speaking engagements, Serita has been at the forefront in changing and impacting people where it counts in their personal lives.

Carol Kent
Port Huron, Michigan

Carol Kent is the author of several books, including the best-selling book *When I Lay My Isaac Down*. She is a popular radio and television guest and has been training Christian leaders in communication skills for two decades. "You can be an inspirational speaker, an informational speaker, and a *transformational* speaker," she says. "As Christian women in leadership, we need to communicate biblical truth with authenticity, honesty and personal vulnerability."

Beverly LaHaye
Rancho Mirage, California

Beverly LaHaye is the author of over 10 books on family living, marriage, raising children and social issues, including a four-novel series on family written with Terri Blackstock. She is also chairman of Concerned Women for America, which she founded in 1979 to protect and promote biblical values for women and families. Today, Concerned Women for America is a vibrant organization with over 500,000 members in all 50 states, who are coordinated by a dynamic staff from the national office in Washington, D.C. Beverly is the wife of well-known pastor and author, Tim LaHaye, who cowrote the best-selling *Left Behind* series. They have been married for over 50 years and have four grown children and nine grandchildren.

Sheri Lerner
Kissimmee, Florida

Dr. Sheri Lerner is the founder of Celebration Family Chiropractic in Celebration, Florida, and is the author of *Bouncing Back from Pregnancy*. An inspiring Christian woman, she speaks with encouragement and enthusiasm to churches and women's organizations around the country on how women with hectic and harrying schedules can experience the energy and time they need to live the life of their dreams. "Imagine feeling more energetic, more fit, more *alive* than ever before!" she says. "Imagine this kind of vitality is easier to attain than you ever dreamed! Now stop imagining and start experiencing." Sheri's husband, Dr. Ben Lerner, is the author of the *New York Times* best-seller *Body by God: The Owner's Manual for Maximized Living*. They are the proud parents of two children.

H. B. London, Jr.
Colorado Springs, Colorado

H. B. London, Jr., has 31 years of pastoral experience and currently serves as vice president of church, clergy and medical outreach for Focus on the Family in Colorado Springs, Colorado. He has coauthored several books with Neil B. Wiseman, including *Pastors at Greater Risk, The Heart of a Great Pastor, They Call Me Pastor* and *The Shepherd's Covenant for Pastors*. H. B. London and his wife, Beverley, have two married sons and four grandchildren.

Lynn Mathison
Montgomery, Alabama

Lynn Mathison is the wife of Pastor John Ed Mathison of the Frazer Memorial United Methodist Church in Montgomery, Alabama, where she has given leadership to the women's ministry and has also been a speaker for women's retreats and seminars. At Frazer Memorial United Methodist Church, every member volunteers to serve, and Lynn volunteers as chairman of the one-member committee of pastoral care—

she feels her ministry is to her husband. "I believe we cannot mobilize other women until we are free to soar ourselves," she says. "To be balanced in pursuing the things that God has given to enrich our lives takes commitment and practice, plus the knowledge that God has favored each of us to be a woman and a pastor's wife." Lynn and John Ed also present a daily family devotion on Frazer Christian television. Lynn enjoys traveling with her husband and has a successful career as an interior designer. They have four children and nine grandchildren.

Jeannie McCullough
Bethany, OK

Jeannie McCullough is a pastor's wife, mother and grandmother. She is the founder of the Wisdom of the Word Bible Study series and is a frequent speaker at conferences and retreats throughout North America. Her life and ministry have taken her to Bethany, Oklahoma, where her husband, Mel, is the senior pastor at Bethany First Church of the Nazarene.

Julie Meek
Indianapolis, Indiana

"What does the life sciences initiative really mean?" asked Indianapolis mayor Bart Peterson at his 2003 State of the City address. For one fascinating answer, Peterson looked no further than Dr. Julie Meek, who was seated in the audience. Julie is the founder and CEO of a young life sciences company in Indianapolis, the Haelan Group, which helps businesses cut healthcare costs by using innovative techniques to analyze the health of their employees. The goal is twofold: to improve the health of a given population, and to help companies avoid unnecessary expenditures on healthcare. At the Free to Soar Pastors Wives Conference, she asked, "Do you struggle to take care of yourself so you can better minister to others? Unleash the secrets of a successful lifestyle change and you'll come away with the tools for living well. Identify the common challenges you face when trying to make a lifestyle change and learn the stages of 'readiness to change' and how to get to the next stage."

Teresa Merritt

Duluth, Georgia

Teresa Merritt is the wife of James Merritt, who is the pastor of Cross Pointe Church, the Church at Gwinnett Center in Duluth, Georgia, and the host of the television broadcast ministry "Touching Lives." In June 2000, Dr. Merritt was elected president of the 16-million member Southern Baptist Convention and has served on numerous committees for the Southern Baptist Convention since that time. While his preaching is characterized by his verse-by-verse examination and explanation of the Scriptures, it is his practical, down-to-earth delivery that leads listeners to apply the Word of God to daily living. "There are many pastors' wives who do not feel fulfilled in the ministry," Teresa states. "They need to realize that God wants to do more for them and through them. The Bible offers encouragement and self-fulfillment. If they will focus on their faith, family, fellowship (church) and friendships, God can and will maximize their womanhood in ministry!"

Donna Mullins

Palm Beach Gardens, Florida

Donna Mullins is the wife of senior pastor Dr. Tom Mullins of Christ Fellowship Church in Palm Beach Gardens, Florida. She has influenced the lives of many people, young and old. Cofounder of Place of Hope Children's Home, Donna has helped provide homes for neglected and abused children in the community. She is also the Director of Women's Ministry at Christ Fellowship Church, where she is able to impart to other women the knowledge, wisdom and love of Christ. Donna is the mother of two children.

Cheryl A. Reccord

Alpharetta, Georgia

Cheryl serves alongside her husband, Bob, president of the North American Mission Board. Prior to Bob's current role, he served in the pastorate for over 15 years. After raising three amazing kids, Cheryl is now an author, speaker, life coach and the president/CEO of Total

Life Impact (totallifeimpact.com), an organization that equips and energizes people to impact their sphere of influence through maximizing their unique gifts, talents, passions and experiences to make their lives count.

Joyce Rogers
Cordova, Tennessee

Joyce Rogers is the wife of Adrian Rogers, the pastor of Bellevue Baptist Church of Memphis, Tennessee. She is the author of several books, including *Becoming a Woman of Wisdom* and *The Bible's Seven Secrets for Healthy Eating*. As a leader in women's ministry, Joyce has served on the advisory board of Concerned Women of America and the Council of Biblical Womanhood. She has participated in the White House Meeting of Christian Women Leaders and is on the board of Global Pastors Wives Network. She speaks at women's retreats and conferences, most recently speaking to pastors' wives at the Beyond All Limits 2 Conference (GPWN). With all of these interests, Joyce still keeps her focus on her home and the local church. She is the mother of four grown children and has one child in heaven. She and Adrian have nine wonderful grandchildren.

Gary Smalley
Branson, Missouri

Gary Smalley is one of the country's best-known authors and speakers on family relationships. He is the author or coauthor of 28 best-selling, award-winning books and several popular films and videos. He has spent over 35 years learning, teaching and counseling. For 40 years, he has been married to his wife, Norma, who works side by side with her husband at the Smalley Relationship Center and who has coauthored several books as well. Gary and Norma have three children—Kari, Greg and Michael—and eight grandchildren.

Melanie Stockstill
Baker, Louisiana

Melanie is the wife of Larry Stockstill, senior pastor of Bethany World Prayer Center in Baton Rouge, Louisiana. Under their direction, Bethany

World Prayer Center has grown to its present size of approximately 10,000 members on three campuses. The Stockstills' emphasis has always been on prayer, cells and missions, and their guiding principles are simplicity, sincerity and sacrifice. Melanie assists her husband in all aspects of pastoring the large congregation, with a special ministry to the women of the church and community. As director of the First Lady Network, she is actively involved in preaching, teaching and training other women. Founder and executive director of the two Centers of Hope for Women, she supervises community outreach to women and children in the Baton Rouge area. Melanie and her husband have six children.

Devi Titus
Youngstown, Ohio

Drawing from 41 years in the ministry, Devi Titus is a leader of leaders. She serves on the advisory board for *Ministries Today* magazine and on the Board of Directors for both the International Foursquare Church and the Global Pastors Wives Network. Devi is among America's most recognized Christian conference speakers and authors, and her life's passion is helping women to live to their full potential. In addition to conference speaking, she has now opened The Mentoring Mansion, an 8,000-square-foot, stunning historical home in Youngstown, Ohio, where she trains women during a four-day Home Mentoring Intensive on creative home management and vital relationship skills, with the goal of restoring the dignity and sanctity of the home by teaching women how to make their homes havens of rest and sanctuaries of love. Devi has also partnered with her husband, Larry Titus, to establish five churches. "Follow me as I follow Christ—building the kingdom one person at a time" is the theme of their lives. They have two children and six grandchildren.

Ruth Towns
Lynchburg, Virginia

Elmer and Ruth Towns live in Lynchburg, Virginia, where Elmer is cofounder and college/seminary professor at Liberty University. He has authored more than 70 books, many of which are used as college textbooks. Ruth has also taught at the university. She is well known for her compassion and her counseling ministry to women and families and for her books *Joined Together* and *Women Gifted for Ministry: How to Discover and Practice Your Spiritual Gifts.* Elmer and Ruth Towns have been married for 52 years and are loved and appreciated for their continuing efforts toward church-growth and church-planting around the world.

Elisabeth Tson
Oradea, Romania

Elisabeth Tson married Dr. Joseph Tson when she was 25 years old. From July 1972 until September 1981, Dr. Tson was a pastor and Bible teacher in Romania. During those years, they went through many hard times: house searches by the police, arrests, interrogations and threats on their lives. But they also experienced the presence of the Lord in their lives as never before. When the government exiled the Tsons from Romania in 1981, they came to the United States and served with the Romanian Missionary Society. In 1990, after the fall of communism, the Tsons moved back to Romania to carry out the ministries and projects of the Romanian Missionary Society. Elisabeth is a contributing author to *Lydia* (a Christian women's magazine published in Germany) and also speaks at women's conferences in Romania and surrounding countries in Europe. The Tsons' present ministry is in Romania and in the United States.

Togetta Ulmer
Inglewood, California

Togetta Ulmer is the wife of Bishop Kenneth C. Ulmer, senior pastor of Faithful Central Bible Church in Inglewood, California. He is one of the most prolific and sought after speakers of this age. Since his arrival at the Faithful Central Bible Church more than 15 years ago, the congregation has grown from 350 to more than 12,000. Togetta leads the women's ministry and is faithful in supporting the ministry that God has called her husband to oversee. Married for 25 years, the couple has three children and one grandchild.

Jelly Valimont

Griffin, Georgia

Jelly Valimont and her husband, Randy, have been senior pastors at First Assembly of God in Griffin, Georgia, since 1993. During this time, their congregation has grown from 450 to several thousand after seeing more than 9,000 people come to Christ, and their leadership team has grown from 2 to more than 14 pastoral staff members. Randy is involved in state, national and international church leadership. Jelly desires to see staff members function as unified families, and as administrative consultant she seeks to balance church calendars and events while maintaining family life for the staff.

Mary Jo Williams

Lansing, Michigan

Mary Jo Williams and her husband, Dave, are the pastors of Mount Hope Church in Lansing, Michigan, which has grown in attendance from 226 to over 4,000 in 20 years. Dave has written more than 65 books and has started branch churches in North America, Africa and the Philippines. He sends trained ministers into unreached cities to establish disciple-making churches, and he is the founder and president of Mount Hope Bible Training Institute, a fully accredited institute for training ministers and lay people for the work of the ministry. Mary Jo and Dave established The Dave and Mary Jo Williams Charitable Mission to provide scholarships to pioneer pastors and grants to inner-city children's ministries. A gifted teacher in her own right, Mary Jo says, "God has given us all we need for life and godliness. He has made us to be more than conquerors, given us the mind of Christ, and desires to abundantly meet all of our needs."

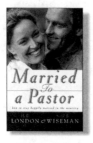

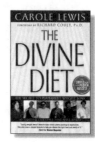

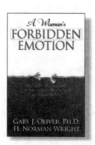